The Sailfish and the
Sacred Mountain

Will Johnson with his son Kailas at Dolma La Pass, Mt. Kailas, Tibet, 1994.

The Sailfish and the Sacred Mountain

*Passages in the Lives
of a Father and a Son*

WILL JOHNSON

Inner Traditions
Rochester, Vermont

Inner Traditions
One Park Street
Rochester, Vermont 05767
www.InnerTraditions.com

Library of Congress Cataloging-in-Publication Data
Johnson, Will, 1946-
  The sailfish and the sacred mountain : passages in the lives of a father and son / Will Johnson.
    p. cm.
  ISBN 0-89281-193-5 (pbk.)
  1. Johnson, Will, 1946—-Travel—China—Kailas, Mount. 2. Kailas, Mount (China)—Description and travel. 3. Spiritual
biography—China—Kailas, Mount. I. Title.
  BL73.J646A3 2004
  204'.092—dc22

                              2004001314

Printed and bound in the United States at Lake Book Manufacturing, Inc.

10 9 8 7 6 5 4 3 2 1

Text design and layout by Rachel Goldenberg
This book was typeset in Sabon with Caslon Open Face as the display typeface

*This book is dedicated to the memory of my father,
David Z. Johnson, a great backgammon player
who taught me about life by teaching me
the rules of the game he so loved to play:*

1) First and foremost, perfect your skills.

*2) Maximize your gains when the dice are rolling in your favor;
minimize your losses when they begin to roll against you.
In this way you will come out ahead in the long run.*

*3) Don't play results. Make the best decision you can with
the full awareness that dice are mysterious and fickle.
If things don't work out, don't torment yourself
into thinking that you did the wrong thing.*

4) It's also helpful to know how to count.

Contents

Acknowledgments

I would like to make mention of some of the many people in my life who have assisted me in my journey and who appear, visibly or invisibly, on these pages: my mother, father, and brother, Kailas, Jamie, Lyn, Vassi, Aimee, Jonathan, Ellen, Cindy, Faye, Kesar, Jennifer, Jean, Bill, Gigi, my extended family through the Institute for Embodiment Training, and my many formal and informal teachers. I hope that in some way I have been able to assist them in their journeys, as they have assisted me in mine.

With one exception, the events and people that are described in this book are all real. The exception is the fishing-boat captain. I have heard that he is now quite elderly and enjoying the solitude of his retirement. In deference to his privacy, I've changed his name and altered some of the details about his life. I have also taken some small liberties in reconstructing the story of his transformation into a fishing-boat captain from the information he shared with us. Other than that, everything that I have described on these pages is true and is as close an approximation to what actually occurred as language and the interesting telling of a story permit.

Part I
Passages and Prayers

The Sacred Mountain

EVERY MOMENT IN LIFE is a moment of passage. Everything I can perceive to exist is continually shifting its shape and altering its appearance from one moment of perception to the next. The sounds, the sights, the thoughts, the sensations, the tastes, and the smells: all of these change with the most astonishing rapidity through the passage of the most insignificant amount of time. The ringing of a bell hung around the neck of a mountain goat, the last glimpse of the setting sun as it sinks beneath an ocean horizon, an insight that resolves a particularly thorny impasse between friends, the richness of sensation that fills the body after love, the taste of the finest wine or the most bitter medicine, the aroma of a well-cooked meal coming out of a kitchen window: everything arises only to pass away a moment later. Where do these phenomena come from, and where do they go?

Change is the only constant in life, and its effects are irreversible. Once something has passed, it is gone forever. Today's pleasure, as much as I might like to hold onto it and make it last forever, is destined to take up residence as a shadow of its original self in the storehouse of my memory. Like some once-valued object that has now acquired a permanent layer of dust in the basement of a museum, I may visit it from time to time and even try to restore it to its former splendor, but never again will it possess the vibrancy and thrill that accompanied its spontaneous entrance into my life. If I spend too many long hours in the dark storeroom of my memory attempting to resurrect something that no longer exists, I eventually cut myself off from the possibilities continually being presented to me on the ground floor of my life, and something in me begins to wither. If I come to find the truth of change unbearable, I withdraw and become disconnected, a bystander rather than a full participant in life, and everything appears to pass me by. Of course, everything that has caused me sadness and heartache will eventually fade away as well, although often the effect of these events appears to linger for a longer period of time than does the effect of their more pleasurable counterparts.

Much of the pain we feel in our lives can be directly traced to our unwillingness or inability to honor and acknowledge the inevitability of passage. We cling to the pleasurable moments in the attempt to make them last forever. We try to protect ourselves from the unpleasant events and are at best only partially successful. We try to freeze a moment of our lives or hold something to its current form only to find that, like water, it has already slipped through our fingers. Even though everything we can experience passes away from one moment of awareness to the next, we shore up our sense of self, our "I," and in the process delude ourselves into thinking that we can somehow remain immune to the inexorable law of passage. In the long run, however, we know that death is destined to get the upper hand, and that we too will pass away. Living our life in fear of this great certainty, however, is not to live our lives at all, and paradoxically something inside begins to die. If we truly want to participate in this great game into which we've been born, then we have no choice but to accept the inevitability of passage.

While the great majority of moments pass one into the other with an ease and deftness that borders on invisibility, a handful of these moments may be truly, and quite literally, momentous. These moments are occasions of the greatest and most profound change. Some time later, when we may have the luxury to look back on the passage of our lives, we will recognize that these momentous events signaled a turning point in our lives, as though the winds we were running with inexplicably changed direction, and we had no choice but to respond and follow the new impulse. With the passage of these kinds of moments, we intuitively know that something fundamental has changed in us and that we will never again be quite the same. Our first moment of awareness, our first taste of love, our successes and failures, the births and deaths of those we love: how can we ever again be the same after any of these?

In my earliest memory I am sitting on the linoleum floor in front of the refrigerator in my house. I'm playing with a jigsaw puzzle that has large interlocking pieces painted on both sides with parts of figures. I experience what I will later call elation at my ability to put the pieces together and watch the completed picture take shape. There are four figures, but they're all at right angles to one another, as though their legs emerge from the center of the puzzle, and their individual torsos and heads then extend outward in the four directions. I take the pieces apart and put them back together again. Every time I do so, the pieces fit together effortlessly, and yet every time I do so, the pieces go together differently. No matter how I put the pieces together, they always fit perfectly. A different head might appear on a different body. Different legs might appear under a different torso, but everything always fits, no matter how the pieces are placed together.

Over the years I have often thought about this moment and wondered how it could be possible that such a puzzle existed, how the pieces could possibly have been designed to be so interchangeable. Nonetheless, I know that it did exist, and that it did work this way. Everything fit together into a perfect and seamless whole, and it did so time after time, no matter how the pieces were placed.

What kind of effect does an earliest memory have on a child's life? Is it *just* an earliest memory, or does this first moment of awareness and recognition count for something more? Does it constitute what might be called the seminal moment of passage, and does it signal and determine a fundamental direction in which the course of that child's entire life will move?

It is, of course, impossible to answer questions like this with any kind of certainty, and yet as I grew into an older child and then became a young man, the major dilemma that gnawed at me was the apparent lack of interconnection that appeared in the world at large. Everywhere I looked I found division and discord. Nothing seemed to fit together harmoniously, and yet I knew that, appearances notwithstanding, everything was all of a single piece. Does an earliest experience like the one I've just described make me a person who would even ask these kinds of questions?

In acknowledgment of the power that moments of passage have on our lives, we have created rituals for our sons and daughters in hopes that these events will confer some of the transformational powers that true moments of passage possess. The baptisms, bar or bas mitzvahs, and confirmations of Western religions all attempt to confer a rite of passage on the participant and to raise him or her to a higher level of maturity or understanding. The ritualistic markings and piercings of the body, the exposure to the world of spirits, the quests for visions that are sought by youths of non-European cultures serve essentially the same purpose. A young girl becomes a woman. A boy is a boy no longer, but can now participate as fully as he is capable in the activities of the men of his culture or tribe. Marriages are consecrated everywhere. Births and deaths, even divorces, are treated with highly prescribed rituals that reflect the belief systems and hopes of the individual tribe or culture.

The problem with creating artificial rites of passage is that there is no guarantee that the desired effect will occur. Only a very wise shaman can foresee if the time is indeed auspicious for a youth to set out on the quest for a vision that will clarify the direction in which the youth's life should subsequently move. A thirteen-year-old Jewish boy may perform his bar mitzvah only to find that nothing has changed, that he is still a boy and is not yet treated like a man in the way that the ceremony originally promised. The hopes and vision of eternal union that are spoken of with such optimism on the day of a wedding are often not sufficiently powerful to protect a man and a woman from the vagaries of fickleness or the loss of affection. Nor can they assure that each partner will be able to face the inevitable fears and shadows that deep partnership naturally draws up to the surface of prolonged and committed companionship. If these fears and shadows are not embraced and dealt with, the marriage falters, and the bond that carried with it so much hope begins to come undone.

Neither are there any guarantees that the culturally created rite of passage will provide protection from the fateful changes and occurrences that can truly turn a life upside down. A young Catholic acolyte may one day be inexplicably drawn to the teachings of an esoteric form of Korean Buddhist practice. A beautiful, young woman who has entered into a formal engagement to be married may one day innocently turn a corner and collide with a slightly older man, whom in some distant part of her memory she knows she has been looking for all her life, whose name has been encoded in a strand of her DNA. What will she do? Which moment of passage will she acknowledge to be the one richest in importance and deepest in meaning? Artificially induced moments of passage run the risk of diluting the potency of the mystery that true moments of epiphany naturally possess into a dose that has no real effect.

Humans are the only animals that attach so much meaning to the abstraction of meaning. We value meaning for its own sake, independent of whether that parcel of meaning actually has any real and significant effect on our lives. Often, of course, meanings have no such effect at all, but rather serve just the opposite purpose. We often use meaning to justify the creation of ever smaller circles of communities and to separate ourselves from the larger sphere of humanity with whom we share the planet. Perhaps the rites of passage that we have created and to which we still attach so much meaning and importance once possessed a real, organic significance, like the ritual urination by which a wolf communicates to the world the boundaries of his territory. In the time of Jesus, for example, the bar mitzvah ceremony meant that the boy could now enter into the temple as a full adult and begin discussing and arguing over interpretations of scripture that were so important to the lives of the men of the community.

Even though we know instinctively that God knocks at our door in Her own time, according to Her own schedule and unfathomable agenda, we still attempt to lure Her in the direction of our sons and daughters. We create rites of passage and attach great importance and meaning to them. Maybe, just maybe, the rite of passage will coincide organically with the very moment at which God decides to reveal Her mystery. Or maybe we are much more realistic than that. Maybe we know that the coincidence of such an interaction is unlikely, but that the rite of passage will somehow prepare the child for the moment, sometime in the future, when true revelation and the moment of epiphany spontaneously occur. Whatever our motives, or the under-standing behind our motives, we keep on creating rites of passage because we love our sons and daughters so very much.

My son was born during one of the most bitter and protracted labor disputes in the history of the Canadian postal system. Just as we expect the cold, northern winds to sweep down from Alaska during the fall and winter months, we expect our mail to be delivered to our mailbox every day of the workweek, and suddenly it stopped being delivered. Businesses could not send out their billing, nor could they collect it. Friends, families, and lovers (e-mail and the fax machine did not yet exist) could not communicate with each other through the mediating veil of cards, notes, and occasional long letters, but were forced into sit-uations that demanded much more immediate honesty of interaction by relying almost exclusively on the telephone.

The strike became ugly. Management brought in replacement workers whom the workers on strike referred to as "scabs," as though they were some kind of tough, unwelcome crust of dried serum and blood that had formed over the sore of the negotiations. Replacement workers attempting to steer their trucks through a sea of protesting strikers ended up coming perilously close to running over them instead. Rocks were thrown, fists were struck against other bodies, blood came close to being drawn.

What this all meant practically for me was that I no longer had to walk down to my mailbox only to have my hopes for some kind of meaningful correspondence dashed by the reality of junk mail, I no longer had to pay my phone and electric bills, and my wife and I were given a period of grace in which we didn't have to comply to the government's regulations that the selected name for newborn babies be registered within two weeks of the birth. This last consequence of the postal strike was a most welcome one for us because, in truth, we didn't have a clue what we wanted to name him. It wasn't a question of disagreement between my wife and me, but rather that every name we tried simply fell flat, like the sound an underinflated basketball might make when bounced on a cement driveway liberally covered with wet, autumn leaves.

Middle names were no problem. My father, who was given no middle name by his parents, had been called into the registrar's office at the University of Minnesota shortly after he began his freshman year of college. Minnesota is one of the high seats in the world for the Johnson clan, and it is a sobering experience for a visitor to Minnesota to look up a listing for a Johnson in the Minneapolis phone directory (at last count there were almost thirty full pages of Johnsons). The registrar informed my father that there were too many David Johnsons already enrolled and, in order to keep their records straight, he needed to list his middle name or initial as well. But he didn't have a middle name or initial, my father tried to explain. But *everyone* has one, the registrar retorted, or at least should have one, and if you don't have one, then choose one! On the spot my father selected the letter Z for his middle initial and walked out. I have always loved him for this decidedly quirky act and have always known that if I ever had a son, I would give him the middle initial Z.

In the spirit of fairness, we decided that we should give our son a middle name after my wife's father, in addition to the middle initial that came from my father's name. Rob, Robert, and Bob got spliced together and brought up to date, and it was easy to agree upon Robin as his full middle name. This now gave him a middle name, a middle initial, and a last name, but nothing even remotely approaching a first name, which is arguably the most important of the lot.

The moment of birth is one of the two most momentous moments of passage in the whole of a life. So much transpires in this one little moment, lives are changed so irreversibly, that it is easy to lose sight of the fact that in terms of conventional time, it takes no longer for a child to emerge out of the mother's tummy, from the first sighting of the crown of the head to the first inhalation that signifies the actual birth, than it takes to prepare a lettuce and tomato sandwich. In the face of such profound change, our awareness of the passage of time becomes extremely altered. Time simply explodes through the intensity of the moment, and for weeks afterward the dust of that explosion coats our lives, constantly bringing us back to the initial moment of explosion itself, like some kind of volcanic ash that reminds us that an extraordinary event has recently taken place.

The world stood still for us for several weeks after the birth. Certainly there was much to do and much to be learned about how to care for and relate to this recent arrival, but everything that transpired seemed to be filtered through the lens of the moment of birth itself. Two months later, as if to wake us from our slumber, my mother pronounced that we couldn't go on calling him "Boy-oh-boy!" for the rest of his life and, mail strike or no mail strike, he had to be given a proper name.

And once again my wife and I were simply stumped. The only name that had had any appeal to us was Kai, and yet we strongly felt that Kai was a shortened version for something else, much as Will is an abbreviated form of William, but for the life of us we couldn't figure out what that something else could possibly be. One afternoon, with the postal strike winding down, a friend from across the road came over to pay a visit, check on how we were doing, and find out if there was anything we needed. Yes, there is something we need and rather desperately, we told her. We need a name for this kid, and so far we've had as much success selecting a name as we might have picking the winning numbers for the following week's lottery! Our friend smiled as she listened and then told us that the same dilemma had presented itself to her and her partner, when their son had been born a year earlier. For several weeks they couldn't decide on a name, until finally one day, out of desperation more than anything, she began paging through the books on her shelves in hopes of finding something that would break the impasse. And it had worked.

It sounded as plausible a way to make a name selection as any at that point, and so after our visit concluded, I walked with her back across the road to her home and library. My wife and I had recently moved to the island, having left behind or given away most of our possessions, even our books. I remembered that our friend's walls were covered with shelves of books and welcomed the opportunity to spend a few quiet hours pouring over her collection.

It didn't take hours. The first book to catch my eye was an old favorite of mine, one that I hadn't seen for many years, but which had been very important for me during the formative years of my early twenties. *The Way of the White Clouds* by Lama Anagarika Govinda is an extraordinary account of an Argentinean-born-German Buddhist's travels through Tibet in the 1930s. Twelve years earlier I had read and reread this book several times, and to this day I credit it with instilling in me a certainty that the path of the Buddhist *dharma* (literally "teachings") spoke to me with more clarity and sanity than anything else I had ever encountered. Standing now in my friend's rustic but comfortable cabin, I opened the book, and the first thing I saw was a diagram of a mountain in southwestern Tibet. The name of the mountain was Kailas.

As I again read the account of Lama Govinda's pilgrimage to this most sacred of mountains, I began to remember:

> There are mountains which are just mountains and there are mountains with personality. The personality of a mountain is more than merely a strange shape that makes it different from others— just as a strangely shaped face or strange actions do not make an individual into a personality.
>
> Personality consists in the power to influence others, and this power is due to consistency, harmony, and one-pointedness of character. If these qualities are present in an individual, in their highest perfection, then this individual is a fit leader of humanity, either as

a ruler, a thinker, or a saint, and we recognize him as a vessel of divine power. If these qualities are present in a mountain we recognize it as a vessel of cosmic power, and we call it a sacred mountain.

The power of such a mountain is so great and yet so subtle that, without compulsion, people are drawn to it from near and far, as if by the force of some invisible magnet; and they will undergo untold hardships and privations in their inexplicable urge to approach and to worship the center of this sacred power. Nobody has conferred the title of sacredness on such a mountain, and yet everybody recognizes it; nobody has to defend its claim, because nobody doubts it; nobody has to organize its worship, because people are overwhelmed by the mere presence of such a mountain and cannot express their feelings other than by worship . . . .

Thus it is that above all the sacred mountains of the world the fame of Kailas has spread and inspired human beings since times immemorial. There is no other mountain comparable to Kailas, because it forms the hub of the two most important ancient civilizations of the world, whose traditions remained intact for thousands of years: India and China. To Hindus and Buddhists alike Kailas is the center of the universe. It is called Meru or Sumeru, according to the oldest Sanskrit tradition, and is regarded to be not only the physical but the metaphysical center of the world.*

—◗

As the Himalayas slowly rose from the waters to form the imposing seventeen-hundred-mile-long barrier of mountains with which we are familiar today, they created a natural wall that separated the warm and temperate landmasses of the south from the colder latitudes to the north. The natural vegetation in the south was tropical and lush; to the north lay unbroken plains stretching as far as the eye could see and covered in grass. The grasslands formed a natural habitat for animals,

---

*Lama Anagarika Govinda, *The Way of the White Clouds* (Boston: Shambhala, 1971), 197–98.

and where animals wandered, man followed. As the Himalayas continued to rise, however, they began to form a curtain, which effectively kept the vital rain-bearing clouds to the south, and gradually the grazing lands to the north began to dry up and lose their fertility. Even today you can witness this phenomenon. From June through August the monsoon rains threaten to turn the Indian subcontinent back into the watery domain that once occupied this geographical location. What begins as the small, muddy puddles of spring can build to become the most terrifying flood conditions of late summer. Everything in the path of water is swept away. Cross the Himalayas onto the high Tibetan plateau, however, and the clouds simply stop, like some pack animal that refuses to move forward.

As the northern grasslands became less fertile, the animals that depended on the naturally growing grain for their sustenance became less plentiful. Man had no choice but to begin to migrate in search of more hospitable conditions. From approximately 10,000 BC onward, several distinct tribal groups of people, whom present-day ethnographers refer to as the Alpanoids, Khasas, and Dards, made their way south, skirting both the eastern and western edges of the Himalayas in search of a more permanent home.

The early Aryan peoples who migrated southward across the Himalayas around 2000 BC and settled in what is the northern part of present-day India stand out among these many waves of settlers in that they arrived with an elaborate cosmological and theological vision of the universe on which much of present-day Hinduism is still based. Central to the Aryan cosmology was the account of a sacred mountain that, they were convinced, formed the actual center of the universe and on whose summit Lord Shiva himself was said to live. They spoke of it as "the Mountain of Blazing Appearance," a perfectly formed dome that rose dramatically and unexpectedly from a high, flat plain and out of which the four main rivers of the land flowed like petals from the center of a flower. They were speaking about Mount Kailas. The grandiloquent metaphors of shape and centrality and the image of the mountain as the source of the great sacred rivers all match the actual, geographical reality.

In my early twenties I discovered that my true church had nothing to do with the oversized and self-important houses of worship that man had built. Walking into these structures, I felt nothing. Walking alone into the high mountains, however, I began to feel everything that my soul thirsted for, as though I were waking from a long dream and remembering what I had always known to be true. The enormous churches and synagogues of Western culture made me feel small and ashamed of myself. They made me feel insignificant in the eyes of the greater perspective, as though there was no way that I could ever rise above my humanness to merge with the greater mystery. These structures spoke to me of the glorification of God at the expense of man.

Implicit in their message is that nature should be walled out and excluded from the act of worship. Such an architectural message directly reflects the beliefs of the religious orders that have built these structures—that the human body is somehow less than completely godly and needs to be transcended. Later in life I would come to view this devaluation of the embodiment of nature and the simultaneous overvaluation of the concept of "soul" or "spirit" as the most fundamental mistake of religious endeavor. Yes, there is a greater mystery to be experienced in this very moment and in this very body. It does not, however, come about by denigrating one's humanness.

The mountains glorify both man and God simultaneously. They welcome the traveler into their sanctuary and then proceed to reveal nature's deepest secrets. They became my church, and indeed the earliest religious monuments of Hinduism and Buddhism, *chortens* and *stupas* composed of stacked or carved stones and mud, are sculptural copies of mountains. I would walk into the high Sierras of central California and spend several days essentially doing nothing but enjoying the mountains. I could sit for hours transfixed by a massive rock face. Over the course of several hours, the overwhelming solidity and hardness of the granite monolith would begin to soften, and it would start taking on the appearance of heat waves seen in the distance across a desert plain. As it would begin to undulate and shimmer in this way, so too would my body begin to lose its sense of solidity. Emotional fixations and physical pain alike would start to come undone. My breath would become deeper and smoother. As I would continue to gaze at the monolithic granite face, I would begin to be aware of what I came to call a ground dimension of being, a substratum of experience that seemed to exist just beneath the surface of appearances and out of which all appearances emerge, rock and body alike. Within this deeply merged state, words like body, spirit, soul, and mind had little relevance. Mountain and body, God and man were just different manifestations of the one fundamental ground.

When, during this period, I read *The Way of the White Clouds* and first heard of Mount Kailas, I knew that I would do everything in my power to go there.

So much happens on our journey through life. We may think we're following a river's tributary, only to find that we arrive at a destination entirely unexpected and unforeseen. The perception of goals, dreams, and purpose changes over time. Some goals turn into other goals. Others just never take root and disappear into the ground on which they were sown. By the time I stood in my friend's library, I realized that I had completely forgotten about Mount Kailas. I hadn't even been on a backpacking trip in years. Reading Lama Govinda's description of his pilgrimage to the sacred mountain, however, a long buried memory began to wake up from its hibernation, as though it were slowly reviving itself around the warmth of a late winter fire.

Many of our friends had already commented that our son did not even look particularly Occidental. His face was round, his ears long, his eyes shaped like elongated almonds. He didn't look unlike pictures of Tibetan babies that I've seen. The coincidence of my pulling that particular book off the shelf at that particular moment and turning to that particular page was not lost on my wife either, and our son had his name at last.

And at that moment, warmed by the blood of memory, a new dream began to form. How wonderful it would be, not only for me to rekindle my dream and travel to Mount Kailas at some point in my life, but to take my son with me as well. And how wonderful it would be to do that around his thirteenth birthday as a rite of passage into adulthood.

I remembered back to when I was that age, and I underwent the bar mitzvah ceremony, the Jewish rite of passage for a young boy into adulthood. I remembered how I had enjoyed the ceremony, but had also felt let down by it, as though it hadn't fully delivered on its promise. I remembered further back to an event in my life that had occurred totally outside the domain of organized religion, and how I'd always considered that event to have been my true rite of passage into adulthood. I knew that a journey to Mount Kailas would challenge a young boy at physical, emotional, and even spiritual levels that he would likely have never been challenged at before. Certainly it is through the successful completion of challenges like this that a young boy can undergo the transformation into adulthood.

Even as I visioned it, however, I knew that there were problems with this dream and that the doubts accompanying it were real. In 1959 the armies of the People's Republic of China had invaded Tibet and claimed the Tibetan landmass as their own. For more than twenty years now, no Westerner had been allowed into Tibet, and there were no signs that this situation would change in the future. Even if that situation were to change, I also realized that a journey of this magnitude would be enormously expensive to undertake. Although my work as a body-oriented psychotherapist could often be extremely gratifying, the riches I received from my work had much more to do with personal satisfaction and the opportunity for real intimacy and service than they did with any actual monetary reward. I would joke in later years that Joseph Campbell's famous cry "Follow your bliss!" should have been required to carry a cautionary warning to the effect that following your bliss may prove hazardous to your bank balance. Still, thoughts and visions are like seeds planted in the mind, and the dream began to dream itself.

Nighttime

TO UNDERSTAND MY MOTIVATION for wanting to choreograph a decidedly nontraditional rite of passage for my son, we need to travel far back in time into the years of my childhood. My parents and brother have said goodnight to me. I have climbed into my bed. I lie down on my back, tired but expectant, hoping that what in later years I will look back upon as the single most important event of my childhood might occur one more time again. I love this event more than anything I know. I wait.

It would happen at night, as I would begin drifting into sleep. I remember entering into the comfort of my bed, a stuffed bear in either arm, the warmth and security of the sheets and blankets that covered me, the softness of the pillow on which I lay my head. I remember feeling secure, warm, content. I remember my body settling into the softness of the mattress. I remember my body feeling wonderfully relaxed, as it settled into the softness. And then I remember it dropping and settling even further, and then further again, as though it had passed right through the mattress itself and entered into a whole new dimension of experience.

Mostly what I remember is the feeling, the extraordinarily soft feeling, whose sensations would start spreading through my body from my head to my toes. The feeling always came first, and I always knew that it was happening again, when I began to recognize the unmistakably pleasurable taste of the feeling. It's difficult to know how one tastes a feeling, but it always reminded me, more than anything else, of the first time I tasted a pear. It was served one day during luncheon at the school I attended. I eyed it suspiciously, but was drawn to taste it nonetheless. It was like nothing I had ever tasted. Its sweetness, its wetness, its pearness thrilled me, and all I wanted to do from that moment was to eat pears.

The feeling state that I would begin to drop into was not unlike the taste of that first pear. It felt delicious and unhurried, as though I could savor its taste forever, and indeed the first stage of delicious warmth and pleasure would last for five or even ten minutes. Only after I felt as though I was completely satisfied would it begin to shift and deepen, and I would sometimes feel a slight shudder coming from deep within my body.

Suddenly the feeling of settling down or sinking would intensify. Like iron filings in the presence of some mysterious magnetic force, I would feel my body being summoned or drawn deeper, right through the mattress into a dimension that permeated the level of conventional reality, but bore little resemblance to it otherwise. There were no objects or names here, only a seemingly limitless expanse of sensation. However, the deeper I was drawn and the closer I was pulled to the source from which this magnetic force emanated and pulsed, the more difficult it became to fathom or make out what this source actually was. All I knew was that it was vast beyond anything I had ever known to that point, far beyond the ocean's horizon I had seen in Florida, far beyond the valleys of the Grand Canyon that from the South Rim appear to go on forever.

The warmth and pleasure of the initial level of entrance were entrancing and delicious, but the pleasurable nature of this second level of sinking made the initial pleasure seem almost superficial or coarse in comparison. I would feel magnetically pulled and drawn to some central source to which I could only yield. Holding back would have been impossible. And as I was pulled ever deeper into this dimension of experience, I would simply begin to disappear. A sense of presence would inevitably remain, but it had nothing to do with the conventional boyhood me. There was only presence, authentic and simple, extension that seemed to move outward forever, and a feeling of wonder and rightness that I had never otherwise tasted.

As I would keep sinking ever more deeply, a third level of experience would begin to appear, in which my body began to undergo the most distorting kinds of awarenesses. I would feel my right arm way off in the left side of the room. I would feel my left arm ten feet outside of the window to the right of my bed. My body would begin to feel as though it were turning itself inside out. The inside of my body could be felt out in the room far beyond my physical form. The skin of my body collapsed in on itself, as though it occupied the smallest point in space at the very center of my body. I would sometimes feel spacious and vast, as if I went on forever, lightly floating in space. At other times the body became very small and felt as though it must weigh five tons. At these moments I would experiment and attempt to move, but it was never possible. Not even a little finger could be called on to move a single inch. The windowsill next to my head felt as though it were a mile away. The trees from across the field felt as though they were standing firmly rooted in the center of my body.

Every time I felt this experience beginning to occur, I would tell myself that I would observe what was happening with as much precision as possible, so that I would be able to go to my mother the next morning and describe to her what had happened. Every time that it would occur, however, I would be taken to a place where words don't exist, and I would never be able to describe a thing. I sometimes felt that I could work my way back into a dimension in which words could function, but I never once had even the slightest inclination to do so.

I entered into this dimension of experience on a regular basis several times a week between the ages of five and eleven. No one knew anything about it because I could never communicate what was happening. I feel fortunate that I was never inclined to respond to this unusual event with any fear whatsoever. With no fear to block its emergence, the experience would simply continue to deepen from one day to the next. After a certain time, perhaps twenty minutes, it would begin to reverse itself. The feeling state of my arms would once again return to their anatomically correct position. The trees would recede back across the lawn. The windowsill returned to the location next to my pillow. The vast intensity and spaciousness would subside. My body would begin to feel very comfortable. I would taste again the deliciousness of the pear. I would become me again. And then I would fall asleep.

~

While I was never able at the time to describe this dimension and the process by which I entered into it in words, I was able after a few years to create an image that captured the flavor of this place as closely as anything that I had been able to come up with. Again it was an image in which sensory modalities were freely mixed.

I began to envision the feeling of this dimension like the sound of silence that permeates a vast desert valley, a sound at once impossible to detect and yet completely deafening in its echoing presence. During the last year of its regular occurrence, I was even able to envision a picture of this vast valley. I would be sitting atop a high, rocky escarpment looking out over a desert valley that extended in every direction as far as the eye could see. About a mile away from me, I could make out the lumbering shape of a giraffe moving ever so slowly and silently across the landscape. I could feel the giraffe's movements, as though it were moving through my own body, not across the landscape. I could feel the giraffe's movements, as though I were hearing them from a close distance, but not feeling them. I knew that if there were a God, He was the sound and the feeling of this valley.

And then, quite suddenly one day, these experiences disappeared, never to return again. As I became engrossed in normal childhood pastimes, I gradually forgot that anything had ever happened to me. The appearance of this dimension as a seven-year-old had felt completely natural to me. Its disappearance at the age of eleven or twelve didn't strike me any differently. I never asked it to occur; nor did I brood over its disappearance. My attention went elsewhere, and I simply forgot that it had ever taken place. Only two decades later, after I began the regular practice of sitting meditation, did I begin to remember what had happened to me at night during my childhood.

~

Even though I lost conscious contact with the memory of this event, it continued to influence and affect me nonetheless. Just as I automatically associated my first, early stirrings of sexual feelings with the image of a woman, I knew that this mysterious event of my childhood must somehow be associated with religion. Although half of my mother's family had made their way to the Roman Catholic Church, my brother and I were being raised in the tradition of Reform Judaism. This meant that we would observe the traditional Jewish holidays during the year and attend religious classes on the weekend. Nowhere, however, did the benevolent God of Sunday school class appear even remotely to resemble the harsh disciplinarian that I read about in the Old Testament. It was as though Dr. Spock had entered the religious arena, and we were being presented with a whole new image of effective religious parenting and childrearing. It ultimately seemed as though Reform Judaism was more of a good and heartfelt strategy for establishing social order and harmony within the family and community than it was a path to encounter firsthand the extraordinary force and organic potency that went by the name of Jehovah.

All the same, I intrinsically knew that the experience of my childhood must somehow be related to the manifestation of that force. I would attend occasional services with my parents and scour the texts of the service for confirmatory evidence of that connection, and it didn't seem as though I had very far at all to look. The most repeated phrase during each and every service (referred to in fact as "the watchword of our faith"), the one sentence that we, the congregation, were asked to repeat over and over again during the service was: "Shemah Yisroael adonai elehanu

Inner Traditions • Bear & Company
P.O. Box 388
Rochester, VT 05767-0388
U.S.A.

BEAR & CO.

BEAR CUB BOOKS

INNER
TRADITIONS

HEALING · ARTS · PRESS

DESTINY
BOOKS

Park Street
Press

INDC
BOOKS

Please send us this card to receive our latest catalog.

☐ Check here if you would like to receive our catalog via e-mail.

Name _____ Company _____

Address _____ Phone _____

City _____ State _____ Zip _____ Country _____

E-mail address _____

Please check the following area(s) of interest to you:

☐ Health ☐ Self-help ☐ Science/Nature ☐ Shamanism
☐ Ancient Mysteries ☐ New Age/Spirituality ☐ Ethnobotany ☐ Martial Arts
☐ Spanish Language ☐ Sexuality/Tantra ☐ Children ☐ Teen

Order at 1-800-246-8648 • Fax (802) 767-3726
E-mail: orders@InnerTraditions.com • Web site: www.InnerTraditions.com

adonai echod." Hear, oh Israel, the Lord our God, the Lord is one.

Within this phrase I believed I had found the key and connecting link I'd been searching for. While in Sunday school class, I had been taught that during the formative phase of Judaism, a great many of the indigenous Middle Eastern peoples worshiped numerous idols and gods. The radical revolution of Judaism, on the other hand, was founded on the belief and understanding that there is only one God, one force, and everything we can perceive to exist is somehow an expression of that single force.

One of the most significant features of the experience into which I would sink, as I lay in my bed at night, was a profound feeling and awareness that, appearances notwithstanding, everything that existed was of a single, fundamental piece. My body, the bed, the room in which I lay, the world outside my window: at the essential core of all these apparently different and separate objects and events was to be found a substratum of experience, a common ground, that was inherently one and the same. It was as though out of this common ground a million objects and events could spring, all with the most convincing appearance of separate individuality, and yet at the core of these objects everything participated in the one, fundamental truth: God, the very energetic source of manifestation of the million different objects and events, is one.

That this experiential recognition of the oneness of the ultimate level of existence and reality was the source of the paradigm shift that differentiated the early Israelite tribes from their Semitic brethren was completely comprehensible to me. I can now look back on my life and realize how different it would have been if I'd never been exposed to my nighttime journeys. A tribe of people, all of whom were privy to this state of awareness, would truly feel removed or alienated from another tribe of people, who had never opened to such a direct experience of this common ground. Eventually they would want to separate themselves and live their lives according to their new understanding and principles in harmony with their other brethren who shared the same understanding and beliefs.

All original religious impulse begins with a new and fresh way of viewing the world in which we live. That this initial gesture of faith and understanding generally transmigrates over time into the burning urgency to have everybody else see things the same way is, of course, one of the most tragic side effects of the religious impulse. All the same, the natural human tendency, quite benign in its initial motive, is to share an experience that you know to be extremely valuable with as many people as possible. Unfortunately, as we remove ourselves in time from the initial moment of inception of the new awareness or experience, we tend to become insecure about the certainty of our new understanding and attempt to placate the insecurity by enlisting the support of as many different people as possible. The next phase of religious impulse, then, is to sign up as many people as possible onto your side. Because we can only do so much at any given time, the continued exploration of the initial profound insight takes a backseat to the missionary work. If this phase is truly successful, a new church is born, and the initial heretical leap in consciousness often becomes ossified in the canon of orthodox belief. At this point, in the words of Carl Jung, "Organized religion becomes a defense against having the religious experience."

Somehow, though, I held fast to the belief that the experience of my childhood could be best explained and explored within the context of Judaism. My genes were overwhelmingly Jewish, after all, and so it only made sense that the nature of this mysterious and revelatory experience that would come to me at night must refer to the original leap in consciousness on which the Jewish religion was based. Now I didn't see much evidence that there was a great deal of interest within the Reform Jewish tradition in exploring anything even remotely like my childhood experience. Nevertheless, I assumed that the intensely personal nature of the experience dictated that it be opened and shared in private, and I began to assume and envision that there existed a branch of the Reform Jewish faith (perhaps with a whole separate room in the synagogue dedicated to just this purpose!) in which this occurred.

The confirmation of this belief came in the form of my family's trumping up the significance of the bar mitzvah ceremony, the Jewish rite of passage par excellence, which occurs around a boy's thirteenth birthday. The ceremony marks the passage of the young boy into manhood, and I knew that in traditional Jewish cultures, this meant that the young boy was now invited into the company of the elders with whom he was now welcome to converse about the most important theological truths and controversies. I so believed that my early experiences were directly related to the most important theological insight of Judaism that I was sure that the company of elders focused relentlessly on exploring the experience of the unified state, for only in the bodily experience of this state was it to be understood.

I threw myself into my studies. I enjoyed learning Hebrew, familiarizing myself with the sculptural shapes of the letters of the alphabet, listening to the sounds of the new letters, some so like the Roman alphabet, others not. I felt proud when I went with my father to his clothing store and bought my first real suit. The great day came. I performed well. I received presents, but refused to allow my parents to throw a party in my honor. I didn't want a party. I wanted to be shown where the secret room in the synagogue was and meet the elders who were experimenting with the experience of primal union. I wanted to tell them of my experiences and ask for their further guidance. I wanted to gain greater understanding of this fundamental truth of Judaism. "Hear, oh Israel, the Lord our God, the Lord is one." Listen, children of the spirit, the world is of one piece.

Nothing changed in my life. I was still treated as before. I was still a boy. The room in the synagogue didn't exist. Nor did I meet any elders engaged in practices oriented toward the exploration of the unified state. I felt deeply let down and disillusioned, as though a promise that had been made to me wasn't delivered. My nighttime experiences had stopped occurring with any kind of regularity. There existed, as far as I could tell, no practices within my religious tradition to guide the seeker back into that primal state of union out of which, I continued to believe, the whole of the religion had emerged and on which it was originally based. I threw myself into my academic studies and let religion go.

Only many years later as a grown man would I find that some of the most passionate and beautiful descriptions of this condition of primal union had, in fact, been expressed by Jewish mystics, many of them European rabbis who lived in the eighteenth and nineteenth centuries. At the time, however, I knew nothing of this. And not until much later in my life would the doubt and disappointment that surrounded the event of my bar mitzvah be cleared up when, during a chance encounter with a stranger, I came to realize what this event had, in fact, signified for me. I have no doubt whatsoever, however, about when my true rite of passage into adulthood occurred. It did not happen at age thirteen, when I was standing in front of the altar of the synagogue singing my haftorah during my bar mitzvah ceremony. It happened, rather, two years before that event on a fishing boat in the Florida Keys.

Fish

LIKE SO MANY OTHER YOUNG BOYS who grew up in Minnesota (the "Land of Ten Thousand Lakes," as touted on its license plate), my primary passion of the summer months was fishing. My family was fortunate to be able to spend our summer months in a small cottage on a lake that was still within driving distance of my father's place of business. In the early evenings, as the intense heat of the summer day would recede with the setting of the sun, I would invariably find myself down by the water's edge, trying to catch the large sunfish that swarmed around the footings that supported the small dock my father had constructed. These fish were my playmates and companions, and in those early years of my childhood, catching and eating my friends didn't strike me in any way as an ethical problem. I talked to my friends as I was fishing for them. I even began recognizing some of the larger ones that I was particularly trying to lure to my bait and concealed hook from night to night and gave them names. I liked how they tasted when my mother cooked them.

> *Fishy, fishy in the brook,*
> *Come and bite on Billy's hook.*
> *Mommy cook you in a pan.*
> *Billy eat you like a man.*

As I moved through the long years of childhood, I became naturally more proficient at my passion of choice. This proficiency not only allowed me to play ever more successfully with my watery friends (i.e., it enabled me to catch as many of the bigger ones as possible), it also led to a greater appreciation for the many different approaches to fishing, and I found myself drawn to the elegance and beauty of fly fishing's motion. I became a fly-fishing addict, practicing my casting technique on the spring lawn in preparation for the thaw that would eventually melt the ice that had formed so thickly on the lake that you could safely drive a car over it. I would do my homework immediately after school and then go downstairs after dinner to tie fishing flies during the long winter nights. I made fly rods from bamboo shafts, and I began devouring any literature I could find about fishing: books on fly-fishing techniques, instructional pamphlets on tying flies, magazines about fishing all over the planet. I became aware of the much larger river and pond beyond the lake of my childhood, and I first heard of tarpon, bonefish, steelhead, the marlin of the Pacific waters, and the sailfish of the Atlantic. I began dreaming of fish, big fish.

Sixth grade had just begun, and the maple trees of central Minnesota were just beginning to hint at the riotous change in color they would soon undergo, when my father came home and announced that we would drive to Florida over the Christmas holidays to go deep-sea fishing and attempt to catch a sailfish. The announcement simply stunned me. All the magazine articles I had ever read about sailfish presented an image of a Neptunian being unequaled in majesty and evasiveness, a watery version of the Himalayan snow leopard. Many of the magazine articles that I'd read actually described the author's *unsuccessful* attempts at catching a sailfish. I had always reasoned that if such an account could still get published, it must mean that this was a very special and elusive being indeed. When a new issue of a hunting and fishing magazine appeared in a store, I would rapidly scour its contents to see if it contained an article about sailfish. I put this animal on a pedestal above all other sea creatures. Fishing for trout in a Montana stream held little allure for me when one could be on a fishing boat in Florida hoping to find and hook a sailfish. They were beautiful fish. They were very large. They represented the pinnacle of fishing, or so I imagined, as I contented myself with the sunfish, pikes, and bass of my backyard.

With my father's announcement, a new dream was planted in the garden of my mind, and it rapidly began to germinate and establish roots. I was going to go deep-sea fishing in the attempt to catch a sailfish. I instantly became obsessed with this idea and this possibility. I was actually going to go out on a deep-sea fishing boat, trolling through the waters where sailfish swim. One thought alone began to take over my inner mindscape and turned itself into a desire so strong that it completely colored the next three months of my life. I knew that I wanted, more than anything that I could think of, to catch a sailfish.

My father's announcement gave birth to my first real awareness of the internal monologue, the silent voice inside my head that carries on a running commentary on my desires and fears, my past victories or defeats, my future possibilities. As the existence of this voice is a function of language, it appears only gradually, as a child matures and learns how to piece words together and to juggle abstract thoughts. The ability to function conceptually is, without question, one of the extraordinary achievements of our species. The problem, however, is that this function, once activated, begins to take over the entire mind, leaving little room or space for the many other parts of the mind to take their rightful turn and contribute their gifts. Like a faucet that has been left running, its pronouncements and commentaries just go on and on, whether we are interested in them or not, and it becomes very difficult to locate the tap capable of turning this stream of thoughts off. No longer are we able to pick up this function at the appropriate time and moment and use it consciously and creatively; we become, rather, the unconscious effect of it.

These unconscious thoughts are very powerful. They are capable of generating the most positive or negative effects, depending on the purity and motivation of their source. The Buddha has said that all action originates in thought. Think positive thoughts, and positive consequences inevitably follow. Lose yourself in negative thoughts, and unwholesome events will naturally occur. Free yourself from the process of unconscious thought entirely, and you may free yourself from the entire cycle of birth, death, and rebirth.

During the fall of that year I became keenly aware of this inner voice as a single thought began to form in my mind and, then, to repeat itself over and over and over again like the mantric repetitions of Eastern spiritual practices or the prayers of Christian monks and nuns. The thought was simple, its message was specific, and it was very loud: *I want to catch a sailfish. I want to catch a sailfish. I want to catch a sailfish.* I couldn't stop it from thinking itself.

The thought clearly possessed a life of its own. I couldn't not think it, and so I welcomed it into my life. It's said that the power of a mantra or prayer, if intoned long enough and with enough conviction, gradually begins to manifest as a reality in the life of the aspirant. I knew nothing about any of this at the time. All I knew was that *I want to catch a sailfish; I want to catch a sailfish.*

I don't remember very much of the first few months of sixth grade. Both my teacher and parents commented that I appeared to be distracted and had little interest in my schoolwork. Until that year I'd been a good student. Now everyone spoke of my inability to concentrate or focus my attention on much of anything. In reality, this observation couldn't have been further from the truth. I was intensely concentrated in a way that I'd never before known. The problem was that it was not on my schoolwork, but rather on the simple thought of wanting to catch a fish. This one thought had come to dominate my mental landscape so thoroughly that there was little room left for me to focus on anything else. I would attempt to read a book, but after a few paragraphs my concentration would be disturbed. *I want to catch a sailfish. I want to catch a sailfish.* I would try to do my math homework, but the number seven looked too much like the dorsal fin of a sailfish, the number one too much like its beak. *I want to catch a sailfish. I want to catch a sailfish.*

Although I was aware of what was happening to me, I wasn't able to do anything about it. The thought appeared to have taken total control over me. I went to bed with the thought at night. I woke to it in the morning. It never left me for more than an hour at a time. If I was fortunate to receive even that much of a break from its constant drone, it was sure to return with a vengeance and repeat itself endlessly. I'd heard that people would occasionally lose touch with the world in which they lived and experience something called "going crazy." There were moments when I wondered if this was what was happening to me.

In spite of my fears about this, I felt even more timid to tell anybody about what was occurring. I was very sensitive about being teased and felt, frankly, embarrassed about what was happening to me. If I were, in fact, going crazy, better to suffer on my own than to have the word get around and be forced to endure the condemning or pitying glances of my neighbors and friends. And so I kept it to myself, telling no one. *I want to catch a sailfish. I want to catch a sailfish.* I began to call this thought "my companion," as though it were an imaginary friend on the mental plane.

By November the thought had become a familiar part of me. Its persistent presence no longer upset me. I decided that I wasn't going crazy after all. I just wanted to catch a fish. No harm in that. It began to seem like a pretty normal ambition for an eleven-year-old boy. As my tolerance for the presence of the thought increased, it began to become less frantically persistent. It no longer hammered away inside my head like a broken record on a phonograph for which the manufacturer had neglected to construct an off button. It would come and go, but only rarely would linger for unbroken hours on end. Perhaps it felt that it had done its job. Perhaps it began to trust me, to trust that I had taken it into my heart and that I wouldn't forget it if a few minutes went by without my hearing the constant reminder of its directive. It never went away completely, but it no longer tormented me either.

By the beginning of December, it had subsided even more. Every ten minutes or so I would hear it quite clearly. It would repeat itself once or twice and then fade away. I couldn't tell if it would disappear totally during these intervals, or if it simply lowered its volume to a level that I was unable consciously to hear. I'd heard that there are frequencies of sounds that only dogs could hear. I began to wonder if my thought was lowering its frequency in such a way that, although I could not consciously hear it, some deeper part of me could still register its message.

During the week before we left to drive to Florida, it began once again to resume the level of persistent intensity I'd experienced in September. I was beginning to get quite excited in anticipation of our departure, our journey, and our ultimate appointment with the ocean. Its reemergence didn't frighten me, however. I recall almost welcoming it back like a best friend whom I hadn't seen for a while. I'd learned how to accept this inner voice and sensed that it was to my advantage to have it. I was able to hear it and focus on my schoolwork at the same time. No longer did I feel so disoriented or distracted by its presence in my life. It had become my friend. I realized it was telling me the truth. *Yes, I do want to catch a sailfish. I really do want to catch a sailfish.*

—⁀

We drove to Florida. The snows of Minnesota and Iowa slowly gave way to the dampness of Missouri and Arkansas. With every passing mile of road, winter changed itself into spring. There still were no leaves on the trees, but there was no bitter chill in the air either. We drove across the twenty-four-mile bridge over Lake Pontchartrain and spent an evening in the French Quarter of New Orleans. People were happy here. Their movements were unhurried. They went around at night with their top buttons opened and no drab outerwear to cover up the brightness of their shirts. I felt as if my family and I had entered into a different world. My only point of reference, the one constant element that hadn't changed, was my companion thought. The journey didn't seem to affect it in any way. Unfazed by its new environment, it continued much as before, unchanged and unchanging. *I want to catch a sailfish. I want to catch a sailfish. I want to catch a sailfish.* Its presence had blended into my life by then. When powdered chocolate is first added to warm milk, the contrast of the two colors is strong and distinct. After the two have been mixed together, however, they form a homogenous presence. The new blend belies their origins as separate substances, and they become something beyond which either on their own was capable of attaining. It was impossible at this point to separate myself from my companion thought.

As we drove across the Gulf of Mexico toward the panhandle of Florida, the sun shone warm and large. It continued to extract the chill of Minnesota and remove it from our bodies, and we began to feel unhurried and relaxed, like the people at play in New Orleans. The miles took care of themselves. We were making good time. We were getting closer to our destination. The state line of Florida was no more than a half inch away now on the map that we had gotten from the automobile association. As we continued to move ever closer to that symbolic boundary line, however, I began to experience a subtle uneasiness. It is one thing to want to catch a sailfish and another to actually catch one. Within this new environment, in which I was essentially a stranger, I was soon going to be awarded the opportunity I had so long sought. The fantasy of looking forward to going out onto the ocean in hopes of catching a sailfish was soon to become the reality of that actual day and attempt. I would return from fishing, go to bed that night, and my fantasy would be put forever to rest in the face of the reality that had occurred on the water. I would wake up the next morning, and my world would be different. I realized that for the past three months I had essentially been living in the future, in the imagined expectation of an event that was now within arm's reach. And for the first time, I began to experience doubts about the outcome of this trip. I remembered all the articles that I had read in which the author had set out to catch a sailfish, but had not been able to do so. Certainly that author must have wanted to catch a sailfish. I began to feel foolish for the obsession I had created. It's only a fish. I began to equivocate on my commitment to myself. Maybe I'll catch a sailfish; maybe I won't. Enjoy your holiday. Don't let not catching a sailfish ruin your vacation. And yet at a deeper level, my companion thought continued as before.

~

The Florida Keys are a strand of small islands off the southern tip of Florida that form a gentle arc reaching out in the direction of Mexico. The individual keys are largely barren and flat. They are the topmost ridge of a shallow, underwater mountain range, whose peaks just barely manage to rise above the surface of the ocean. They are strung together, the oversize jewels of a terrestrial bracelet, by a series of extraordinary bridges that extend fearlessly out into the horizon. Some of the islands are so far apart that you are unable to see land either in front of or behind you when you're in the middle of the low bridge that, like some flying fish mysteriously fossilized in flight, seems just barely to skim above the surface of the water. The body of water that sits between the southern face of the Keys and the northern shore of Cuba is home to one of the most concentrated populations of sailfish to be found anywhere on the planet.

Leaving my aunt's tranquil home just outside of Miami, my mother hesitated before getting into the car and kept loudly calling out, "Goodbye, sister! Goodbye, sister!" A group of nuns visiting a family across the road thought she must be speaking to them and came rushing over excitedly to see why they'd been summoned. Our family is convinced that many years later the continued prayers of a group of nuns in Philadelphia for the health and recovery of my aunt were the main agents that allowed her, time and time again, to defy her doctor's forecast that she had between three and six months to live. I was not so young that I could not enjoy the humor of watching this well-intentioned group of women surrounding our car wanting to know how they could be of help. Nor was I so guileless that I was beyond calculating how I could use this situation to my advantage, and so I closed my eyes and silently asked the nuns to please go and tell God that I wanted to catch a sailfish.

In the last few decades, the Florida Keys have become extremely popular. Driving between Key Largo at the edge of the mainland and the road's end at Key West, you will encounter heavy traffic on the bridges and beach-to-beach condominiums and service businesses on the islands. It was not always this way, however. In 1957 there were very few full-time residents in the Keys and relatively few visitors either. Leaving the mainland, we made our way over long, empty bridges only to come to often-deserted bits of land. It seemed as though the purpose of the land was simply to link the bridges together, and we could not imagine why anyone would have gone to the trouble and expense to construct this magnificent road. Mostly what I remember about the islands we crossed that day was the feeling of solitude and silence. I liked how I felt driving across those empty bridges and islands. I remember telling my family that it felt so big and empty here.

Our destination was Marathon, one of the better-sized keys, situated approximately halfway along the bracelet of bridges and islands that stretched between Key Largo and Key West. Marathon was a fishing center. People came here from all over the world to go out onto the ocean on custom boats that had been designed and constructed solely for the purpose of catching large fish. Marathon was one of the places most often cited in the magazine articles that I had been reading for years. For a place that my young imagination had highly glamorized, however, it didn't appear to have a great deal going for it: a few fishing lodges and assorted motels, a handful of restaurants and gas stations, the expected services, some homes.

We checked into a modest fishing lodge, and my father left us to go down to the docks and arrange to charter a boat to take our family out fishing. It was midafternoon, and the boats would be returning by now from their day on the open waters. He returned a few hours later and said that he'd found the perfect person to take us out. We would spend the next day resting and exploring this small island and then would depart for our day of fishing early the following morning.

‸

Up until just a few years before we met him, Dick Karalis had been an ambitious stockbroker in Hartford, scurrying as fast as he could within the world of dollars and numbers, attempting to create a secure life for himself and his young family. He told us how his initial enthusiasm for this fast-paced world had begun to fade over the years and was gradually replaced instead with a feeling bordering on loathing and despair. He resented that he had to work every day at a job that no longer held any interest for him simply so he could feed his family and pay his mortgage. He resented that he had to be indoors for most of his life. And mostly he resented that his job didn't allow him to go fishing as much as he would have liked.

As a young boy he had gone fishing a great deal with his father. They were some of the happiest memories of his childhood. Now, however, he had to be near his office every day that the New York Stock Exchange was in session. Even a short vacation would cause him to lose the edge of understanding that he had worked so hard to develop in relation to the markets. He had tried taking two-week fishing vacations and had found that it took a full week for his mind to unwind from the world of changing stock quotations and prices. During the second week he began to obsess about what he might have missed while he had been away. The vacations were hardly satisfactory, and yet he saw no way out of the dilemma he'd created for himself.

He told us that when he left home on the morning of what was to be his last day of work, nothing felt different or out of the ordinary to him. It was just another day at the office, no different from any other day that had ever been. He had evidently been looking forward to going to work that day. He was eager to finish working on some transactions that he'd been assembling, which were now almost complete. A recent storm had left the city air feeling fresh and clear, and he felt quite good physically.

He sat down at the desk in his office. It was still early, and only a few people had arrived. He enjoyed this early quiet time before the markets opened and the energy in his office would begin to become ever more frantic. With few distractions he was able to pour his attention over the papers that awaited his completion when suddenly, as he would tell us, he began to experience very unusual sensations in his body.

First his legs began to tingle, and then the tingling slowly rose into his upper body. As he became increasingly aware of these sensations, his body began to experience rapid alterations in temperature. He would feel flushed one moment only to feel cold chills the next. He wondered if he was suddenly coming down with a flu, or even having a heart attack. He became panicky for a moment, and yet he knew he wasn't ill. He described the feeling as being inside, of all things, a fishbowl. Sounds appeared blurred, as though he were hearing them from a great distance. His mind began racing faster and faster, attempting to decipher what was happening to him, and then, just as suddenly, it shut itself off. He felt as if he couldn't move and couldn't think.

The stock market opened in New York. He sat at his desk impassively watching the quotations pass in front of him, as though he were just a spectator in someone else's life. He still couldn't move and was unable to respond to anything he saw. Nor did he want to. The numbers on the screen would ordinarily elicit his undivided attention, but now they just seemed to be laughing at him, and he began inwardly to smile back at them. Life is a game however you play it. Just find the one that works for you. And with this thought he knew exactly what he had to do.

Within a few minutes the unusual sensations subsided. He told us that he watched himself with a good deal of fascination, not quite believing what he was doing, but knowing with a certainty that he had never felt before that he was doing exactly the right thing. He called his secretary on the intercom and asked her to go the storeroom and get a number of large cardboard boxes and then to come into his office and pack all his belongings. He asked to have them sent to his home. He stood up from his desk and walked out of his office never to walk back in again.

On his drive back home that morning he saw clearly what the next step in his life was to be. He was going to sell his house, pack up his family, and move to the Florida Keys. He would buy a boat with his savings, become a charter skipper, and take people fishing. All he wanted to do was to take people out onto the open ocean and help them to have the experience of catching big fish.

⟜

I liked Dick Karalis enormously from the moment I met him, and he genuinely seemed to like our family as well. He was heavily tanned with dark hair and eyes and had to shave all the way down the front of his neck to where the thick hair on his chest began. He seemed to my young eyes to exude health and well-being. He was obviously a very contented man.

The next afternoon we went down to the docks to greet the fishing boats as they returned from their day's outing. The boats would tie up at the dock, and then the first mate would remove the fish that had been caught that day from the holding box at the stern of the boat. The fish were then hung on a display scaffolding for everyone to see. The only people who were in Marathon were people dedicated to the sport of fishing, and so each afternoon an interested and animated crowd would gather around the docks to appreciate what their fellow fishermen had been able to catch and commiserate with those who had had a disappointing outing. The group of fishermen fraternized easily in the company of their peers. Their appreciations and commiserations were vocal and heartfelt.

I made my way through the crowd to get a closer look at the fish that were being transferred to the dock: mostly tuna, barracuda, and a beautiful, iridescent fish with a blunt nose that in later years I would discover to be the mahi-mahi that is served in Hawaiian restaurants, some as long as four feet. Although they were the largest fish that I had ever seen, I was disappointed not to see my first sailfish. I'd hoped that some might have been caught, but no one seemed to have had any luck that day. Occasionally I would overhear a snippet of conversation concerning the sailfish. The conversations seemed unusually subdued.

"None, didn't see a one. . . ."

"We spent almost the whole day in the deep water. . . ."

"They just don't seem to be around."

Twenty boats had gone out that day, and not a one had even seen a sailfish. *I want to catch a sailfish. I want to catch a sailfish.* My father introduced us to Dick Karalis, and he greeted each of us warmly. He encouraged my brother and I to get to sleep that night as early as possible. My father told him once again that our dream would be to catch a sailfish, and he began to beam broadly. Too many people, he said, had been coming lately to Marathon to fish with no such ambitions. Instead, they preferred to stay in the shallower waters all day, where you could easily catch large numbers of tuna and barracuda. Although such a day, just as the bumper sticker suggests, was still preferable to a day at the stockbroker's office, one quickly got the sense that it was the larger game of going after the big fish that had truly motivated Dick Karalis to leave the relative security of his life in Hartford. Staying in shallow water reeling in small fish was the saltwater equivalent of pulling trout out of a stocked pond in Wyoming—no great challenge there. He spoke with us frankly, though, and said that catching the big fish was an uncertain proposition. No one had seen them around for the better part of a week, and yet he was certain they were still there. He told us he knew we would have a good day.

We walked back up to the lodge to have an early dinner. In the bar before going in to dinner, we met a single man who had come down from New Jersey for a week of fishing. I remember him having quite short hair and the most deeply etched facial lines I had ever seen. They ran across his forehead in deep gullies, and between his outer nostrils and the sides of his mouth as well. My father told our new friend that we had come down from Minnesota with the express purpose of going out and catching a sailfish. Our new friend laughed quietly and politely. A grin that in later years I would come to understand could only be described as patronizing caused the lines at the front of his cheeks to become even more pronounced. Evidently, within the fishing fraternity, the desire to catch a sailfish was not something about which you openly spoke. He told us that not everyone who wants to catch a sailfish is able to do so and that, in fact, he had been coming down to Marathon for eight years, fishing every day for a week each visit, and had still not caught his first sailfish. Undaunted, my father continued to express his enthusiasm for our prospects of the morrow. Inwardly, something inside me felt stung by the words of this experienced fisherman. All the articles that I had read about people *not* catching a sailfish began to flash up on the screen of my mind. I checked inside to see how my companion thought was doing with the information of this afternoon and evening. Much to my relief, it continued as before. I got very little sleep that night.

I awoke quite early the next morning to a beautiful, cloudless sky without even the hint of a breeze. It was going to be a very hot day. Back home in Minnesota, the very best fishing always occurred right before a storm relieved the barometric tension that had been building in the atmosphere. I wondered if the same was true here in Florida. If so, it was not a good sign. Not only were there no storm clouds building anywhere, there was not even a tiny trace of white in the unbroken expanse of deep blue that stained the sky from horizon to horizon.

I felt groggy when I first awoke, but I forced myself out of bed, only partially awake, and stumbled clumsily to the bathroom. My parents and brother laughed at my apparent lack of coordination on my ten-step journey from the bed to the toilet. I realized that it must have looked quite funny and joined in the joke. We were all in good spirits. I put on loose-fitting khaki trousers, a beige short-sleeved shirt, and sneakers. The day I had been waiting for had begun.

I had little appetite for breakfast, and just as I was getting up from the table, I had the most discomforting realization. My companion thought was gone! I kept looking inside, probing dark corners and turning over inner stones, and yet it was nowhere to be found. It was simply gone, as though it had never existed or had passed away quietly during the night, and its body had been removed by morning. I remember feeling a moment of panic, certain that its desertion at this particular moment was an omen that today was not going to be the day that I would catch a sailfish. I tried to argue against this conclusion with thoughts that, its preparation completed, perhaps it felt as if it had done its job, and now I needed to deliver on its promise and hope. I began consciously intoning the phrase to myself, but it sounded flat and artificial. Uncomprehending and somewhat dazed, I followed my parents and brother down to the docks.

Dick and his first mate were busy with preparations when we arrived, but they both took time to greet us. Dick was excited. It was perfect weather evidently for deep-sea fishing. When I asked him about the relationship between fishing and storms, he smiled and replied that in Florida, if there's even a hint of a storm, you don't go out. Too dangerous for one thing, and besides, he'd never experienced that bad weather improved the chances of catching a large fish. He asked my brother and me if we had gotten a good night's sleep. We both smiled, and I nodded my head and lied.

Dick's mate was almost his complete physical opposite. Where Dick was short, broad in body, and dark in complexion, the first mate was tall and slender, very blond, with pronounced aquiline features. The contrast between them made each appear all the more striking. They were both very handsome men. I remember thinking that they looked like the lords of night and day, leading their respective armies against the infidel during one of the Crusades. Misguided as those campaigns may have been, I recalled that the fish was a symbol of the cause for which those campaigns had been launched.

At eight o'clock Dick started the engines of the boat, and we moved away from the dock. The boat was named the *Ballyhoo* after the small fish that would be the primary bait we would use that day. It had only a small cabin. The majority of its length was taken up by a spacious rear deck on which were bolted two large, padded chairs that looked like they belonged in a barbershop.

Dick explained that it would take us about an hour to get out to the fishing grounds. We had left from the north side of Marathon, would make our way west for a few miles, and then cross under a bridge out into the open southern waters. The day would end at three o'clock, when we would have to retrace our route back to the docks. Dick explained that it simply wasn't safe to stay out on the open ocean past that time. Even so, we would have six solid hours of fishing, and he assured us once again that we would have a good day.

The movement of the boat through the still morning air cooled me in the hot sun. As I sat back, I kept looking inside, searching for my companion thought. It wasn't there. As we slowly continued to move across the water, I let my upset go. I was on a fishing boat heading out onto the deep ocean. I was enjoying myself. I was happy.

Passing under the bridge that linked the west tip of Marathon with the next key in the chain, we moved out into what Dick kept referring to as "the shallow waters." We could barely see the shore of Marathon from the shallow waters, and I began to wonder what "the deep waters" must be like. *Go deep. Go deep inside. Catch your fish.* I began to think for a moment that I had heard my voice again, but was immediately drawn to Dick's voice instead. He began explaining how the rods and reels and seats worked. Two people could fish at a time, so we would have to take turns. We would be strapped into our seats as a precaution in case we hooked a truly enormous fish. We would hold the largest rod and reel that I had ever seen. Its butt end would fit securely in the metal cup at the front of the seat. As a further precaution against having the rod and reel pulled from our hands, the rod would be fastened to the harness that kept us secured in our seats. The first mate would hook a small fish, a ballyhoo, to a large hook on the end of our fishing line. He would let out a few hundred feet of line and then attach the line to an outrigger on the side of the boat. The outriggers were long, flexible poles, whose ends extended far out past the sides of the boat and onto which something resembling a clothesline on a pulley had been attached. Our fishing line would be attached to a clip on the clothesline. By pulling on the clothesline, our fishing line could then be elevated and extended far above and to the side of the boat. In this way our bait would appear to swim on its own outside the wake that the boat was making.

Dick would steer the boat from an elevated deck. From this vantage point he could watch the bait skip across the surface of the water, as the boat moved at the same speed that a ballyhoo might swim. Wearing strongly polarized sunglasses, he could often see a fish take the bait. When that happened, the fishing line would break free from the clothespin, and he would call out loudly, "Right outrigger, reel!" This would be a signal to the person in the right chair to pull back strongly on the rod to set the hook and then to begin reeling in the fish. Dick suggested that we stay in the shallow waters for at least an hour so that we could accustom ourselves to the equipment and the feeling of reeling in an ocean fish. Once we had all learned the procedure, we could head out into the deep water to see if there were any sailfish around.

"Left outrigger, reel!"

"Right outrigger, reel!"

Back home in Minnesota, as I attempted to coax the small sunfish to my bait, I had had to learn the virtue of patience. Indeed, the cultivation of patience is often cited as one of the most salutary benefits to be gained through the sport of fishing, the justification for doing something that one loved in a world that often looks for philosophical justifications for nonutilitarian acts. Through the action of fishing, we learn to nurture and perfect this valuable, yet so often elusive, human quality. The sunfish would nibble, poke at, and toy with the bait, but would rarely bite into it firmly enough to allow me to set the hook and reel the fish in. I had to be patient if I wanted to catch them. Strapped into the chair on the fishing boat, I was unprepared for how quickly the fish took both the baits. I jerked my rod back and began turning the handle on the reel as quickly as I could. I had to use all my strength simply to hold onto the rod and not have it pulled from my hands. I had hooked a big fish, a very big fish, and I suddenly felt a surge of energy and emotion explode through my body with the recognition that I had not been fishing for more than a minute or two, and I had hooked my sailfish! I could barely hold onto the rod, as it pulled against my arms, and only very slowly was I able to reel the fish closer to the boat. I could feel my arms beginning to shake, and my chest and back began to hurt. But I'd caught my fish, and I wasn't going to let it go. I kept reeling and pulling on the rod. I could feel how the fish was wanting to take the rod from me, but I wasn't going to give in to that wish. I had caught my fish, the one I'd been calling for the past three months. It had heard my call. It had come, and I would reel it in.

Several minutes later the first mate pulled the fish into the boat. I was shocked to see that it wasn't a sailfish. It was a tuna, perhaps two feet long, weighing no more than ten or fifteen pounds! I couldn't believe it. It wasn't a large fish at all. The effort I'd had to expend to reel it in belied its size, and suddenly I felt frightened about the prospect of actually catching the fish that I'd been invoking these past three months. Maybe I really didn't want to catch a sailfish. Maybe I had no idea what I was actually getting myself into.

Another ballyhoo was attached to the hook, and the line was let out and hoisted to the outrigger again. Within ten minutes I had been called to begin reeling again. The next fish was even bigger than the first had been. It took much longer to reel in and caused my arms to shake and my chest and back to ache even more than had the first fish. I was relieved to see that it was a slightly larger fish, a barracuda this time, almost three feet in length and weighing fifteen pounds. Still, it was nothing even close to the size of a sailfish. What foolishness had brought me here, had given me the idea that I wanted to catch a sailfish? I was more than happy to stand up from the chair and give my mother a turn.

~

The shallow waters were home this time of year to large schools of tuna and the barracuda that scavenged off them. Indeed, as I looked out over the waters on either side of our boat, I could see ten or fifteen commercial boats moving among the sport-fishing boats. The commercial boats would drag long nets through the water and bring in large quantities of tuna (and anything else that was unfortunate enough to have joined the concentrated schools of tuna). Some sport-fishing boats would stay in these waters all day, as you were virtually guaranteed to reel in fish after fish with very little patient waiting in between. Dick explained, however, that if we were to stay in the shallow waters, there would be no chance at all of catching a sailfish. They simply didn't come in this close, preferring instead the open, deep, and uncrowded waters. They were solitary animals. Rarely did they move in anything resembling a school. If you wanted them, you had to go and find them. They would not come to you.

Later in the morning, after all of us had caught a number of tuna and barracuda, we made the decision to head out to the deep waters. I had hooked and reeled in several more fish by then and no longer felt so daunted by this new form of fishing that at first had represented such an exponential leap from the worms, feathered hooks, and cork poppers of my backyard.

As we headed further and further away from the shores of Marathon, I once again took my seat. I looked out over the water and watched intently as my ballyhoo skipped across the surface, sending small sprays of water into the air as it moved. We kept moving further and further away from shore. The ocean swells became larger, and the boat rocked and swayed, as it rode up and down the sides of the swells.

The boat moved more slowly now, and both Dick and the first mate gazed out behind us, watching for signs of a large fish, anticipating a first strike. Oftentimes a sailfish will swim up to the ballyhoo and play with it, just as the sunfish in my backyard would toy with the worm on the hook. Once you have spotted a sailfish, you can slow the boat down and let the line out a bit more so that the bait stays right with the sailfish. Everyone on the boat kept gazing at the ballyhoo.

Slowly and patiently Dick steered the boat back and forth across the deep waters. Every mile or so he would turn the boat around and make another pass back across the area over which we'd just come. Back and forth we moved. Back and forth. I experienced a feeling of emptiness and isolation this far out into the ocean. When we had been in the shallower waters, there had been a great deal of activity: scores of sports and commercial boats weaving in and out of one another's path, the wakes from all the boats slapping into one another, churning the water's surface, flocks of seagulls hovering over the major concentrations of the schools of tuna, like lookouts directing the fishing boats to their goal, the deep growl from the diesel engines, and the cries that carried across the water of "Left outrigger, reel!" Out in the deep water, we were alone. The boat was moving more slowly, and you could hardly hear the engine. There was little to talk about, and no birds ventured out this far from shore.

Every half an hour Dick would turn the boat around, and we would make another pass across the expanse of ocean over which we'd just traveled. The boat turned and turned many times. I took a break from the inactivity of the fishing and ate the sandwich and hard-boiled egg that filled the box lunch that had been provided. While my brother and father took turns in the seat on the left, I was sharing the right seat with my mother. She was happy to participate in this adventure, but was also just as happy to let me do most of the fishing. Everybody knew that I was the devoted fisherman in the family and recognized that it would mean a great deal for me to catch a large fish. No one, of course, knew just how devoted I had become to that idea, however. During family discussions that fall, we had all talked about the prospect of catching a sailfish and agreed that we would be like a mountain-climbing team, helping and supporting one another the entire way. If any one of us were fortunate enough to get to the summit, the trip would have been a success for all of us.

At one thirty Dick came down from the upper steering bridge, shook his head sympathetically, and told us that he was sorry, but there just didn't seem to be any fish out in the deep water today. The mood on the boat had become quite somber over the past hour, and he suggested that we move back into the shallower water and have the enjoyment of catching some of the many fish that were to be found there. We all knew it was the right decision, but as he turned the boat back toward shore, I felt my dream begin to sink in the deep waters that we were leaving. My thought had abandoned me on the most important day of its life. It had been a sign. Today was not to be the day. I wouldn't let anybody see the extent of my disappointment, though. It had been a good day all the same. Remember what the gentleman in the bar had said last evening, that he had been coming down for several years, fishing for a week at a time, and he was yet to hook his first sailfish. Remember all the magazine articles that described the author's *unsuccessful* attempts at catching a sailfish. I began to rearrange the story of my life. I was not to be a young boy who had caught a sailfish. It was nothing to be ashamed of. I pretended that I didn't care. I smiled and laughed with my family. And, yet, underneath the smile was a deflated feeling of resignation. My dream hadn't flown.

As we neared the shallower water, we once again began catching fish. Two of the blunt-nosed, iridescent fish hit each of the lines at exactly the same moment, leaping six feet into the air as they did so. It was a beautiful sight. They jumped twice more, clear out of the water, the iridescence of their bodies shining turquoise and purple in the afternoon sun. These magnificent creatures lost their color very rapidly as soon as they were pulled from the water, and I began to feel some remorse at having robbed them of their life and their beauty. Maybe this was my lesson for the day. Maybe fish are supposed to live out the entire course of their lives in the ocean and not have their watery destinies be interrupted for the sake of a human's sport. Still, we caught more fish. We all felt revived after the somber, slow passage of midday. We were enjoying ourselves again. It had been a good day.

At a quarter to three, my father suggested to Dick that perhaps we could take one last pass out in the deep waters before returning back to Marathon. Dick agreed that it was worth a try and turned the boat back around, and once again we moved away from the crowded shallow waters. Dick said that we would have just enough time to make one large loop and could fish all the way back to the bridge that would lead us back to the northern side of the island. By then I'd made my peace with the fact that my wish hadn't been answered. Something had happened to me when I saw the beautiful iridescent color fade out of the snub-nosed fish, and I wasn't sure that I would have wanted to catch a sailfish anyway. I stayed sitting in my seat more because I was too tired to get up than because I was interested in catching any more fish.

Dick steered the boat slowly over the large arc that led back to the bridge. The fishing was much the same as it had been earlier in the day. We watched the ballyhoo skip across the surface of the water, but it couldn't attract a single fish. The ballyhoo began to look forlorn and foolish, a wallflower at its own dance. I remember wishing that we hadn't made this last pass. As we neared the bridge, the waterways became congested. Sport- and commercial fishing boats began to line up, waiting their turn to pass under the bridge. Large flocks of seagulls clamored loudly above it all, attracted now to the fish in the holding boxes of the boats.

We were within a few hundred yards now of entering into the crowded lanes in front of the bridge, and I expected Dick to tell us to begin reeling in our lines. Instead, he turned the boat around and headed back out to the open waters. At first I thought he was simply avoiding the traffic jam. I looked over at the first mate. For a moment he too appeared perplexed, but didn't say anything. No one on the boat spoke. We stayed in our harnesses, our rods fixed in our hands. We were going fishing again. I fixed my attention on my bait, as it skipped across the surface of the water.

Whatever sense of hope may have been rekindled through Dick's unexpected decision to return to the deep water was quickly dispelled over the next half hour, as the fishing was no different than it had been all day. There was still no sign of any fish anywhere. The advancing afternoon transformed the open ocean. The sun cast a light that was far less glaring and bright than it had been just a few hours earlier, and the heat of the day finally began to abate. The large swells of midday had now subsided as well. As the light continued to soften and the water settle, birds began to appear. They would call out to each other and come to rest on the now-less-turbulent surface of the water. It was all very beautiful. And still there were no fish.

After a half hour Dick turned the boat again, and we headed back toward the bridge. Birds followed the boat now, calling down to us, asking for a small sample of our catch. The air was almost cool now. To experience the ocean at this time of day felt like a special treat. Dick had given us a gift by taking us on this last, final loop.

As we neared the bridge, I looked and saw that rush hour was over. In fact, there were no other boats anywhere in sight. It was now almost four o'clock. We were out on the beautiful ocean alone. It had been a great day.

And then quite suddenly, and again without a word, Dick turned the boat around and headed back out to the deeper water. His earlier decision to return to the deep water had made sense in light of the option of queuing up to wait our turn to pass under the bridge. Now, though, there was nothing to hold us back. I felt confused, and Dick clearly did not want to speak to us. I looked up at the first mate, and he calmly told me to just keep watching my bait.

Traces of high cloud began to appear. The birds appeared delighted that the heat of the day had passed. They were flying, playing, dipping down abruptly onto the ocean surface, calling out raucously. We all watched the ballyhoo as they bounded across the water. Their floppy movements didn't look particularly convincing to me. Would a large fish actually be fooled into thinking that this was a serendipitous snack?

And still nothing changed. We were going for a beautiful boat ride, nothing more. After another half hour had passed, Dick abruptly changed the course of the boat. I expected that he would turn back, but instead he headed out even further away from land. I looked all around me, and all I could see was water. The drone of the engine was soothing. The intense heat from the sun that had toasted my body during that long day left me feeling happily tired.

The sailfish hit my line at half past four. It came from nowhere. We never saw it saunter up to the ballyhoo and toy with it like a cat playing with a mouse. Instead, it must have come at the bait from below at a tremendous speed, taking it fully in its mouth, the momentum from its run carrying the whole six feet of its length entirely out of the water. Dick screamed at me to set the hook, and I pulled back on the rod that I felt being pulled from my hands with all the strength I had. I could feel that the hook had settled deep in the fish's mouth and that it was secure. A sound came out of my throat that I'd never heard before. It was a cry of sheer bewilderment. We were all shouting. The first mate hurriedly took my brother's rod and reeled in the line, lest the fish become entangled.

The fish began a series of runs with my line that I had no way of stopping. It began jumping completely clear of the water, scuttering across the surface on its tail. I could see its long beak and the full length of its body. However, its huge dorsal fin that could extend to form the shape of a sail, and from which it gets its name, was folded in on itself, giving it more the appearance of the mane of a fast-moving horse. Still, it was the most magnificent animal I had ever seen. Again and again it jumped, as though it were walking on the water, its head jerking back and forth in panic, trying to eject the pain from its mouth. Dick called to me to begin reeling the line in between jumps, but it was all I could do simply to hold the rod in my hands. The fish began running away from the boat, darting from one side to the next, jumping in alarm, taking line from my reel that I had no chance of taking back.

The rod was pulling me far forward over the front of my seat. I had caught my fish. I knew I wouldn't let go for anything, but I also realized that I couldn't reel any line in either. Just holding on to the rod, letting the fish strip line away at will, was more demanding than anything I'd ever been asked to do in my life. I had never pulled against anything like this before. I had never been asked to find this much strength. I had never been challenged in this way. As I kept pulling against the fish, my arms became rubbery. It was too much. I couldn't hold on. The fish was too strong. After ten minutes of struggling simply not to let go of the rod, I started to cry.

My father looked up at Dick and called out to him, "Dick, we've got to help him!" I will never forget Dick's response. Very calmly and slowly he answered back, "No. He caught the fish. Either he lands the fish, or the fish goes free."

The tone of his words settled me. My tears stopped. I became more focused. I pulled on the rod now in answer to the fish, showing it that I too had strength. By now the sailfish had taken almost a thousand feet of my line. Its jumps were less frequent, its runs from side to side less forceful. It too was beginning to tire, and as it was forced to rest, I began to gain back some of the line that it had taken. Every revolution of the reel handle felt like the most physically demanding task I had ever performed. With every turn of the handle I let out an involuntary grunt like a martial artist attempting to split a board with his hand. It was still all that I could do to keep holding the rod.

The fish was now swimming, and sometimes resting and lying, close to the surface. It was tiring. It could jump no more, but it could still find spurts of strength and pull more line away from me at will. When it rested, however, I was able to gain some of it back. It was so far away now that we could scarcely see it. It was resting at the surface of the water. Suddenly the first mate cried out in alarm, "Dick, is that a shark out by the fish?! Can you see?"

We all looked out and could see a small fin cutting through the surface of the water in the vicinity of the fish. But the fish was so far away, we couldn't determine for certain what it was. It was impossible to tell if it was a shark coming to scavenge the distressed sailfish, or if the fish was lying on its side or back and one of its smaller fins was sticking up in the air. One moment we all thought it was a shark. Then we thought it must be the fish itself. A moment later it once again looked like a shark circling in the distance. All I knew was that I hadn't come this far to have a shark take the fish I'd been given. I was filled with rage toward the shark and began reeling in line with a newfound strength and fury. I had been fighting the fish now for thirty minutes.

Slowly, foot by foot, the line came back onto my reel. The fish still had reserves of energy that let it make forceful runs away from the boat, but they were much less frequent now. I kept retrieving line. We still didn't know if a shark had gotten the fish, but began to think that perhaps that hadn't happened, as the fish was still able to fight against the force that was pulling at it. I kept reeling. Ten minutes of reeling.

Twenty minutes. More line came in, and then more line still, and suddenly we could see the fish. He was getting closer and closer to the boat. I saw him swimming no more than fifty feet away. He was much bigger than I'd imagined. The extension on his upper jaw that formed the pointed sword so characteristic of this kind of fish was much longer than I'd thought it would be. He was still capable of darting suddenly away and taking line with him. But it was easier for me to take it back now. At one point I thought I saw him looking over at the boat, straining to see who was in it, as though he knew exactly what was happening. He made another strong run and took fifty more feet of line with him. There had been no shark. His body was fully intact and magnificent. I kept bringing him closer and closer to the boat. His movements by now were slow and sluggish.

The first mate put on a pair of heavy gloves and positioned himself at the stern of the boat. Dick began maneuvering the boat to bring the fish over to where the first mate was standing. The fish was now just a few feet from the boat. He was exhausted. The first mate took the fishing line in one hand and told me to keep reeling very slowly. He reached down with his other hand and grabbed hold of the beak of the fish. In one fluid, strong, and very quick movement he clutched the upper body of the fish with his other hand and pulled the fish over the rear railing of the boat and down onto the deck. As the fish lay dazed on the deck, an intense spasm rippled through the muscles of its body. It jerked itself violently in one last explosive bid for freedom and life, and then it relaxed and, I believe, looked directly over at me. Our eyes met. For the briefest moment something seemed to pass back and forth between us, and then it was over. I broke down and started sobbing.

I have no memory of the next few minutes. My father told me later that I was crying and calling out as though I'd entered into another world. When I became once again conscious of what was happening, I was panting through my tears and clutching my mother, my father, and my brother. It took several more minutes for my crying to stop and for the gasping of my breath to calm itself.

I collapsed back down onto the chair, completely spent. I became aware of my body for the first time in an hour. It was a mass of exhilarated ache. I could hardly move or speak. The first mate had gone down into the cabin and emerged back up with sodas for everyone. We all sat and drank our sodas in silence.

We all looked around at each other and at the fish. In the light of the late afternoon it lay glowing on the deck. We went over to look at the fish. It was magnificent, the most beautiful animal I had ever seen. We stood and gazed at the fish in silence.

The silence was abruptly broken by the sound of the boat's radio. Dick ran to get the call. It was now almost five thirty, and we were more than two hours late returning back to the docks. Over the last hour the marina had been trying to phone us to find out why we hadn't returned. Shortly after we'd hooked the fish, Dick had turned the radio down, so that we wouldn't be distracted. Unable to contact us by radio and fearing that something had gone badly wrong, the marina was just about to dispatch a number of boats to look for us, when Dick answered the call. He thanked the people on shore for their concern and assured them that we were fine and would return to the docks in a little over an hour, flying the flag that indicated that a sailfish had been caught.

The first mate drove the boat back to Marathon. Dick sat in the back of the boat with us. We were all laughing and feeling almost giddy by then. At one point Dick abruptly rose from his chair, came over to me, and extended his hand. I took it in mine, marveling at the strength of grip of this man I had so come to admire.

"Congratulations, young man," he said. "A boy couldn't have landed that fish."

We talked about our family and our good fortune of the day and about luck in general. I had always been considered to be the lucky one in the family, the one who won raffles and found money on sidewalks. With a sense of good-natured resignation, my brother proclaimed, "It looks like luckbox did it again." In truth, though, I recalled that it had been him and not me who had won at bingo at the school fair. The fishing rod that I brought home with me from the fair that day had been the result of his generosity, when we went up together to choose our prize. He knew that I wanted it and had always looked after me with the kind of protective love that an older brother often feels for a younger sibling. Later in life, when he was able to create a remarkable international business with offices in more than a dozen cities world-wide, while I floundered, often aimlessly, in my attempts to discover where I could most profitably commit my energy and enthusiasm, there would be cause to reassess whether the family assignation "luckbox" truly belonged on his shoulders, not on mine.

The shallower waters into which we moved and the bridge under which we passed all seemed strangely familiar in the late light of the day. As we made our way along the north shore of Marathon, I rested in my chair. Too exhausted to be truly excited, I did look forward to getting back to the docks. I anticipated that they would be crowded. Word had been radioed that our boat had caught a sailfish. Evidently no one else had caught one that day, and this was the first sailfish that had been taken in more than a week. I felt that the whole fishing fraternity of Marathon would be waiting for us.

As we motored slowly into the marina past the rock safety wall, I saw that I was right. Thirty or forty people were milling about at the end of the dock awaiting our return. They crowded around our boat, tossing out questions before the engines had even been turned off.

"How big a fish?"

"Where did you have to go to find it?"

"Who caught it?"

Dick put his arm around my shoulder and informed a person standing close to the docked boat that it had been me. I was aware of a chain of conversation passing through the crowd like a trick billiard shot in which one ball strikes another, which, in turn, strikes another, until all the balls on the table are in motion.

"The little boy?"

"I'm telling you that's what he said."

The mood in the crowd was at once congratulatory and a bit incredulous. A few individuals came up to me to offer their personal congratulations. We hoisted the fish we had caught onto the display scaffolding and brought the sailfish out last for everyone to admire. In photographs that I still have of that moment, I look too tired to be proud, and indeed I slept well into the next morning, and felt achy and exhausted all through the next day.

As the crowd began to thin, I happened to look up at the elevated lawn just below the fishing lodge. People were walking back to the lodge slowly, returning to their dinners. The sun had now dropped beneath the water. My eyes landed on one solitary figure who had not come down to the docks to greet our boat. His stiff and unmoving body was silhouetted against the softening colors of the evening sky. He stood there staring far out into the ocean. He looked stunned. It was our friend from the evening before, the gentleman in the bar with the deeply lined face who had been coming down to Marathon for so many years, but who had still not caught his first sailfish.

Was my brother right? Had it simply been a matter of luck? Or had the determination of my wish, expressed through the constant repetition of my companion thought, called that fish to me? And why had Dick Karalis stayed out on the water so long that day? We asked him about that on the ride back to the dock, and he replied that he couldn't really explain it himself. He said that he'd had a feeling about our family when he first met us, that somehow he felt that we were supposed to catch a large fish. He'd had that same feeling again at three o'clock, as we were about to join the line of boats waiting their turn to pass under the bridge. He said that since his experience on his last day of work in Hartford, he'd learned to honor these kinds of intuitions, as crazy or even unwarranted as they might turn out to be. He shrugged his shoulders and confided quietly that he'd never stayed out so long on the water before. He didn't understand what had motivated him to make that final pass back out into the deep water or what reflex had influenced him so suddenly to turn the boat out into the even deeper water. It was more of a hunch, he said. It wasn't anything that he'd seen. Sometimes he felt that the fish were calling to him.

There are now studies that demonstrate that a patient who prays and is prayed for by his or her family and friends has a better chance for a speedy recovery from a serious illness or surgery. Over the years I have often returned in my mind to the events of those months. What happened to me goes by many names that all amount to the same thing: prayer, mantric repetition, affirmations. Whatever it's called, the formula and explanation for the power of these kinds of practices are identical. By fixing the mind on a single thought or vibratory sound, we encourage that thought or quality of sound to manifest as a physical event. Somehow we set up the conditions that allow and attract that thought to become real. I have never, either before or since the events of that fall and Christmas season, been conventionally religious in the sense that I regularly engage in the activity of prayer. For one moment in my life, however, the power of prayer was incontrovertibly demonstrated to me.

I have also spent much time thinking about the stunned gentleman from New Jersey, the seasoned fishing veteran who was forced to watch a young boy, on his very first day of deep-sea fishing, accomplish what he himself had been unable to achieve in eight years. I would think about the aura and tone of pessimism that surrounded this man and colored his speech. What part was cause, and what was effect? Had the pessimism entered this man's life because of his inability over all these long years to catch a sailfish? It's reasonable to conclude that this could be so. Or had the pessimism over the prospects of catching a sailfish been with him from the beginning? Had it even preceded the first moment he ever stepped aboard a deep-sea fishing boat? Perhaps his companion thought had been more along the lines of *I don't think I can catch a sailfish. The chances aren't good. It's so unlikely.* If this were so, then these words too, if repeated often enough and taken deeply enough into the heart, would function as a form of prayer. The effect of such a prayer, however, would be defeat, not victory.

My tears and hysteria on the fishing boat were the effect, I assume, of simple physiology. Once the fish was in the boat, my body could finally relax, and the endorphins that had been stimulated through the intense physical effort could then release themselves and explode through my body. Even top athletes in Olympic games have been known to experience similar, intensely emotional responses to successful efforts, in which they pushed themselves beyond anything that they had formerly believed to be possible.

Something had also happened to me, however, when the fish was brought into the boat and gave up its life. It looked at me just before it let its life go. It wasn't a look of anger or hatred. It was more a look of curiosity, as though it needed to see and know who its partner in this last chapter of its life had been. Our gaze met at that moment, and something passed between us. As strange as this may sound, I felt at that moment that the fish loved me, and I know that I very much loved the fish. That love between two beings should end in the death of one of the participants horrified me at that moment, and it continues to horrify me to this day.

True hunters and fishermen are supposed to keep moving on to ever new challenges in their sport. It wasn't that way for me. Something had started happening to me when I saw the color fade from the gorgeous body of the iridescent, snub-nosed fish. Whatever had begun at that moment was completed when I then viewed the life force depart from the body of the sailfish, clearly the most magnificent being I had ever had the privilege to know and interact with. Whatever the explanation, my passion for fishing began to leave my life. When we returned home from our vacation, I turned my attention back to my schoolwork and became interested in other childhood hobbies. I didn't tie fishing flies that winter in anticipation of using them in the summer. I fished some that year, but it was halfhearted. Within a year or two, I didn't fish anymore at all.

Prayers are powerful forces. Like a floating iceberg, whose tip is visible but whose greater bulk lies hidden from our sight, they possess many hidden levels of influence when invoked. Perhaps, when they're answered, they give us much more than the specific request we may have asked for. Perhaps they even demand something of us in return. On that day on the fishing boat I was given a direct experience of the ties that bind us together, humans and animals alike, into an inseparable unity that we all participate in. Individually, we act out different roles in our passage through life. Some of these roles are happy ones, others not. But underneath all the roles is the inseparable unity that, by whatever name you call it, is the agent to whom all prayers are addressed. Listen, children of God, the world is of one piece.

Part II
Journey to Kailas

Water and Elephants

YEARS PASS. DREAMS LOSE THEIR WAY. Like clouds that form and dissolve, they sometimes come to fruition in the life-giving rain of their promise. Just as often, they simply evaporate into the sky, leaving no trace of their existence. New dreams form only to be forgotten again.

A young boy returned from Florida and, through his experience there, never quite felt like a young boy again. Over the passing years, however, the promise alluded to in his transformation began to collide with the realities of his life. Successes were followed by failures, occupations were begun and let go of, relationships were entered into and dissolved. A child was born, and old dreams were rekindled. And then another child. Two children and two parents: the world in the middle felt comfortably secure and stable. Even so, I knew that within the cocoon of that relative comfort, I was denying some of my strongest yearnings and holding back on some of my deepest wishes. And then my father died, and things began to come undone.

Denial may work well enough in life, but it comes up miserably short in the face of death. In my case I felt its hold on me begin to come apart, just as my father's body began slowly to disintegrate before my eyes, during those last painful months leading up to his passing. It's hard to maintain the feigned dignity of a lie in the face of the certain knowledge of the finite nature of our lives. As I watched my father's strength slowly leave his body once and for all, I too began to experience the strength of my denial slipping away, like a pulse that gradually loses its vitality until you simply can't feel it anymore.

My father died in April, barely two months before my son's thirteenth birthday. For many years I had not thought seriously about my dream of taking my son to the mountain after which he was named as a rite of passage into adulthood, and suddenly I couldn't keep the thought out of my mind. It was not so intense and persistent in its recurrence as had been the thought of my youth to catch a sailfish. And yet it was there. Time was running out on my dream. If I wanted to do this with my son, we needed to do it now. If we waited, we would miss the moment.

When I had first planted the seeds for this dream so many years earlier, the possibility of its ever coming true seemed exceedingly remote. In 1981, when my son was born, China was not allowing any Westerners to visit Tibet. Permission to travel into that country had only been reestablished a few years before my son's thirteenth birthday. The first trickle of Westerners had once again begun visiting what was left of the sacred sites of Tibet after the Chinese invasion and systematic destruction of the shrines of worship and the people who worshiped there. I remember having seen an article in a *Smithsonian* magazine a few years earlier about Mount Kailas and was thrilled to realize that Westerners were once again being allowed to travel to the sacred mountain, but the dream of my son and I going to the mountain ourselves did not at that time strike me as particularly realistic.

Dreams aside, I knew that a trip of this nature would be very costly, and I was just barely able to cover mortgage payments, taxes and insurance, clothes for my family, food, the occasional meal at an interesting restaurant, toys, and outings. There was no way that I could pay for a trip to Tibet.

But then my father died. Although he left the entirety of his modest estate to my mother, I was unexpectedly named as the beneficiary of two small insurance policies that he had taken out on his life. I could scarcely believe it. The money I inherited was enough to buy a small car. We could also pay down the mortgage on our home and substantially reduce our monthly payments. Over the years, however, my wife and I had discussed my dream of taking Kai to Tibet, and finally she put to rest any notions of using the money in a "practical" or "responsible" manner. She said simply that in twenty years' time, Kai would not come to visit us and say, "Hey, Mom and Dad, remember that car that you bought and that underground sprinkling system that you installed? Well, they really changed my life."

The next morning I phoned friends in California who had organized trips to Mount Kailas in the past and who had, over the years, been particularly supportive of what I wanted to do with my son. Yes, they were planning another trip there in the fall. Yes, it was expensive, but the money that I had inherited would just cover the expense of the trip! They put me on hold, as they checked to see if there was still room for any more people to join the journey. A few minutes later they came back on the line. Yes, there was still some room for more people to go on the trip; in fact, there was room for just two more people. It would be wonderful if we wanted to join. Did we want to come? Yes.

Later that afternoon my wife and I went to pick Kai up from school. He knew that I was phoning the people in California that morning to find out if the trip was possible. In talks with him about the trip, he'd always expressed a great deal of excitement about the possibility that we might be able to do this together. Something about the prospect of the journey had infected his soul as well. In the way that small children become very possessive of their stuffed animals, he would often refer to the mountain as "his" mountain and would keep asking me matter of factly when we were going.

I was talking with a friend when I saw Kai walking across the lawn toward us. I turned away from our conversation and walked slowly over toward him. He stopped and looked at me questioningly. I hesitated for only a moment and then slowly nodded my head yes. A reluctant, and somewhat disbelieving, smile began forming on his face. As the smile picked up momentum in its passage across his cheeks, however, a loud shriek erupted from his mouth, and he jumped on top of me. Even at thirteen, he was big enough to knock me over.

My father loved Kai very much, and it has always struck me as particularly tender and ironic that his death permitted Kai and me to attempt to journey to Mount Kailas. It was the final gift from this man whom I loved so much in life and continue to love in death.

There exist only two small windows of time during which it's possible to travel to the remote, southwestern regions of the Tibetan plateau where Mount Kailas is located. Some pilgrims prefer to approach the mountain in the late springtime after the winter snows have ended and before the monsoon from India spills across the Himalayan barrier and shrouds the region in constant cloud and occasional showers. The potential problem with spring pilgrimages, however, is that one never knows when winter has truly ended. Storms can form rapidly and unexpectedly on the Tibetan plateau. Like everything else on the plateau, they can be extremely intense. The two most popular traditional routes into the region are westward across the plateau for the Tibetan people and northward across the Himalayas for the Hindus and Jains from India. Both routes involve the constant fording of rivers and streams. Depending on the severity of the winter snowfall, the waterways that one consistently encounters can range from small, trickling rivulets to the most treacherous, cascading torrents. The constant presence of water prevents many pilgrims to Mount Kailas from ever getting anywhere close to their destination.

Another window opens in September and early October when the monsoon begins to lose its power and recedes back down the Himalayan crest where it will eventually evaporate over the Gangetic plains of India. The wild card to a fall pilgrimage is, once again, water. A severe monsoon that manages to spill itself over the ordinarily protective barrier of the mountains onto the plateau can wipe out all traces of roads that, in temperate weather and at the best of times, are never much better than a logging road in the Pacific Northwest and rarely even that good. Such a monsoon will also cause the rivers over which these roads routinely cross to swell, sometimes to an impassable size and force. On top of this, no one knows for certain when the first winter storm will appear.

Many stories of pilgrimages to Mount Kailas, not unlike the earlier accounts I had read as a boy of attempts to catch a sailfish, recount how the pilgrims never reached their goal. This is as true in current times when the preferred mode of transportation is Chinese buses or Toyota Land Cruisers as it has been for centuries when people would walk to the mountain or, if they were fortunate, ride on horses with yaks carrying their supplies. Other than the few short weeks in the spring and fall, it is not realistic to attempt a pilgrimage. It is difficult enough then. During the rest of the year, movement across the plateau and the mountains simply stops. The nomads move their tents and flocks to lower pastures, and the small cadre of Buddhist and Bon-po practitioners who spend the winter in the *gompas,* or monasteries, surrounding Mount Kailas cannot travel far from the life support of their monastery.

The trip that Kai and I would attempt was slated for September. It was hoped that we would be late enough to avoid the tail end of the monsoon, but early enough to miss the bitter turn in temperature that could catch late pilgrims by surprise. Our friends in California kept cautioning us about the hazards and uncertainty of the journey. We would all do our very best to reach the mountain, but there were no guarantees that we would even be able to get close within the time frame that we'd allotted for the trip.

In addition to the uncertainty of washed-out roads and overly swollen rivers, there is another major wild card that can unexpectedly undermine the best intentions of travelers to Mount Kailas. That card is the altitude. At fifteen thousand feet the Tibetan plateau is the highest habitable landmass on the planet. The altitude makes the plateau exceedingly inhospitable, however, for any human or animal that hasn't grown up there. In comparison with the saturated air of the lowlands, the air at high elevations has an extremely low concentration of oxygen.

The progressive thinning of the air, as one keeps climbing to higher and higher altitudes, causes a variety of problems and symptoms in the unconditioned traveler. These may range from moderate fatigue and lightheadedness to the most severe and debilitating physical pain and disorientation. Simply to take a step at high elevations can tax a person's stamina, and for this reason we were advised to spend the summer getting into the best aerobic and physical shape of our lives. Kai and I immediately began a routine of long, aerobic walks in the morning, exercise in the afternoon, and repetitive noontime hikes up and down the steep hill at the bottom of our property.

Preparing yourself physically can offset the inevitable fatigue and physical challenge of high altitude, but it can in no way guarantee protection from the sometimes life-threatening effects of full-blown altitude sickness. Typically this illness will begin with a mild headache that rapidly turns severe and causes extreme dizziness and vomiting. At its worst, the fluids bathing the soft matter of the brain begin to swell dangerously. Tissues can rupture and the body die.

To make matters worse, no one knows what causes this illness. Physical conditioning and the vitality of youth are no guarantees of protection from a sudden onset of altitude sickness. It strikes the young and fit as readily as it affects the old and infirm. The one precaution that can be taken is to increase elevation gain very slowly, ideally no more than a thousand feet a day once you have climbed above eight or nine thousand feet. It's thought that this gradual increase in altitude allows the body time to acclimate itself to the thinner air. Certainly, climbing too high too quickly is a known tempter of altitude sickness and is almost universally avoided if at all possible.

If, while climbing a mountain, a person begins to experience any of the preliminary symptoms of altitude sickness, the prudent response is to descend several thousand feet as rapidly as possible. As the concentration of oxygen in the air once again thickens, the most severe symptoms of altitude sickness begin to subside. Although this works fine if you're climbing a mountain, the Tibetan plateau offers no easy escape route. If you begin to experience symptoms of altitude sickness in the middle of the plateau, it would take several days to travel to an elevation that was significantly lower. For this reason many cautious travelers to the Tibetan plateau will include a Gamow bag in their inventory of equipment. At first glance a Gamow bag looks like a normal mummy sleeping bag. Once you've zipped yourself in, however, a device is activated that effectively alters the atmospheric pressure and oxygen conditions so that in a relatively short time the body is fooled into thinking that it has descended back down to a much lower elevation. Over a period of several hours, the worst symptoms of altitude sickness may gradually subside, and the person can emerge back out again into the more rarefied air. The pressurized and oxygenated cabins of modern-day airliners that customarily fly at elevations above thirty thousand feet are not unlike large-scale Gamow bags.

Although no one knows for certain why this illness occurs and how to prevent it, research in recent years has focused on the prophylactic benefits of consuming large quantities of water as a safeguard against the onset of altitude sickness. The reasoning behind this is that the medical community is increasingly viewing altitude sickness as a function of dehydration. By constantly overhydrating the body, it's hoped that some degree of protection may be created. It isn't that easy to sleep soundly at high elevations anyway, and waking in the night two or three times to urinate is looked upon as a small, and not that inconvenient, price to pay to protect the body from the devastating effects of altitude sickness. Once we got onto the Tibetan plateau, we would be drinking as many as eight quarts of water a day. It struck me as particularly ironic that water, the element that was most likely to derail our journey and make it impossible for us to get anywhere near the mountain, could also provide us with the greatest protection and support in our attempt to do so.

September 2 and 3

The flight to Bangkok, and then on to Katmandu, makes for an almost impossibly long day. As you fly west across the Pacific, the earth turns

opposite to the direction in which the plane is flying. These two opposing motions come close to canceling each other out, and clock time
almost stands still. I would occasionally look down at my watch and
realize that I couldn't even remember what time zone it was set for or
even if it was night or day.

Two dear friends, Tim and Laurice, had stopped by unannounced
the night before we left to wish us well on our journey. We had finally
just finished packing when they arrived. Although we were genuinely
pleased to see them, both Kai and I realized that their visit and warm
wishes were likely to be two of the last familiar events we would experience for the next month. We told them that we were almost uncomfortably excited in anticipation of our departure early the next
morning. When pressed to elaborate on what that actually meant or felt
like, Kai said that it felt as though he was 90 percent excited and 10
percent terrified! Laurice teased him, "Gee, Kai, maybe you should
have just had a regular bar mitzvah after all."

During our months of physical conditioning in preparation for our
journey, I had often spoken to Kai about his religious heritage. I had been
raised Jewish, whereas Lyn had been raised in a family whose religious
orientation can best be described as "devout agnostic." Like his mother,
Kai had never gone to a Sunday school of any denomination. Unlike his
mother and father, he'd been raised in a home in which both his parents
were committed meditation practitioners. Over a period of several days,
we carried on a conversation about the values and perils of organized religion. Kai was simply dumbfounded to hear about the internecine rival-
ries, bickering, and even hatred that existed among different religious
groups. He inquired in some detail about my religious upbringing and
whether that automatically conferred the status of being Jewish onto him.
I tried to speak to him about the visions and impulses that were common
to the creation of all the different religious traditions and of the trouble
that the subsequent followers of those traditions would get into as they
lost sight of the original revelation and became preoccupied instead with
the more superficial symbols of their faith. The Bible tells us that "life can
only be found in the spirit, never in words alone," and yet followers of

all religions continue to battle one another over the words and symbols of their respective scriptures. I knew that our multilayered conversations about religion had been successful when, after an extended period of silence and thought, he turned to me one day and said simply, "Well, I'm either all of them or none of them." He liked the idea that we would be traveling first to Nepal, a Hindu country, where we would then embark on what a friend of mine in Arizona had dubbed a Buddhist bar mitzvah.

Two nights before our departure, Kai had broken down and cried. He'd felt quite vulnerable to me during that entire day. He hadn't had any solid food to eat that day as part of an anti–jet-lag diet we were experimenting with, and we'd both felt a bit wobbly from the last two inoculations, immunoglobulin and menningococcal, that we'd taken earlier in the day. I sensed that the prospect of what we were about to do was finally becoming real for him, and I felt his fear of the unknown beginning darkly to surface, adding a whole other shadow dimension to his excitement. I felt it too and kept reminding myself that this was the whole purpose of this trip. It is youthful folly, the attitude so typified by the Fool of the tarot deck, to enter into the unknown without a healthy amount of fear as one's companion and guide. I kept reminding myself that people who move ahead in life are able to do so not because they feel no fear, but because they aren't paralyzed by their fear. They include it as a necessary component and companion and move forward just the same. Even so, this sadness at leaving the familiar and excitement about moving into the unfamiliar that mingled with each other in almost equal parts seemed a strange mix, a bit like the emotional equivalent of combining oil and water.

As we settled into our seats on the 747, Kai opened a book he'd brought with him to find a card that Lyn had hidden. In it were two pictures, one of Lyn and his younger brother Jamie and another of Jamie and Rhodo, the family cat. Kai began to read the card out loud, but faltered when Lyn suggested that he look at the pictures if ever he felt homesick. He and I both began drinking large volumes of water to counteract the dry atmosphere of the plane's cabin and to replenish the water that seemed to leach out of us in tears.

We had requested seats in the far back of the airplane to be near the lavatories. My cousin, a steward for Northwest Airlines, told us repeatedly that the best way to weather multiple time-zone changes and the dry air of airplane cabins was to consume as much water as possible, at least one eight-ounce glass an hour. Kai and I joked that we were starting our high-altitude regime early and began to familiarize ourselves with the constant shuffle back and forth between our seats and the nearest lavatory. Over the weeks ahead, we knew we would become very familiar with this shuffle, except that there would likely be no lavatory to which we would be shuffling.

Our flight was one of the first-ever transpacific flights that was designated nonsmoking. We watched with self-righteous mirth the jittery antics of the Chinese smokers who, halfway through the flight, were sneaking cigarettes in the back of the plane and even in the lavatories, in spite of the captain's sternly repeated announcements reminding everyone that this was a nonsmoking flight. Kai and I joked that maybe the stewardesses thought our frequent excursions to the lavatory were for the purpose of sucking nicotine.

The passage of time on the airplane was mostly marked by the succession of movies that were shown. It seemed that every single movie we saw was a tearjerker. In the last movie the main character was a young man named Will, who was facing an impossible choice and an impossible task. My tears seemed to reflect my knowledge that, not just for Kai but for me as well, this trip was signifying a change in the direction in which my life had been moving. I'd been feeling quite empty for several weeks, and I knew that this trip was a journey away from the known routine and rut that had become my life. More tears. So many tears.

⟿

September 4

A friend once described Katmandu as a giant, 360-degree television screen more than six stories high that was connected to a satellite dish capable of receiving more than three hundred channels, all of which were being broadcast simultaneously. What he failed to mention was that the sound track for every channel was blaring at full volume from a huge stack of tinny speakers. Nor did he mention how the dirt and dust and exhaust fumes from too many vehicles with no emission controls tend to hover and cling to the moist air of the late monsoon season. Many pedestrians routinely don handkerchiefs to cover their nose and mouth, protecting their lungs from the noxious air. Tied securely around the neck, this functional and widely used accessory gives the impression that a subcaste of colorful bandits is walking everywhere.

Nepal is an almost completely agrarian nation. Travel even a short distance outside of the city centers, and crops can be seen planted everywhere: in spacious gently rolling fields, along narrow paths and lanes, and in spectacularly engineered terraces cut into the sides of mountains like gigantic stairs leading to the peaks and stars. Every square foot of arable land appears to have something growing on it. The nonagrarian modernization that has come to Nepal is mostly confined to its few major cities. Nowhere is this more visible than in Katmandu.

Katmandu has become the primary drawing card for the youth of the Nepalese countryside who want to leave their rural lives behind, climb atop a motor scooter, and be transported into the twenty-first century. In the last two decades, the population of Katmandu has grown precipitously and dangerously. The pace of growth has far eclipsed the city's ability to service its expanding population. The roads are clogged to standstill. Water supply is questionable. Garbage proliferates like the water buckets of Disney's sorcerer's apprentice. Large mounds of discarded refuse materialize once again on street corners within hours after garbage collectors have been by to remove the previously existing piles. Many street corners are not serviced by garbage collectors at all.

Like a child who has wanted, or been forced, to grow up too quickly and don adult's clothing and manners, Katmandu projects mixed messages at every corner. The innocence and dignified beauty of its cultural heritage and architecture clash loudly with the painful hustle and accelerated rush toward urban maturity. Unfortunately, the model on which this vision of modernization is based appears to be places like Delhi, Bombay, or Calcutta, none of which are exactly exemplars of urban life at its best.

In a sheltered, recessed courtyard of Durbar Square where many of the oldest and most ornate buildings are found lives a young girl who is revered as the Kumari goddess. She occasionally makes appearances to the public from a distance. She does not look real. She is dressed in the most expensive and elaborate saris, and the amount of makeup applied to her face would make the complexion of a Bombay prostitute look pallid in comparison. This young girl will retain her status until she begins to menstruate. The onset of her monthly cycle renders her impure, and her reign comes to an end. She is then awarded a modest pension and forced back out onto the streets of Katmandu where no man will marry a former Kumari goddess, her life over at age twelve. A younger, uncontaminated version is found to replace her, and the cycle begins again. The plight of this young woman spoke to me more strongly about the incongruities of Katmandu than anything else Kai and I would experience. Any way you look at, listen to, see, smell, taste, touch, or think about it, Katmandu is a sensory glutton's smorgasbord, a buffet that leaves even the most temperate diner coming away from the table feeling as though he'd eaten too much.

The anti–jet-lag diet appeared to have worked. We arrived in Katmandu tired, but by no means exhausted. We had slept reasonably well in Bangkok the evening before and had caught an early morning flight to Katmandu. The airport is relatively new and modern, and it was only when we began driving to our hotel that Kai began to realize, as he would convey many times that day, that "this ain't Duncan," referring to the sleepy town of loggers, Natives, and middle-class house-holders ten miles away from our home back in Canada. The air was hot and muggy, and my body felt covered in a thin, invisible film of moist dirt from the short ride to the hotel. The very first thing we did when we checked into our room was to head for the shower. Reasonably refreshed, we decided to set out on foot toward the main old square in the city, a twenty-minute walk away.

The noise of the city and the heaviness of the dirt-laden air hit us like unexpectedly large waves in waters we somehow had assumed would be shallow and windless. Within a block of leaving our hotel, we both felt rattled enough to join the cadre of pedestrian bandits and tied handkerchiefs over our mouths and noses. During the past year Kai had reached an age in which I would watch him teetering back and forth between being a mature man one moment and a young boy again the next. The closer we got to the square, the younger Kai appeared to become. As the streets became narrower and narrower and the people became more and more numerous, he clasped my hand tightly and kept requesting that we move ever more slowly. We couldn't move very fast even if we'd wanted to, as the empty spaces between bodies became smaller and smaller. The further we ventured, the more it felt as though we were leaving the twentieth century behind. With every corner we turned, the city seemed to become more and more compacted as though twice and soon six times the volume of activity was being forced to exist in a space large enough for a single event at best to transpire back in Canada. The increase in visual density was mathematically matched by an increase in the level of clatter. CLANG!!! GHAWWWUUNNNNKKK!!! AING! AING! AING! Automobiles honked at bicycles. Bicycles honked at pedestrians. Pedestrians loudly cursed the vehicular horns. Starting off from the pleasant garden in front of our hotel, it now seemed as though we'd walked out of the pastoral spaciousness of an Italian Renaissance painting into the *horror vacuii* (literally, "the fear of empty space") of something from Hieronymus Bosch.

Everywhere we looked people were selling something: used clothing, incense, brass pots, ornate tassels made from silk embroidery thread, legumes, green bananas, everywhere green bananas, religious *thangka* paintings, carpets. Kai and I were obvious marks, and people began swooping down on us with objects for sale and guide services to offer. It didn't seem to matter whether we were interested in what they were selling or not. They were determined to give us the very best price and get it from us in return. As we rounded a corner, I saw a group of seated men on makeshift chairs take notice of us and immediately call out to a friend just down the street who was carrying wooden flutes for sale. He quickly descended on us for the hoped-for sale, apparently unable to understand that we might not want to buy one of his flutes. Later a young European man looking much older than his years, his pupils badly dilated, the whites of his eyes streaked with lines of blood, would come up to us and try to sell us the identical flutes.

As we entered into the center of Durbar Square, a young and particularly persistent man kept trying to convince us that Kai's brand new Nike sneakers were badly in need of repair. As much looking for haven as rest, we climbed up the steps of a sixteenth-century temple in the shape of a ziggurat and sat down exhausted.

"Dad, this ain't Duncan."

From across the square a carved and painted wooden sculpture of Radha and Krishna, the eternal Hindu lovers, looked out from a rooftop opening in an elaborately carved wooden screen, gazing serenely down at the frantic activity below. Her right arm was draped over his right shoulder. His left hand was gently cupped over her left breast. Where do lovers find privacy to play in this world, I wondered? As we would discover over the next few days, personal privacy, whether in matters amorous or religious, is not so much of a prerequisite for the Nepalese people as it is for us in the West.

Half an hour later, we began to make our way back to the hotel. I had been to India twice before, and so the shock of this new culture with its intense display of colors, sounds, and smells didn't feel too foreign to me. Not so for Kai. He was clearly ready to be back in our hotel room. He kept saying that he'd seen enough on this first outing. When we finally reached the hotel, we were both very hot and tired. Kai felt understandably overwhelmed, and the first thing he did on entering our room was to become teary. He said he missed Lyn and Jamie. I tried to support him in his response and told him that there would be many tears for both of us during this journey, that tears were normal in the face of what we'd just experienced. We both lay down for a nap before dinner and awoke two-and-a-half hours later.

Kai said he was still tired and didn't feel hungry, so I showered and went downstairs alone for a meal of rice and cooked lentils, the staple dish of Nepal, in a restaurant that embodied many of the contradictions of Katmandu itself. Beautifully carved, free-standing wooden screens were strategically placed to hide neon lighting. The overly friendly waiters wanted mostly to practice their English. A Stevie Ray Vaughan tape played loudly from large speakers behind the bar.

When I went back up to the room, Kai, more curious than hungry, asked me how dinner was.

"Kai, this clearly isn't Duncan!"

We both slept very soundly that first night in our new world.

—❧

September 5

I woke early to the sound of the monsoon rain tap-dancing on the rooftop of the hotel and the screened windows of our room in a series of crescendos and lulls. It was a very welcome sound, both soothing to the ear and cooling to the atmosphere. Yesterday's steamy and oppressive conditions, so laden with the stagnant pressure of positively charged ions, had been washed clean. The colors outside appeared richer, the sounds clearer.

I walked over to the window and looked out. I could see great sheets of rain, one after the next, careening convulsively toward the hotel, completely engulfing it in water, and then disappearing as quickly as they'd arrived. Between the downpours, billowing clouds would slowly form out of the uniform grayness. Occasionally the clouds would lift, and for a brief and tantalizing moment I would catch a glimpse of spectacular snow-covered peaks off in the far distance north of the city. Just as rapidly, the clouds would collapse back down on themselves, and the next silhouetted sheet of rain would come lurching toward the hotel, a meteorological drunk out for a morning walk. Mountains, clouds, and rain all appeared to be playing hide-and-seek with one other.

By the time we'd finished breakfast and cleaned up, the clouds and rain were gone. The growing heat of the sun caused the puddles of collected water to steam. I realized that it wouldn't be long before the accumulated exhaust from the unmuffled cars, trucks, and buses would saturate the steam with carbon monoxide emissions. We donned our handkerchiefs, made jokes about being outlaws from the Wild East, and took a fifteen-minute rickshaw drive to the Pashupatinath temple complex on the outskirts of Katmandu.

Despite its popular association with Tibetan Vajrayana Buddhism, Nepal is primarily a Hindu country. Pashupatinath sits on a steep hill leading down to a shallow river of perpetually gray waters and consists of an impressive sprawl of pagoda-roofed, weather-stained temples and shrines built haphazardly one on top of the other. It is a very holy site for Hindus, a Nepalese version of Varanasi far to the south. One of the highest aspirations of many devout Hindus is to die in Varanasi and be cremated on the banks of the Ganges. If one can't get to Varanasi, Pashupatinath will do just as well.

The inner temples of Pashupatinath are strictly off limits to non-Hindus, and so we made our way across a stone bridge to the other side of the river where numerous, small stone shrines offered shelter to the wandering Hindu holy men known as *sadhus*. Gazing back across at Pashupatinath, we could watch the comings and goings of the hundreds of devout Hindu pilgrims who mingled on the stone promenade and steps that led down to the water's edge. Death and dying is the major, visible preoccupation and industry of Pashupatinath. Merchants had set up tables under makeshift plastic tarpaulins where you could buy the flowers, shrouds, fruits, and sacramental rice that are used in the elaborate ceremonies leading up to cremation. The steps leading down to the water were occasionally truncated by broad, flat landings, large enough to lay a shrouded, recently deceased body on. The bodies were mostly concealed under saffron-colored sheets, which were then covered in flowers. Hindu priests with shaved heads and white *dhotis* covering the bottom half of their bodies would sit for hours around the dead bodies, chanting prayers and performing rituals with pans of rice and containers of water or oil, before the bodies would be set ablaze. Groups of pallbearers could be seen walking in the shallow waters of the river, carrying another shroud-covered body on a simple wooden stretcher, bringing it to another platform to await its ceremony and disposal. On the far side of the bridge, the promenade and steps were much less elaborate. It was here that the poor people, who could not afford the services of the priests and the adornments of the merchants, could be placed and burned. Either way, rich or poor, everybody turned to ashes. Temple monkeys roamed freely about on both sides of the river.

Kai had never seen a dead body before, and we sat in silence for some time, watching the drama of death and final disposal slowly play itself out over and over again. As we began to move about, exploring the rows of small shrines and observing the sadhus who had taken up residence in them, we were once again struck by the multiple incongruities of Katmandu. In the center of most of the shrines that now housed this small community of supposedly celibate sadhus were smoothly carved stone sculptures of Shiva lingams emerging out of softly rounded openings depicting the yoni, the lingam's female counterpart and place of completion. In Hindu cosmology the eternal manifestation and dissolving of the universe is likened to an act of sexual play between the masculine and feminine forces of nature, and yet the phallus and vulva of the temple shrines stood in stark contrast to the mostly emaciated sadhus who consulted their books and administered blessings to the people who sought their services.

Being a sadhu has become for some an occupation and business like any other, a way to make one's living and provide oneself with housing and food. As with entrepreneurs in the West, many of the younger sadhus appeared to be searching for ever more creative ways to promote and draw attention to themselves. One highly photogenic young sadhu looked resplendent in a pink dhoti, a large amber necklace, designer sunglasses, and a black leather jacket. The small headphones in his ears were connected to a Walkman that he was carrying. His flashing smile and undulating movements would not have looked out of place in any Western discotheque. For a price, another sadhu would take people behind a stone wall and with his penis lift a fifty-pound rock to which he'd attached a rope.

The final touch of surrealism was provided by the steady stream of large, commercial airliners that flew over the temple complex at low elevations on their descending flight path into the Katmandu airport. The new airport had been built less than a mile away. With a simple turn of the head, you could move your attention from the late twentieth century back in time to a medieval scene that probably hadn't changed for hundreds of years.

Leaving Pashupatinath, we made our way once again by motorized rickshaw back across town to the Buddhist shrine of Swayambhunath, an enormous rounded *stupa*, or religious monument, overlooking the Katmandu valley. To reach the stupa you have to walk up 365 steps. Kai wanted to count every one. Some of the steps are short and steep. Others are long, extended landings on which are built statues of the Buddha, smaller stupas, and open shrine rooms housing prayer wheels both enormous and tiny. As you pass the shrine rooms, you can turn the brass cylinders and send the energy of the prayers out to the world. By the time we reached the top of the staircase, we were both out of breath. Although Katmandu's altitude, approximately 4,500 feet, offers some degree of physical challenge to sea-level dwellers, it was sobering to realize that the highest pass that we would need to cross in our walk around Mount Kailas was almost two-and-a-half miles higher! I decided not to share this thought with Kai.

No one knows for sure when this stupa was originally built, but it's thought to be more than two thousand years old. It probably originated as a natural dirt mound that was gradually fortified over the centuries with brick, clay, and water to secure its hemispherical shape. Today the regularly whitewashed stupa supports a tall, conical spire of elaborate copper gilt. At the base of the spire, resting on the very top of the mound itself, is a ten-foot-high cube of carved stones on each of whose faces are painted the famous all-seeing eyes of the Buddha. When we finally made our way to the top of the staircase, Kai looked for a moment at the round white dome topped by the elaborate face and eyes and commented that it looked like a cross between a miniaturized Seattle Kingdome and an enlarged Jabba the Hut from *Return of the Jedi.*

The atmosphere of the Buddhist Swayambhunath felt completely different from the Hindu Pashupatinath and seemed to reflect the stereotypical differences between the two Indian religions. At the Hindu temple complex, everything had been buzzing with activity and crowded to overflow. The air was thick with the smoke of the funeral pyres and the heady redolence of the sweetly floral incense that tried to mask the smell of burning flesh. In spite of the apparent dignity and unhurried solemnity of the ritual activities, one sensed that nothing wanted to stand still for very long at all. The Buddhist stupa was far more tranquil. Situated on a high hill, it seemed to float serenely above the rush and bustle of downtown Katmandu. The air was clean and fresh. We could gaze off into empty space for scores of miles in all directions. Nowhere were there the crowds and frantic commerce we'd experienced in the morning. It was also considerably quieter.

Hinduism exults in the proliferation of matter, the infinite ways and variations in which particles can interact, the appearance of the divine in all His and Her myriad forms on Earth, whereas Buddhism is more interested in the empty space between those particles. Both orientations are, of course, valid and provide completion to the other's path of inquiry as reflected in the famous statement from the *Heart Sutra*: "Emptiness is form; form is emptiness." When observing an incompletely filled glass of water, Hinduism will see it as half full, Buddhism as half empty. Certainly the opportunity for dogmatic confrontation between the two religions looms large, but for some unexplained reason, Hinduism and Buddhism have mostly managed to live side by side in remarkable tolerance over their long centuries of coexistence. Directly mirroring the recent Western attempts at healing the wounds that Christianity and Judaism have inflicted on each other through the proclamation that Jesus was originally a Jew, we would see T-shirts for sale in the marketplaces of Katmandu that heralded the reminder: BUDDHA WAS A HINDU.

Kai became fascinated with the monkey families that moved easily about begging for handouts of food, grabbing impatiently and skillfully if the food wasn't immediately offered. His mood had completely shifted from the overwhelmed young boy of just twenty-four hours earlier. He was clearly enjoying himself, excited by the monkeys and the view across downtown Katmandu. He liked the stupa and wanted to meander around the maze of smaller buildings and votive shrines that surrounded it. At one point he walked into a building and then came out quickly, motioning for me to follow and join him. Inside a large shrine room, a ceremony was being presided over by a young Tibetan boy his own age, probably a *tulku* who had been recognized as the reincarnation of an important earlier teacher. The young boy was seated on a raised platform with older attendants positioned on either side. On the floor sat fifty mostly older, purple-robed monks rocking slightly back and forth to the singsong rhythms of the prayers. Kai was fascinated by the chanting. When we left the ceremony, he took me over to a small stall that had Tibetan artifacts on display and insisted that we each buy a *mala*, a long string of beads not unlike a Catholic rosary that is used for counting recitations of mantras or prayers.

When we returned in the late afternoon to our hotel, Kai wanted me to show him how to use the mala. We each lay in our beds to rest, and I instructed him to repeat a simple Tibetan mantra: om ah hum. With every repetition of the phrase, his fingers skillfully manipulated the beads until he had made his way through one circuit of the mala, 108 beads in total. He then reversed direction and kept intoning the mantra. His voice grew softer and softer, and he commented on how relaxed he felt, just before he fell off to sleep for a much-deserved afternoon nap.

At six o'clock we went downstairs to meet the other people who would be accompanying us on our journey to Mount Kailas. Kai has always been comfortable in the company of adults, and most everybody appeared quite taken with the ease and maturity of this aging boy and with the story behind our desire to get to the mountain. I felt proud as we all went around the table, taking turns to introduce ourselves and express our hopes and fears for the weeks ahead, as he spoke comfortably to this group of strangers about how he had been named and about his special relationship to the mountain. Everybody at the table had their own personal dream about reaching the sacred mountain and about the role it had played in their lives.

Among the people whom we met that evening were Jennifer and Jean who, with the same Seattle address, turned out not to be a female couple, as I had thought when I first saw their names, but rather a young American woman and her elegant, considerably older Swiss husband. Both had traveled extensively in the Himalayas, but had never gotten to Mount Kailas. Cindy was a CNN camerawoman specializing in hot spots. She had been a member of the film crew in Baghdad during the first Gulf War and had gone on to cover the elections in South Africa, the American occupation of Somalia, and the killing fields of Rwanda. Faye, with the appearance of the goddess Kali's younger but somewhat more conventional and well-adjusted sister, was a hairdresser from Michigan who, years earlier, had fallen under the spell of the Himalayas. This would be her fourteenth trip into the region. Ellen, a medical doctor from San Francisco, was initially quite reserved as she introduced herself, but her warm smile almost immediately gave her away as someone very large in heart and deeply committed to Buddhist practices. Jonathan was a delightfully witty Jewish Buddhist from New York, who couldn't seem to navigate his way through a single sentence without introducing at least one pun, almost all of which turned out to be miraculously original and funny. He had tried unsuccessfully to get to Mount Kailas three times in the past and sincerely expressed his hope that this trip would end his jinx. We had no way of knowing at the time that Aimee, a lovely young woman halfway in age between Kai and me, would turn out to feel like a dear and very closely bonded sister to both of us by the end of the trip. Vassi, a rugged Greek-born American who is one of the Dalai Lama's official photographers, would function in the role of group leader. He had traveled extensively in the high mountains all over the world, but also had never yet been to Mount Kailas. He'd arrived in Katmandu several days earlier to make sure that the arrangements for vehicles, equipment, and support staff were in order. It felt like a wonderful group of people.

In addition to meeting everybody, the meeting had been called to brief everyone on the schedule, routine, and jobs that we would all need to perform to ensure that the trip would go as smoothly as possible. Mostly Vassi went out of his way to put the fear of God into everybody. He spoke at great length about the perils of altitude, describing the possible complications in gruesomely detailed vignettes drawn from his personal experience, and kept reiterating the need to consume large volumes of water and to walk very slowly and leisurely. His stories were at once entertaining, effective, and unsettling. He also cautioned us again that although we would do everything possible to reach the mountain, our chance of success was by no means guaranteed. He admitted honestly that the preliminary reports from southern Tibet were not favorable, that the monsoon was lingering longer than had been hoped, and that some of the roads we would need to drive over might turn out to be impassable. The only two things that he could guarantee were that we would have an incredible adventure together and that we would all lose weight.

While many of the people went out together for a last night in Katmandu, Kai and I decided to stay at the hotel and have dinner with Jonathan, Cindy, and Faye. Vassi's speech had definitely worked on Kai. He was visibly unnerved, especially about Vassi's account of waking up alone in the middle of the night at Everest base camp with a terrifying headache, unable to stand, having to crawl on his hands and knees in the darkness two thousand feet down the mountain trail. We looked at the menu, but Kai had lost his appetite. Suddenly tired and a little shaky, he excused himself to go up to the room. Within ten minutes, however, he came back down to be with us. We all talked to him about Vassi's strategy to paint the worst possible scenario as a way of scaring people into staying healthy. I told Kai about my very first trip to India twenty years earlier. Before landing in Bombay, my traveling companion had gone out of his way to depict a chilling tableau of what was waiting for me when I stepped off the plane: air so dank and foul that I would feel sick to my stomach when I first inhaled it, and thirty barefoot beggar children dressed in filthy rags who would climb all over me and claw viciously at one another for the privilege of carrying my luggage in hopes of receiving a few pennies for their efforts. When the air turned out to be passably breathable, and I was met by only a small handful of children, I felt relieved.

The stories calmed Kai's fears, but he still wasn't hungry. He was definitely enjoying being in our company, though, and was happily content to listen and watch, as the rest of us began getting to know one other. Later, before bed, he would say of our companions at dinner, "Dad, it's weird, but it feels like I already know them."

At one point during dinner, the conversation turned to rites of passage. Everyone by then knew of Kai's and my purpose for being here. I told Jonathan in particular about how my bar mitzvah had left me with feelings of bitterness and disappointment, how it had always felt for me to be the antithesis of a true rite of passage. In the middle of Jonathan's and my accounts of our respective Reform Jewish childhoods, Faye interrupted.

"No, Will, I don't agree. I think you're missing something here. I think your bar mitzvah was a true rite of passage. It just wasn't the one you thought you were going to get. You needed to experience that to know that organized religion wasn't for you. How truly important an event that must have been for you."

With this one simple statement from someone whom I had just met, I felt thirty-five accumulated years of hurt begin to come undone in a moment. It felt as though I'd been holding my fist tightly all these years, shaking it bitterly in the face of my religious upbringing and heritage, and through this moment of recognition and this simple act of forgiveness, I was able to release my reactive grip, and the blood began coming back into my fingers. I felt deeply grateful for Faye's comment and knew immediately that I would come to like this woman very much.

Back in our room after dinner, Kai and I were almost uncomfortably animated in our banter and physical play with each other. We commented jokingly that our sliding emotional scale was currently hovering at about 70 percent excited and 30 percent terrified. We packed and repacked and kept fussing about every little object we would take or leave behind. Even though we knew that we had to get up very early the next morning, we had difficulty settling down to sleep. We kept talking into the night, remembering back to details and replaying the events of the day over and over, as though they were recordings on a tape, until in the middle of an unfinished sentence, we both finally dozed off.

At two o'clock in the morning Kai was up with diarrhea. We had been told that, of all the places we would visit during the trip, Katmandu was the most likely place in which to fall ill, and we had tried to be doubly careful with the food we allowed ourselves to eat and the liquids we drank. I tried to comfort him, assuring him that it was a common response to the adjustments we were having to make to this new culture. He didn't look reassured, however, and I found that I too couldn't stop my mind from fretting over whether this was the beginning of something serious or just normal nerves before embarking on our journey. Certainly, he had been quite scared earlier in the evening during the meeting. Then again, Kai rarely ever would have diarrhea at home, unless he was really ill. My thoughts began playing mental ping-pong back and forth between the opposing camps of hope and worry, and I found it impossible to fall back to sleep and instead dozed fitfully for the rest of the night. I kept listening every time he would turn in his bed, knowing that any further need to use the bathroom would be a bad sign. Much to my relief, however, his tossings and murmurings didn't appear to disturb him any further. He slept soundly through the night, much better than I, and awoke in the morning saying that he felt fine.

At one point during the night I was woken from my semisleep by the sounds of dogs barking and fighting in the courtyard next to the hotel. I opened my eyes. The air was still and clear outside, no monsoon tonight. In the darkened space of our hotel room, I watched with fascination as red, blue, green, orange, and yellow beads came languidly floating together out of the corners of the room to form into the image of the Tibetan eternal knot. As it hovered and danced in the air above me, a brilliant white light suddenly burst forth from its center. Over the course of several seconds, the light gradually formed into the features of the face of the Buddha. My only thought was that, please, let Kai be well.

~~

September 6

We awoke at five-thiry, had breakfast at six fifteen, and loaded our luggage and sleepy bodies onto a waiting coach by seven o'clock to begin the drive east and north to the Tibetan border town of Zhangmu. The Chinese government, of course, claims Zhangmu as their own, but the Nepalese map that we were given, while acknowledging the current political realities but also deferring to the sentiments of the large population of Tibetan refugees living in and around Katmandu, optimistically declared that "the delineation of international boundaries on this map must not be considered authoritative." Over the next few days, as we would gradually make our way up onto the Tibetan plateau, we would have to gain more than ten thousand feet in altitude. Zhangmu was our gateway to the land of rarefied air. Situated at an elevation three thousand feet higher than Katmandu, it was the obvious choice for our first day's destination. The strategy for the coming week was to "hasten slowly," balancing our conflicting needs to get to the mountain in the small window of time we had allotted with giving our bodies as much time as possible to become acclimated to the higher elevations. If we went too slowly or encountered too many unforeseen delays and obstacles, we could run out of time and be forced to turn back. If we pushed too rapidly, however, we could all too easily compromise our health. If even one person from our small group came down with severe altitude sickness, we would almost certainly have to return to Nepal.

Rush hour in Katmandu resembles Russian roulette on wheels. The roads leading out of the city were impossibly jammed with pedestrians, bicycles, wooden carts with cages of chickens and baskets of legumes, rickshaws, automobiles, trucks, and buses. Everybody kept sounding their horns, and apparently nobody listened to them. The white lines in the center of the roads were laughable. The rule of thumb here was: if a space opens in front of you, move there immedi-

ately, because if you don't, someone else will, and you will be left far
behind, paralyzed by a tangled mass of humanity, whose efforts to
move themselves to their morning destinations would make the morning ritual of the San Bernardino freeway seem positively orderly and
uncrowded in comparison.

Our driver was dexterous and unflinching. He would stare down
anyone in his path foolish enough to try to lay claim to a bit of space
on which he had set his sights. It helped that our coach was larger than
the smaller, mostly Indian-made automobiles that clogged the roads.
Like a tidal pool on a rocky island beach in the Pacific Northwest, the
roads here were ruled by crab mentality. The larger crabs mostly took
what they wanted, swatting the smaller crabs out of their way in the
process. The adrenaline rush of getting out of the city in the early morning traffic, stoked by the multitude of near misses, woke us up quickly.

Leaving the downtown core of Katmandu, the traffic began
thankfully to thin. It didn't take long, however, to realize that the anxiety we had all felt as our driver had ruthlessly negotiated his way
through the downtown maze wasn't going to be alleviated by the relative lessening of traffic along the suburban and country highway.
Relative was the operative word here. The roads were indeed less
crowded, but everyone was moving much, much faster, and any
unwanted contact in this new arena would not just amount to an
inconvenient fender bender. It felt as though we'd suddenly entered
into a more advanced level of a fast-paced Nintendo game. The speed
was greater, the monsters lurking in the wings bigger and nastier, the
surprises waiting around the next corner even more surprising, the
prospects of saving the princess even more remote.

Drivers in Nepal don't appear to be bothered by the decision-making
processes that force most of us back in North America to determine
whether it's safe to pass a car in front of us. If our driver came up to a
slower-moving vehicle, he wouldn't so much as slow down for a
moment's reflection, but—quite the opposite—would simply put his foot
to the floor, point the coach into the other lane, and lean on the horn. It
didn't matter if he were coming to the crest of a hill that he couldn't see

over, if he were rounding a blind bend that he couldn't possibly see around, or even if there were a monstrous, exhaust-belching truck barreling and lurching straight toward us from the opposite direction at a speed that was clearly too high for the driver to control. I quickly gained a new appreciation for all the Hindu gods and goddesses, whose brightly painted images routinely adorned the fronts of all the buses and trucks in Nepal. I also began questioning how sane it was to be traveling in a country whose primary religious doctrines are so strongly fatalistic.

Miraculously enough, this traffic roulette seemed to work, and the chamber never came up loaded. Oncoming traffic simply got out of the way, and we all had to admit that none of us had yet seen a single accident. The thickly trafficked road led us further into the countryside with every turn and began to narrow. We passed the medieval town of Bhaktipur, where many of the ancient scenes from the movie *Little Buddha* had been filmed. In the distance we could see the tall roofs of its pagodas beautifully silhouetted against the even more distant mountains. With every mile we covered, we seemed to be moving back an equivalent distance in time. Buildings became progressively smaller, more primitively constructed, and less numerous. The dense streets of the city were now far behind, the countryside opened wide as if to swallow us, and the landscape became stunning. Following now along the course of a river, we began to move through valley after pristine valley. Every square inch of arable land on the steep hills that rose from the valley floor was terraced into rice and millet paddies. The late monsoon, preharvest season had painted the hills in lush shades of green. It looked as though it would be a very rich harvest this year.

Rounding a corner in the road, our driver quite abruptly hit the brakes. Everyone was jolted forward in his seat as the coach skidded to a halt. Kai turned to me and said he thought that was the first time today our driver had used the brakes. A line of parked trucks stretching as far as we could see had slowed traffic once again to a crawl. Drivers were milling about their vehicles, sharing food and drink, sitting in groups (sometimes right in the middle of the road) playing cards. Clearly they were in no hurry to reach Katmandu. We found out later that they were part of a nationwide truck strike protesting high tariffs on the roads. It actually felt good to be moving more slowly, as we passed miles of trucks parked in protest, thankfully facing in the other direction.

Four hours after leaving Katmandu, we stopped in a small town to share a boxed lunch: hard-boiled eggs, Cadbury chocolate bars from India that looked as though they had been sitting too long on the shelves in a Delhi warehouse and had begun to turn white at the edges, chapatis (the national flatbread of India and Nepal) that had been cooked earlier that morning, pieces of hardened cheese. Vassi only half-jokingly suggested that we all enjoy it, that it just might be the best meal we would have for several weeks. Kai began speaking wistfully about guacamole and chips, but was hungry enough to appreciate what was offered.

After lunch the road began to rise steeply. The valley walls became progressively sheerer and higher, more closely pinned to the river and road. Waterfalls came cascading down from cloud-enshrouded peaks. The coach moved slower and slower, as our driver kept shifting down to lower and lower gears. As we neared the border, the road deteriorated into a single lane of dirt. Every couple of miles there were mud slides around and sometimes through which we had to drive. Occasionally we would have to stop and move the mud and loose rocks out of the way. Finally the road itself became a rocky streambed. We had reached Tibet.

After clearing customs, we reloaded all our gear and bodies onto a waiting truck on the other side of the suspiciously named Friendship Bridge and began the slow, lurching crawl up to the town of Zhangmu. The mud path up to the town was intimidatingly steep and pitted with holes that looked as though they'd been created less by natural processes of erosion than by land mines. In the back of the truck we were jostled around from side to side. Luggage and the occasional body were comically tossed into the air like Mexican jumping beans.

Halfway up the road we were met by our Toyota Land Cruisers. To attempt to reach Mount Kailas, our group would need three Land Cruisers and two large, canvas-covered support trucks that would carry all our food, fuel, and supplies. Our Tibetan drivers had come down from Lhasa a few days earlier, and we were happy and relieved to see them. Toyota has the monopoly on travel in Tibet, as well as the track record to justify that position. Jeeps and Land Rovers are evidently not able to sustain the constant beating that the roads of the Tibetan plateau routinely mete out. The Toyota Land Cruisers carry on as though indestructible, hundred thousand miles after hundred thousand miles. As we climbed down from the truck, its tires now mired a half-foot in mud, we looked up to see our three Land Cruisers, immaculately clean and resting on a hard rock road. They looked like a fleet of Rolls Royces.

The border town of Zhangmu stares down gravity and clings insouciantly to the side of a gorge steep enough to induce vertigo. The roots of dense undergrowth scrub growing everywhere appeared to be providing the major support for the rows of buildings that seemed more suspended above the earth than anchored securely to it. If there were ever any major deforestation here, the town would simply slide back down into Nepal. Like border towns everywhere, Zhangmu is home to several distinct ethnic groups with no clear sign of who is actually in charge. Chinese officials and soldiers in uniform walk past traditionally dressed Tibetans who have ventured down to Zhangmu to sell their wares, mostly artifacts and yak wool. Nepalese youths in blue jeans with Walkmans congregate on street corners like bored teenagers anywhere else in the world.

Exhausted, but exhilarated, Kai and I poked our way through a light supper and fell immediately asleep in our room in the Zhangmu Hotel. He was more amused than irked to find that the television in our room had been put there as decoration and was completely nonfunctional. The attached antenna had actually been placed in a vase of plastic flowers! The private bathroom had a flush toilet, a concrete floor, and a large bathtub with no running water. The floral patterned wallpaper was bubbling and coming undone; the flowers depicted on the paper weren't ones that I recognized. The carpets under our feet, the blankets on the beds, even the carved wood of the chairs and tables: everything was unfamiliar.

Kai looked over at me before we turned off the light beside our beds.

"Dad, to say that 'this ain't Duncan' doesn't even come close anymore."

I was wakened in the middle of the night out of a deep and dreamless sleep by the sound of Kai retching violently in the bathroom. In between convulsions he would whimper like a domesticated animal caught in a leg-hold trap. I fumbled in the darkness until I'd found the light, switched it on, and rushed over to the bathroom.

He was standing in the doorway shaking, as though he'd just stepped out of a freezer. His torso was slumped. I reached out to touch his forehead. He was very hot.

"Kai, are you okay?"

"No, lamebrain, I'm not okay! Isn't that obvious? And, Dad, don't come in! I couldn't find the toilet and hurled all over the flo. . . ."

Before he could finish the word floor, he was vomiting again. It seemed to go on for minutes this time, rising and falling in uninterrupted waves that built to a final sickening crescendo, and then, as suddenly as it had all begun, the vomiting subsided. I knew that he was finished retching for the night. Between the diarrhea from the evening before and the round of vomiting he'd just undergone, there was nothing left inside him.

He was scared and upset, but also relieved to be finished. As he cleaned himself up, brushed his teeth, and realized that there was nothing more to vomit, he told me how much better he felt. We chatted about yesterday's drive up to Zhangmu, as though nothing whatsoever had happened.

We went back to get in bed, and he asked to tuck in and snuggle with me. From the time he was a baby until he was six or seven years old, Kai had mostly slept with Lyn and me. We had opted for the family bed from the moment of his birth and had enjoyed long years of cuddling and nuzzling. We had also endured equally long years of thrashing and flailing, his little body as often as not ending up perpendicular to ours by morning. When Kai had begun to learn the names for the parts of the body, he would point to and name my hand, arm, and elbow. When he got to my shoulder, however, he would only half facetiously say "pillow." One of the hard lessons of parenthood that Lyn and I learned as the years went on was that if you opt for the family bed when your child is a baby, you can't opt out until he's ready to get out. When Kai was six, he began sleeping in his own bed.

As we settled under the covers like two stacked human spoons on their sides, I told him again how normal it was for him to be feeling this way. I reminded him that our bodies were going through an enormous upheaval, that everything that they had known up till now as normal was being challenged. Remarkably, my words appeared to reassure him, and he gradually fell into a deep and restful sleep.

My kind, fatherly words didn't reassure me, however. First diarrhea, now vomiting. I wanted to believe that he'd managed to expel whatever had been poisoning his system, but didn't feel very confident in that belief. Like a helium balloon that loses its air and becomes limply deflated, I collapsed down into worried-father mode and began agonizing over whether I'd made a terrible miscalculation about taking Kai on a trip like this. I remembered back to illnesses that I had had to endure while traveling in India that were worse than anything I had ever experienced in my life. On top of his troubles, I was starting to feel quite woozy myself and wondered whether I might be coming down with the same flu. My throat felt scratchy, I was beginning to sneeze, and I had a mild pressure in my head that felt like the first, early stages of vertigo.

As the hours went on and he continued to sleep comfortably, I was able finally to relax, and my raging inner monologue of worry slowed down into a trickle of concern. If this were the end of his illness, then all would be fine. His sickness and my fatherly alarm were both perhaps part of the price that Mount Kailas was asking of us for permission to enter into its domain. Somehow I found that thought comforting, the resolution to the predicament of our evening, and drifted off into an easy sleep.

When we awoke in the morning, Kai was fine.

⟿

September 7

After a breakfast of dried toast, hard-boiled eggs, and Bournvita (an updated English version of the Ovaltine that Captain Midnight had urged me to get my mother to buy when I was a young child, after my parents inadvertently invited him, through the medium of our very first television, into our home), we set out in our Land Cruisers for the town of Nyalam. We were only planning on driving a few hours that day, but it was almost all straight up. At 12,400 feet, Nyalam was nearly a mile higher than Zhangmu.

Only rarely during the entire drive were our Land Cruisers able to shift into high gear. Mostly they lumbered along in first or second gear, their engines straining past the red line of the tachometer much of the time. Our drivers seemed unconcerned, evidently believing their cars to be immortal. All of our drivers were Tibetans from Lhasa. As owners of their own vehicles, they would be considered wealthy and prominent citizens within their Tibetan communities. They were clearly very proud of their cars. Whenever we would stop to rest, they would break out worn chamois cloths and proceed to clean as much of the accumulated dirt and mud from the hood, sides, windows, and back of their cars as possible, before we would once more set out on our way. It was a ritual that would be repeated over and over again.

The steeply terraced growing fields of the Katmandu valley with their rich soil and crops had given way to rock and scrub growth. With every mile the ratio of grayish-brown to green in the coloration of the landscape became larger. The green growth became sparser, the individual shrubs less densely grouped. The presence of rock was everywhere.

Our road continued to follow the course of the Bhotia Khosi. It is one of the few river systems that has cut a significant pathway through the Himalayan barrier that separates the fifteen-thousand-foot Chang Tang plateau of Tibet from the great Gangetic plain of

India several hundred miles to the south and more than two-and-a-half miles lower. The massive upward thrust of the Himalayas is only a relatively recent geological phenomenon. We ordinarily think of this area in terms of earth and rock, but in truth the element of water has been most historically predominant. For countless eons the landmass of the Himalayas had been the floor of a great ocean, and remnants of seashells and ocean-based fossils are still incongruously found buried next to rocks on the high mountain passes and plateaus of Tibet. As the great island that we recognize today as India kept floating northward, it eventually collided with the beaches of southern Asia and, with almost unimaginable force, caused the surface of the earth to buckle and rise through the compressing impact of the collision. The result of this contact was the Himalayas, which are still rising, even today.

The Bhotia Kosi is thought to predate this cataclysmic encounter of landmasses as an established, southern Asian river system that flowed gently to the sea. As the mountains continued to rise, it just as persistently kept carving its way down through the rocky soil of the earth's slow upward thrust to form the spectacular gorge that now forms the main trade and travel route between Lhasa and Katmandu. Water is like the shadow or invisible counterpart to the Himalayan earth. Like the minister who advises the king in matters of importance, its controlling, yet unseen, presence is never far away. The mountains first emerged out of water, and it is water that both gives permission to enter into the mountains and just as indifferently takes it away.

On the drive to Nyalam, the presence and silent power of the water could be felt and seen everywhere. As it had done for millennia, the river's churning motion from below and the rain's relentless descent from above kept eating away at the rocky cliffs, and periodically large chunks of rock wall would come tumbling down as a result. Like the children's game of rocks, scissors, and paper, it wasn't hard to see that the moist and slowly dissolving action of water appeared to have the upper hand over the permanence and solidity of the earth.

Occasionally snow-covered peaks would show themselves in the distance for the briefest of moments between a gap in the cliffs on either side of the river. The peaks we could see each looked to be progressively higher and more spectacular than the one before. Waterfalls bathed the cliff faces in broad bands and slight ribbons of clear, falling water. Rainbows would appear out of the morning mist, their colored bands weakening and then disappearing, as they reached upward into the clouds that hovered just at the top of the cliff faces. As the Land Cruisers kept straining over the steeply inclined road, it wasn't hard to imagine that we must be climbing through successive layers of paradise. And then, just as suddenly, we came over a crest in the road, and the vegetation simply ceased. The trees were gone. Even the low-growing greenery had mostly disappeared. The rock began to lose its hard-edged definition and softened into sandy slopes. We drove for just a couple more miles and entered into the Tibetan settlement of Nyalam.

Nyalam's reason for being is apparently linked to this abrupt change in geography. It is a kind of halfway house, the median point between the austere and barren emptiness of the Tibetan plateau and the profuse and dense vegetation of the Nepalese valleys to the south. A half hour ago everything was green and lush. Now we could see only sand stretching for miles in all directions over rolling hills. Nyalam must have grown over the centuries as a last staging area for Tibetan traders before they dropped down into the valleys below, where they would exchange their wool for salt and butter.

The clouds that hung to the sides of the cliff walls and peaks in the lower valley had now evaporated, and we had our first introduction to the harsh sun and blinding brightness of the Tibetan plateau. Even though we hoped we wouldn't encounter any snow on our journey, we had been advised to wear glacier glasses with their protective side coverings on the plateau at all times. We got out of our cars and rested in the welcomed warmth of the sun. If we simply walked around a corner into the shade, however, the air would turn immediately frigid, and we would need to put on a sweater or parka to stay warm. As we turned another corner and came out of the shadows, we would need to remove our parkas as quickly as we'd put them on.

We arranged to have a restaurant prepare lunch for us. While we were waiting for our meal to be served, a group of small children came over to gawk at and play with us. At first they stood back and watched us from a distance, peeking out from behind poles and the sides of buildings, but gradually they overcame their shyness and came to sit at our sides. The naturalness of their smiles was contagious. They spoke to us casually in Tibetan, as though we should be able to answer back. All we could do was return their smiles. They became fascinated with Kai's Casio watch. They would erupt in laughter, as he would push buttons and cause beeps to sound, and would jump back in startled delight when he made the display mode on the clock face change. As my body warmed to the sun, I removed my sweater and sat next to Kai with the sleeves of my undershirt rolled up. The Tibetan children gasped, when they saw the dense black hair on my arms. Their shyness had by now completely disappeared, and they raced over and began rubbing my arm. They would laugh hysterically and put their hands to their mouths in apparently sincere amazement, as they swirled my hair into spirals. Most indigenous Tibetans have little body hair, and so my arm must have provided quite a sight and amusement to them. I imagined that they must have perceived me as some kind of benign, lowland ape and enjoyed letting them play, until our lunch was ready. I remembered back to being just their age and playing with the hair on my father's arms in much the same way. I always found it endlessly fascinating. In the way in which children learn to tease and pester loving parents, I would often try to apply spit to his arm and then rub his hair briskly in quick circles until it would form into knots. It was a little game we had. He would let me play with him in this way, but would almost always swat me away before the knots could form. Once or twice I actually managed to form significant knots that he had to cut out with a scissors.

Nyalam's single street looked more like a stage set than a real town, a Hollywood set designer's vision of a cross between a Tibetan village and a frontier town out of the Wild West. The neatly squared and brightly colored fronts of the buildings left me with the uneasy feeling that, were I to walk through their doors, I would step right out onto the sandy hills behind the town. I mentioned this to Kai, and he joked that maybe if we stayed in this one spot long enough, a Tibetan version of Clint Eastwood would come slouching out of the doorway across the street, squinting in the high noon sun, a virtueless scowl etched on his face, mischief or worse on his mind.

Lunch was delicious, a steamy soup filled with vegetables and noodles. A number of the people in the group decided to explore the town and the surrounding hills, but Kai was still a bit shaky and tired from his ordeal the night before and wisely announced that he needed to rest. We went upstairs to our modest hotel room, much simpler and more utilitarian than our room in Zhangmu, and fell immediately asleep.

When we woke at four o'clock, Kai said he was feeling much better, and so we went downstairs and drove off with a few of the other members of our group to a low cement building two or three miles outside of town. A hand-painted sign announced that this building housed both the waterworks and electrical generator for the town, and indeed it had been built right on the banks of the river. We went inside the building, paid a blushing Chinese girl the equivalent of a quarter, and enjoyed what we knew would be our last lukewarm shower before we returned to Katmandu. It felt as though we were back in summer camp with a tattered plastic curtain separating the girl's shower from the boy's.

By the time we returned to the hotel, however, Kai suddenly began feeling much worse again. He raced up to the toilet in our room and proceeded to have another bout of severe diarrhea. He complained of a headache that he described in the teariest of voices as "someone trying to drive a nail through my head," and crawled back to the bed. He pulled all the covers over him, but began to shiver in fits that reminded me of the sheets of monsoon rain that had engulfed our Katmandu hotel one moment and then disappeared the next. His forehead by now was burning. I had never seen him so miserable. He began sobbing between shaking fits and disclosed to me how much he missed and wanted his mother. At the end of a round of shivering, he abruptly bolted out of bed, raced back to the bathroom, and began vomiting much as he had the evening before. I watched as the muscles of his stomach would cramp and release and then cramp tightly down again. At the end of one last extended, undulating spasm, his belly relaxed, and it was clear that he was finished. He wobbled back to the bed, said that he felt a bit better, but it was obvious that he was extremely ill. As soon as he pulled the covers over his body, he began to shake again.

There was a knock on our door. Out in the hallway Vassi had heard Kai vomiting and came down to our room to see how he was doing. After a short consultation in which I detailed the events of the previous evenings, we all decided that it was time for Kai to begin taking Cipro, an antibiotic that was particularly geared to stomach disorders. Within a half minute of swallowing the pill, however, Kai vomited it right back out. He simply wasn't able to hold anything in his stomach.

Vassi left the room to summon Doctor Ellen, while I stayed with Kai and tried to comfort him. Ellen arrived a few minutes later with an anal suppository designed to relax the digestive tract, inserted it, and told us that hopefully in a half hour or so his stomach would settle sufficiently to enable him to keep the antibiotic down. She too agreed that it was very important for him to get the pill into his system.

The next half hour was very rough. Kai would alternately moan, cry, and writhe. The cold shakes would come in waves and then pass away, leaving him burning in their absence. At times he would mutter snatches of incoherent phrases that made no sense. I would ask him what he'd just said, and he would be unable to answer or not remember that he had said anything at all. News of Kai's illness spread through our small community, and a stream of well-wishers showed up at our door. Jonathan brought in a book of Tibetan folk stories. Kai couldn't even acknowledge the gift. Faye brought him a pair of magnificent yak horns she'd found on her walk. Even in his semidelirium he managed to mumble in the weakest of voices, "Thank you. . . , thank you." The next morning he couldn't remember Faye's visit at all and inquired where the wonderful yak horns had come from.

A half hour after Ellen had inserted the suppository, his body quit convulsing. I took this moment of relaxation as our window of opportunity and had him attempt to swallow the pill again. Within five minutes he wanted to throw it up again, but I kept urging him to try not to. I began reading aloud some of the Tibetan folk stories Jonathan had given us and virtually held my breath, as the minutes passed slowly by. I read to him about the young man who had gone into the world and sought his fortune, only to realize that the practice of meditation offered the highest wealth. I read about a woman who made healing potions from the sands and sparse vegetation of the plateau. I kept trying to distract him, to keep his attention from wavering to his body as I read. I read rapidly and dramatically, trying to entertain him as much as possible with the turns and twists of the stories.

An hour later he was comfortably asleep, and it was now my turn to let go. I wept softly for him, telling him in tones that would not wake him how much I loved him, how important it was for him to rest now and let this illness pass out of his body. I'd been through many childhood illnesses with him, but never had I seen him anywhere nearly so sick as he'd been that afternoon. I told him how it was necessary for all of us to purify ourselves, as we made our way to the sacred mountain. And then I too fell asleep. I slept through dinner and into the night.

We both woke up around eleven thirty that night. I turned to him immediately, as soon as I sensed he was awake.

"How are you doing, honey?"

"Dad, I feel fine! Honestly, I really do. It's over."

Never had words sounded so good to me. We both fell easily and quickly back to sleep and slept soundly until the morning light.

September 8

Our wake-up call was for seven thirty the next morning, Mao time. If China followed the rest of the world's system of multiple time zones, the gentle knock at the door actually would have come at five thirty.

But China has decided to set its clocks according to its own priorities, which are determined by the daily schedule of officialdom in Beijing. It is here where all the important government officials reside and work. It is here where the major decisions affecting every facet of Chinese life are made. And so it is here that the clocks are set. In this vast country that spans more longitudes than all but three other countries in the world, all the clocks are set to match the pulse and rhythms of life in Bejing. It makes for very strange days almost everywhere else.

Over yesterday's lunch we had deliberated at length about our options for the next few days. One very attractive option was to rest and spend two nights in Nyalam where, at 12,500 feet, we could slowly begin our acclimatization to the higher altitudes. We didn't know, however, whether we could truly afford the luxury of taking such an extra day. We had no knowledge of what condition the roads across the plateau were in, whether they had deteriorated from the late monsoon and would slow us down considerably, or whether they were even passable at all. There are not exactly rush-hour helicopters hovering over the dirt tracks that constitute what is known as the Southern Route, relaying back messages of road conditions to the harried commuter. The road that we would be traveling on would leave the main road to Lhasa about sixty miles past Nyalam. Our drivers had heard rumors that the Tsangpo River, which we would have to drive our cars and trucks across, was flowing briskly and deep with late monsoon rains, but even they admitted they were only rumors. They simply didn't know for sure, and there was no source of reliable information that we could contact to confirm or deny the rumors.

Our decision to travel on was sealed when one of our drivers said that he knew of a sheltered, hidden valley on the Tibetan plateau, not far from the base of Shisha Pangma, the fourteenth highest mountain in the world. This valley was relatively close to one of the possible places where we might cross the Tsangpo, just beneath the town of Saga, and it was supposedly situated at a much lower elevation than the rest of the plateau. Furthermore, to get to this valley we would make a cross-country detour (our drivers assured us that the indestructible Land

Cruisers would have no trouble negotiating the route) that, if everything worked out, could save us at least a day's travel.

Everyone was relieved to see that Kai's illness appeared to have passed. He was quite weak when we came downstairs (he already looked as though he had lost five pounds), but he was feeling so much better than he had felt the previous afternoon and evening and was in incredibly good spirits. He greeted everybody with smiles, hugs, and toilet jokes. He especially appeared to enjoy seeing whether he could gross everyone out with the most explicit and graphic descriptions of what were immediately dubbed the four C's: the Consistency, Color, and Constitution of the undigested Contents of his stomach that had come hurling out of his mouth and behind. We loaded our gear into our cars and trucks and set out under a beautifully clear sky, the sun already blindingly bright.

The road continued to climb, and the valley surrounding the Bhotia Kosi became much broader. The sheer valley walls of the lower river system looked almost as though they had been tilted on their sides. The bases of the valley walls kept moving further away from the river itself, and the peaks of the valley walls became rounder and softer. Gradually the valley floor kept rising higher, until there was very little difference in elevation between the river valley and the immediately surrounding hills. Our Land Cruisers kept straining upward for the first hour of travel, and then gradually the road began leveling out. We had reached the Tibetan plateau.

My first thought was that there was little wonder that the Hindu cosmological system had always struck me as extremely dense and compressed, as though too much matter or information was being poured into too small a container, whereas the Tibetan Buddhist teachings were based on images of spaciousness, voidness, and emptiness. It was all right there in the land itself. The Nepalese valleys are overgrown and lush. Traveling through them, one feels like a baby swathed securely in bunting. As one climbs out of the valleys onto the plateau, the protective blankets fall away, and one stands naked before a landscape that has no sense of boundary or containment whatsoever. The spaciousness and sheer expanse of the Tibetan plateau make the open, rolling landmass of Montana seem almost insignificant in comparison. Indeed, the whole of Montana could get swallowed up into a corner of the plateau and not be found for days.

What greenery that we could see was now almost entirely confined to a narrow band that hugged either side of the life-giving banks of the river. A few hundred feet away from the nurturing water there was nothing growing at all. The light beige of the dunes surrounding Nyalam had now turned slate gray. The hills leading leisurely up from the valley floor were covered with loosely strewn boulders, as though invisible gods had been out lawn bowling. Kai and I commented on what appeared to be another complete change in the landscape and tried to count how many different worlds it felt as though we'd already ascended through.

Just at the edge of the plateau, we entered into one of the most radiantly beautiful valleys I had ever seen in my life. The residents of the valley had crafted a highly efficient irrigation system, and the entire broad, flat expanse of the valley floor was covered in crops, mostly rice and barley. The plots of different shades of yellow and green looked like an intricate jigsaw puzzle in which differently shaped pieces, mostly triangles and trapezoids, abutted and fit snugly next to one another. The color and vibrancy of the vegetation stood out against the backdrop of the surrounding gray hills and distant snow-covered peaks. In the very center of the growing fields, just at the river's edge, was the concentration of buildings in which the residents of this valley community all lived and which, like the fields themselves, looked as though they all grew out of one another.

I had traveled before to Arcosanti in central Arizona, where the Italian visionary architect Paolo Soleri is building what he believes to be a city for the future. Within that city the dwellings and places of commerce and culture are all massed closely together. This allows the communal land outside the city center to remain accessible and relatively untouched, open and free for the residents to roam about and explore or to be farmed as necessary. Soleri speaks of how his vision is a return to the traditional ways of living and sharing land and a departure from the fast-spreading urban sprawl that, like a proliferating virus that covers over and infects everything in its path, threatens to make our untouched wilderness areas a memory from the past. Surely, I thought, this gentle valley was exactly the kind of place on which Soleri had built his vision.

We could see the inhabitants of the valley in the distance working in their fields. Everything seemed unhurried, in rhythm with the natural cycle of the sun. At the northern edge of the valley was a simple, but lovingly reconstructed gompa, almost certainly rebuilt in the last decade since the Chinese destruction. We learned that the name of this community was Zhanggang and that it was a sacred pilgrimage site for Tibetan Buddhists. Next to the monastery there was a small, protected cave in which the revered yogi and poet Milarepa (1040–1123 AD) had spent time during the cold winter months. It seemed both fitting and propitious that we would encounter the legacy of Milarepa just as we entered onto the plateau, because our destination, Mount Kailas, is the other major site associated with the life of the great yogi. In the area surrounding the sacred mountain, many of his most well-known and magical exploits had occurred. It was there, legend tells us, that he engaged in daily psychic battles with a host of black magicians. The accounts of these battles sound as though they could have been lifted from the pages of J. R. R. Tolkien. The south face of Kailas, for example, is scarred by a famous series of striations that actually do resemble the steps of a staircase. In one of his fiercest encounters, a sort of sumo wrestling match at high elevations, Milarepa is said to have thrown his most evil opponent down from the summit of Kailas. As his body bounced against the sheer face of the mountain on his fall to the valley floor, large gouges were cut into the rock, and the staircase was formed.

The day passed mostly in silence. The immediate effect of the vastness and austerity of the plateau was to reveal, by comparison, the size and significance of small talk as mostly wasted energy. I had had a similar experience as a young man walking into the cathedral at Chartres. I just stood and gaped, unable to speak. When I was finally able to begin talking again to my companion, I was only able to whisper in the softest of voices.

The land was empty. Occasionally we could see a dusty cloud sprouting up like a mushroom on the distant horizon and knew that it belonged to one of the trucks from Lhasa that would soon pass us on its way to Katmandu, its driver and passengers good-naturedly waving and gesturing before we entered into the cloud of thick dust that trailed behind it like a broad, vaporous tail. Other than the occupants of the trucks, there were no people to be seen anywhere. Every couple of miles we would pass the destroyed shell of what once must have been a shrine or monastery. It felt as though we had entered into the country equivalent of a ghost town.

In the early afternoon our drivers pulled over to the side of the road to confer with one another and consult a primitive map they carried. After five minutes of consultation, their decision apparently made, they got back into their cars, and we turned left off the main highway into the countryside. This was evidently the route to the Shisha Pangma valley, and soon we found ourselves moving slowly over a very primitive dirt road. At times the road would simply disappear, and we would follow the imprint of tire tracks from vehicles that had passed this way before us over the gravelly earth and low grasses that increasingly grew wild over this region of the plateau.

Everywhere we looked there were low clumps of green, yellow, and brown grasses covering the rocky soil of the plateau like an intricately woven wool blanket. The grass was able to grow again, because water was everywhere along the ground. Sometimes it would form into actual streams that we would drive right through, as though they were nothing more than puddles on a city street; at other times the water appeared as seepage that trickled and spread aimlessly across the flat plateau. The water came from two main seasonal sources, a combination of the monsoon rains that had spilled over onto the plateau and the runoff from the melted snows of winter. Mostly it had nowhere to go. Our drivers told us that the streams on the plateau change their course and direction constantly. Eventually the water might make its way to one of the major rivers that carves a path down through the mountains into Nepal or Bhutan, but mostly the land of the plateau doesn't incline enough to form river systems that are consistent in their flow. Our drivers went on to explain that it is for this reason that it would be impossible to build a sophisticated paved road to traverse the plateau. The continually changing course of water would keep on washing the road away, unless the entire road was built on a trellis of elaborate, elevated stilts that would be prohibitively costly to construct. Even then, there could be no guarantee that one of the stilts might not one day end up right in the middle of a raging stream.

The magnificent spire of Shisha Pangma kept growing in size, the sharp peak of its summit completely covered in snow and intermittent cloud. I realized that Shisha Pangma and its neighboring peaks, now starkly silhouetted against the southern sky, formed the series of great peaks that I had seen several days earlier from my hotel room in Katmandu, as I gazed northward during lulls in the morning monsoon rain and clouds. Starting out from Katmandu, we had driven first east, then north, and now west. We had encircled three sides of Shisha Pangma as we had made our way up onto the plateau and pointed ourselves in the direction of Mount Kailas.

As we kept nearing Shisha Pangma, we began to see our first signs of life and habitation. In the distance we would see an occasional black canvas tent with a trace of smoke rising out of an opening in the center of its roof. This would be home to a nomadic family who grazed their animals on the plateau during the relatively temperate summer months. They might move their home several times during a season and then dismantle everything, seeking shelter at a lower elevation to sit out the bitter cold of winter. Outside the tents we could see sheep, wild horses, and an occasional yak.

We came to a makeshift bridge, where several nomad men were standing silently, their gaze intent on the rushing water below. We got out of our cars to greet them, but they didn't acknowledge us. They just kept staring down, their eyes fixed on an object in the river. We looked down with them, but at first couldn't figure out what we were actually looking at. Only gradually did we realize that we were looking at a human leg, quite swollen, with a red low-top tennis shoe still attached to the foot. Our drivers spoke to the nomads. They told us that some-one had gone missing several days earlier. He had been known to drink too much *chang*, the local barley-based alcohol that was brewed on the plateau. Now the people knew what had become of him.

They appeared quite unfazed in their discovery and acceptance of their comrade's death. For the devout Buddhist nomads of the plateau, death is an integral part of the great cycle of life, a moment of passage not necessarily unlike or more significant than any other. Their de-ceased friend had evidently led a very troubled life, and they expressed their hopes that his death would release the dark spirits that had attached themselves to his soul.

We set up camp in a magnificent green meadow just at the edge of a gently flowing stream that wove its way through the rich grasses and supplied them with their source of life. Just as our drivers had indicated, the meadow was situated in the middle of a large valley cradled on three sides by the sheltering flanks of snow-covered mountains. Contrary to what they had assured us, however, the readings on our altimeters indicated that we were at almost fifteen thousand feet, alarm-ingly higher than we had hoped to be. There was nothing we could do about this. We alerted everyone in our group about the unanticipated increase in altitude, and we all agreed that it would be prudent to rest and conserve our energy as much as possible and definitely not to set off on long, ambitious walks.

Save for the occasional murmur of the stream or a sudden gust of wind moving through the grasses, our campsite was completely devoid of sound. True silence possesses a palpability that affects the body more as though it were a quality of touch than a feature, even in its absence, of sound. We could all feel it deeply. The silence was humbling. The val-ley was also completely deserted. Other than an occasional bird that would light down on the meadow, looking lost and out of place, as though it had taken a wrong turn somewhere, there were no living beings anywhere to be seen.

And then, suddenly and mysteriously, as though they had sprouted directly out of the earth or stepped out from behind a shrub that could not possibly have concealed them, our campsite was filled with more than a dozen nomads. Mothers and small children were soon followed by their men, some of whom walked into our camp, while others rode in on horseback. Everyone appeared supremely curious about these strange visitors to the meadow with their cars, trucks, and state-of-the-art tents. They were also completely unself-conscious in the expression of their curiosity. They would come right up to us and poke and touch us as though they needed to make sure we were actually real and not just a group of phantoms come down from the mountains or heavens. The women were dressed in black double-breasted dresses that were covered in layers of wool aprons with brightly colored rainbow stripes. Several of them sported impressively strung conch shell bracelets on their wrists which at first looked out of place, but ultimately spoke to the watery ancestry of the plateau. The men's long black hair was tied up in a single braid that was then secured to their head with a silken red sash. Both the men and women had on brightly colored canvas sneakers that looked like something the Boston Celtics might have worn in the 1950s. A baby, no more than a year old, was bundled in striped wool sweaters and leggings and attached by two cords to her mother's back. In an ingenious solution to dealing with a pre–toilet trained child in an area of the world that had probably never seen or even heard of a diaper, the bottom of her leggings had been cut out large and round, and her bum was fully exposed.

The nomads were as curious about our tents as they were about us. As the *Sherpas* traveling with us began helping us set up our tents, the nomads raced over to examine them. They poked at the fabric and made clucking sounds with their tongues, as the tents were quickly erected. Certainly the space-age alloy support rods and ultralightweight rain-resistant material of our tents must have appeared magical to them in contrast to the hefty wooden poles and multiple sheets of heavy black canvas that they used to construct their tents. Our tents could be set up and taken down in a matter of minutes. It would take the better part of a day to dismantle or reassemble their structures.

When we went inside our tents to lay down and rest before dinner, the nomads hurried over and squatted excitedly just outside our doors. Savoring the best of both worlds, they could continue to observe us, but still touch and probe the mystery of our tents. It was clear that they were more in awe of our tents than of us.

As I watched them, I realized that they were completely at home in this pleasant meadow. Unlike us, nothing about this land was unfamiliar to them. The plateau was their home and extended living room. They had nothing with which to contrast the vast space and openness of the plateau, and they were certainly not awed into mute silence by its presence and size. Quite the opposite, they chirped like spring birds and cried out excitedly back and forth between one another as they came across a new member of our group or rushed to watch another tent go up.

Just before dinner Faye emerged from her tent and waved for the nomads to come over to her. Faye is large in bosom with features like a Hindu goddess, and the men raced over to see who could be the first to stand at her side. She reached into a bag and began freely passing out plastic-coated, colored pictures of Tibetan deities. Seeing what she was distributing, the women too ran over, leaving aside their jealousies about this buxom newcomer who held such a fascination for their men. The nomads cherished their pictures, as though Faye had been dispensing gold nuggets. Some of them cried. All of them wanted us to take pictures of them displaying their new gift. Faye brought out a book richly illustrated with pictures of the Tibetan pantheon of gods and goddesses, and the nomads dropped to their knees to bow to it and lovingly touched each other's heads with it.

It is foolish to romanticize the lives of the nomads and pilgrims whom we met during our time on the plateau. It is a very hard life. Many people die at a young age. And, yet, the people of the plateau are extraordinarily open in heart, genuinely childlike and friendly. The culture shock that I was to experience on this trip did not occur in Asia, but was waiting for me when I stepped off the plane back in Canada and was driven back to my comfortable, but modest, home that was larger and more luxurious than any dwelling I had seen in weeks. But mostly it was the people. Back home in the West, I could see our fear and mistrust, the way in which we shut our hearts, cramp our bodies, and hold our minds to patterns of judgment and suspicion. I also grieved over the churches that dot the valley in which I live and that open their imposing doors for a few hours on Sunday for their congregations to bring prayer into their lives, as though spirituality were a muscle that could be exercised on the most infrequent basis and still remain firmly toned. On the Tibetan plateau spirituality is as natural a thread in the woven fabric of daily life as are the acts of eating, sleeping, and laboring. It is not something that is compartmentalized off into a few minutes or hours of the day or week. The people on the plateau, like the mountains, the air, and the earth itself, radiate the most natural and unselfconscious sense of spirit that I have ever seen. I am also clear that I am a child of the West and could not, even if I wanted to, appropriate the naturalness of spirit that I found in the people of the plateau for myself. As Westerners, we have been born to other opportunities and other challenges. And still I felt I had so very much to learn from these simple, decent people who greeted us so warmly into the living room of their meadow.

＿＞

Dinner that evening was a delicious broth of lentils and squash, white rice, and freshly baked chapatis. We were all a bit giddy from the altitude and our meetings with the community of nomads and had fully recovered our tongues, lost earlier in the day to the austere majesty of the plateau. We'd become quite close as a group in a short amount of time, and over dinner we began searching our collective memories for jokes that might even remotely be related to our journey. Most of the jokes poked innocent and good-natured fun at the foibles of the human animal. A few were just awful. Occasionally someone would pause before the punch line and ask me to cover Kai's ears. He seemed to find this action as funny as some of the punch lines he was missing. On a number of occasions we toasted the altitude for suspending our discrimination and rendering us light-headed enough to enjoy a story that would very likely have induced pained groans at sea level.

I told the story of the Catholic priest who was the only passenger traveling from Nepal to Tibet aboard a small propeller plane that developed sudden and severe engine trouble high above the Himalayas. As the young Nepalese pilot wrestled to keep control of the aircraft, first one engine, and then the next, sputtered into silence. The plane began quietly gliding downward.

In the thickest of Nepalese accents the pilot turned to the priest and informed him, "Father, Father! All is lost! The plane is going to crash, and there is only one parachute! Certainly you, a celibate priest, will understand that I, a family man with a devoted wife and many children to feed and care for, must take the parachute and save myself."

The priest replied, "Yes, my son. You must save yourself, and I will have to make peace with my Maker. I have always believed in the power of prayer, and perhaps if I pray forcefully enough, I will be saved. Dear God, please help me in my hour of. . . ."

But the Nepalese pilot interrupted before the priest could proceed any further in his prayer. "Father, Father! Your prayers to your Christian god will be of no avail! We are flying over the land of the Buddha! If you want to have any chance of saving yourself, you must show proper respect and address your prayers to the Buddha himself! I wish you every good luck! Bye, bye!"

And with those words the pilot jumped safely from the plane. As the horrified priest watched the parachute open far beneath him and felt the plane continue to plummet, he thought to himself, "Well, maybe that young man has a point. And certainly, in this hour of predicament, I have nothing to lose."

And so he decided to invoke the Buddha and ask for His help.

"Oh, Buddha, Buddha, please help and save me in my hour of need. Oh, Buddha, Buddha, please help and save me in my hour of need."

And with those words a giant hand came floating upward from far beneath the clouds, its palm facing in the direction of the heavens, and caught and cradled the plane and began shepherding it down safely.

The priest couldn't believe his eyes. Drenched in perspiration, with tears of great gratitude streaming down his cheeks, he cried out, "Ohhh, thank God, thank God!"

And with those words the giant hand slowly turned itself over, and the plane once again began to fall. . . .

With those words we ended our evening meal, wished each other a good night's sleep, and made our way out into the darkness. Unfamiliar stars covered the deep blue-black of the sky like grains of salt that had been spilled from a picnic basket onto a black sand beach. The nomads were still gathered in the meadow, milling about as though it were a town square in a Mexican village on a Friday night. They came up to us holding their pictures once again to their foreheads and nodding their heads in deeply felt thanks. When we awoke in the morning, most of them were still there. They had slept in the meadow all night, oblivious to the dampness of the grass and the light drizzle that fell during the early morning hours, wanting to wish us well before we departed.

September 9

It wasn't until we awoke in the morning and began moving about that we started to feel the altitude. Just to stuff our sleeping bags back into their carrying sacks was exhausting, and I had to stop two or three times to catch my breath. Kai had had his first undisturbed sleep in several nights, and it looked as though he was indeed finished with his illness. He was still quite weak, however, and the altitude left him feeling weaker still. Walking across the meadow to have breakfast in our dining tent felt like a major excursion. Our breakfast spoons felt heavy in our hands, our arms sluggish as they lifted porridge from bowl to mouth over and over again. The large jug of heated milk that was passed around the table had to be steadied by two people, as a small amount of milk was poured into a single cup of Bournvita. As we walked back to our tents in the clear morning air, our bellies full but our heads light, it felt as though we were moving in slow motion, and it seemed to take an unusually long time to gather our belongings and supplies together, load them back onto the trucks and cars, say a last good-bye to the nomads, and set out on our way.

Within about two miles or so, we left any semblance of a road behind. The route our drivers were following wound through canyons and mountains and crossed constantly back and forth over riverbeds, some wet, others dry. For more than half an hour the Land Cruisers lurched slowly and jerkily, as we drove along the middle of a dry riverbed that looked as though it would produce turbulent rapids if water were flowing through. Even though the land through which we were moving was beautiful, the russet and deep ochre walls of the canyon still wet from the early morning rain and glistening when touched by the sun, we began to become irritable with the slowness of our pace, grumbling aloud whether this shortcut was going to end up costing us time in the end. What was disturbing us even more, however (even though we were all hesitant to voice such a concern out loud), was the fact that we hadn't passed any trucks or cars coming from the other direction since we'd left the main road the previous afternoon. Admittedly, this was not a heavily trafficked route, but even a single vehicle coming toward us would indicate that the river ahead was crossable. One of the documented, psychological effects of a sudden increase in altitude is that feelings in all their different states of emotional elevation, from the most profound heights of ecstatic expression to the deepest gullies of depression, become magnified. A slight upset becomes tears. A momentary happiness becomes rapture. In our case, as our cars kept trundling over the rocky surface like an extended amusement park ride that we wanted to get off of, we were all becoming cranky.

Suddenly our driver shouted for our attention. He began tapping his finger excitedly against the windshield, pointing to an object on the distant horizon that would appear, disappear, and then come into view again. We strained to see what he was pointing at, tried to catch it in one of its moments of appearance, and then our hearts jumped. It was a dust cloud! A vehicle was coming from the other direction. The canyon land maze through which we had been moving may have delighted us with strange rock formations and combinations of color, but this small wisp of dust on the horizon was the most welcome sight we'd seen all day.

As the cloud kept coming nearer, we were able to make out the features of two vehicles, a Land Cruiser and supply truck similar to our own. We immediately assumed that they must belong to a small party returning from Mount Kailas and looked forward to stopping, visiting with them, and finding out as much information as possible about the conditions of the road ahead. They evidently wanted to speak with us as well, for as our cars converged, they gestured to us and asked us to stop.

Three Austrian men emerged from the Land Cruiser. They spoke passable English, and the story they told us was not what we had wanted to hear. Our spirits plunged. They were not returning from Mount Kailas, as we had assumed. They too were trying to get to Mount Kailas. The Tsangpo River was impassably flooded, swollen in size from the unseasonably late monsoon rains. There was no way that a car could drive across it. They had been waiting at the crossing below the town of Saga for three days, hoping that a ferry the Chinese officials kept promising would arrive would actually materialize. They had been told that morning that the ferry would not appear after all and were advised to travel several hundred miles to the east in hopes of finding a ferry that might take them across just outside the town of Lhatse. As if this news weren't bad enough, they then told us that they had already waited at this other ferry crossing for thirteen days before being advised that it was not likely that a ferry would appear in Lhatse this year and that they should drive over to Saga to see if a ferry might show up there!

Their news simply stunned us. If we couldn't get across the Tsangpo, our trip would be over. The Southern Route would be effectively blocked, and there would be no realistic way for us to reach Mount Kailas. The only other possibility, to drive to Lhasa and take the Northern Route out to the mountain, would add at least ten days to our travels, far more time than we could afford. The Austrians told us that they were going to go back to Lhatse for one more day and, if a ferry did not magically materialize, head back to Katmandu.

I'm sure that the altitude aggravated the emotion, but I have rarely felt so depressed in all my life as when we got back in our cars and turned around to head back over to Lhatse. Like a Roman candle that fizzles instead of soars, it looked as though Kai's and my dream was over before it had even gotten off the ground, its hope unrealized. I felt foolish for pushing ahead with this trip that, except for my small inheritance, I clearly couldn't afford. Before we had left North America, everyone had cautioned us that the roads might not be passable, but I hadn't wanted to hear or believe them. I had put Kai through the worst illness of his life. Some rite of passage this was turning out to be.

The other people in our party were all far more affluent than I am. If they really had their hearts set on reaching Mount Kailas, they could come back next year and try again. Not so for us. I was overdrawn at the bank as it was. Jonathan moaned that maybe he was bad luck for everybody, that maybe he simply wasn't destined to get to Mount Kailas in this life. Talk turned quickly to what our other alternatives might be. Perhaps we could drive to Lhasa or visit the Everest base camp before returning to Katmandu. My hopes for pilgrimage and questing were rapidly turning into just another tourist trip. We would wait until we reached Lhatse the following morning before making any decisions, but realistically we all knew that those decisions would have to be made. Someone in our car reminded us all of Yogi Berra's famous credo for optimists, "It ain't over 'til it's over," but somehow holding to the vision that a ferry would actually show up out of the ethers felt, under the circumstances, like grasping at the most weakly rooted straw in hopes of breaking one's free fall down a Himalayan cliff.

As if the drive back over toward Lhatse was not going to be gloomy enough, a high layer of clouds slowly formed out of the south and covered the sun. The drive back down the dry riverbed felt even more jarring than it had an hour earlier. The canyon walls, so wet and shining just a few hours earlier, were dry now. They looked dull and flat, as though all the color had been leached out of the stone. They'd been alive with the presence of spirits when we had passed through earlier. Now it looked as though they'd turned back into rock. Most disheartening of all was the appearance of the meadow in which we had camped the evening before. It had been so beautiful and magical when we first saw it, but now it just seemed to taunt us and remind us of our failed efforts. We had left it this morning, commenting aloud that we would never again see this magnificent place, and now suddenly here we were again, five hours later, back to where we had started, half a day wasted. There was no sign of the nomads anywhere.

We decided to camp for the evening on the Tingri plain beneath Mount Everest, perhaps a two-hour drive from Lhatse. It is reported to be a particularly beautiful area with spectacular, unobstructed views of some of the highest peaks on the planet. By the time we arrived in the early evening, however, the high, light clouds that had formed earlier in the day had dropped low and thickened. In some places it looked as though they touched the ground. We stepped out of our cars into something halfway between a mist and a light, persistent drizzle. The mountains, like the nomads a few hours earlier, were nowhere to be seen. As soon as we set up our tents, it began raining in earnest.

Kai and I rested in our tent, not saying much to each other. We were both clearly upset, but doing our best not to show it. Better to say nothing than to voice our truth. The wind outside the tent sounded like a whimpering animal. In the distance we heard the clear tone of a bell cut through the gusting sounds of the wind and rain. It was dinnertime. We put on warm clothes and boots, and began to leave our tent. Suddenly, Kai called out to me, "Dad, I just remembered. It's Lord Ganesh's birthday today!"

As we walked over to the dining tent, my mind began to play with this information and its associations. Ganesh is the Hindu god of good fortune and had long been a favorite of mine. He appeared in the form of a seated elephant, and I had always loved elephants. I remembered back to when I was a toddler in nursery school and for months would shuffle around the house with my arms extended out together in front of my face, loud bleating groans erupting from my throat, pretending I was an elephant king. I puzzled over why Kai would even know that it was Ganesh's celebration day (later he would tell me that he overheard some of the Sherpas talking about it with Jonathan several days earlier) and pondered over the bitter incongruity of finding ourselves in what I viewed as the most unlucky predicament of my life on a day in which hundreds of millions of devout Hindus only a few hundred miles to the south of us were celebrating the god of good fortune.

The gathering inside the dining tent felt like a funeral wake. Small talk went nowhere. Punch lines to jokes fizzled like the earlier Roman candle of my dreams. The food tasted particularly bland.

At the end of the meal I spoke up and told everyone of Kai's reminder before coming into dinner. I talked of Lord Ganesh and told everyone everything that I knew about him, which was admittedly not very much. I lamely suggested that perhaps, when we went back to our tents, we should all pray to Ganesh to help us to get across the river tomorrow. Vassi then added that Ganesh is one of Lord Shiva's sons, and I commented that within Hindu cosmology, Mount Kailas is known to be one of Shiva's favorite abodes. Looking around the table, I felt a faint sense of hope entering back into our group for the first time since turning around earlier in the day. People were at least looking at each other again and nodding their heads to the story of the beneficent elephant god. As we got up to leave, I drolly reminded everybody to make sure that they prayed to Ganesh and not to God. When we walked out into the night, I caught the first light sounds of laughter that I had heard since the morning.

Back in my tent, snuggled into my sleeping bag, I felt like the Catholic priest from my joke the evening before. I felt awkward praying, let alone to an exotic Hindu deity, but closed my eyes and silently began asking Lord Ganesh for help. Over and over again I called to him, spelling out as specifically as possible what I needed from him. I told him of my love for elephants and of my respect for his abilities and ministry. I told him of my love for Kai and how we had hoped to journey together to the sacred mountain of his father. I kept silently invoking him in this way for ten or fifteen minutes. As with the repetition of a mantra, my mind began to slow and my body relax, when suddenly an image of Ganesh burst forth in my mind. I could see him very clearly. He was orangish red, draped in a checkered dhoti that hung over one of his shoulders, his trunk resting in his lap. His body was soft and smooth. The texture of his hairless skin reminded me of the orcas I had seen in the waters off Vancouver Island. His head rocked slowly from side to side. His eyes were slowly blinking, and he was smiling. Much as in my vision in Katmandu several nights earlier, a blindingly bright white light then erupted from the center of his body. As the brightness of the light dispersed into fragments and settled like snowflakes in a paperweight, I could clearly see the features of the snow mountain of Kailas emerging through the storm. I couldn't honestly tell whether I was forcing a fantasy or if this was a promising sign, but I welcomed it all the same and fell quickly asleep.

At four in the morning I awoke from a dream in which I was reading the opening page of one of my favorite books written by one of my favorite authors. *Return to Greco* is an autobiographical novel by the great Greek writer Nikos Kazantzakis. Even in translation there are phrases on virtually every page that take the breath away. *Return to Greco* was the last book Kazantzakis ever wrote, a consummate and deeply personal ode to the path and progression of spiritual practice by an enormously gifted writer who had one last gift to share. On the opening page he lists three different prayers for three different types of people, all of them addressed to the ultimate archer.

The first prayer for the first type of soul says simply, "I am a bow in your hands, Lord. Draw me, lest I rot." The second prayer for the second soul implores, "Do not overdraw me, Lord. I shall break." The third prayer for the third type of soul reads, "Overdraw me, Lord, and who cares if I break!"

In my half-sleep my thoughts turned to prayer and to the occasions in my life when prayer had touched and affected me. I looked over at Kai. He was sleeping peacefully. I thought back to myself as a child and saw myself in Kai. Many people have commented that pictures I have of myself at Kai's age resemble Kai more than they currently do me. I remembered back to the trip I had taken with my parents to the Florida Keys and of my dreams and hopes of catching a sailfish. And then, suddenly, I remembered my vision of Ganesh just before falling asleep. I began praying again to the elephant.

And then the words came, "Dear Ganesh, I am an arrow to your bow. Please shoot Kai and me across that river tomorrow!"

September 10

We left early the next morning in nervous anticipation of what was awaiting us down the road, only the slightest strands of hope threading their way, like the faint morning sun, through an overwhelmingly large cloud cover of resignation. We knew our chances were not good. Vassi had taken one of the Land Cruisers and gone on ahead even earlier. Of all the people in our party, he had had the most experience dealing with Chinese bureaucracy, and he thought that perhaps he might be able to bribe a Chinese official into producing a ferry for us. We had all agreed that if bribery would produce results, we would pay whatever it cost. But the abundance of destroyed buildings that we passed, their architectural carcasses littering the sides of the road, did not exactly inspire a great deal of hope that a Chinese magistrate might look favorably on the requests of a small group of Westerners trying to get to a sacred Tibetan site.

The mood in the car was curiously calm. It reminded me of the accounts of embattled politicians who make peace with their destiny and become almost serene once they've made up their mind to resign their position. As we neared the inevitable river crossing, the sun finally managed to peer through the heavy layer of clouds.

Rounding a bend, we saw Vassi standing by the side of the road. He motioned for us to stop. I held my breath. He spoke to the passengers in the car in front of us for several minutes and then ushered them on. I wouldn't let myself believe that this might be a favorable sign, but then he turned to our car, flashed a smile that would have given the Cheshire cat competition, and gave us the thumbs-up signal. Our whole car erupted into repeated shrieks of "Yes!" Fists pumped and shot high in the air, and we all hugged each other roughly, the pent-up emotional energy of the last twenty-four hours pouring out into the force of our touch.

We were barely able to hear his story as we kept shouting our mixture of relief and exhilaration. Vassi said he could hardly believe the story himself. The ferry had shown up yesterday afternoon for a convoy of army trucks that were coming the other way. The officials with whom he spoke would give him no guarantees that it would run longer than a day, and they were limiting who would be allowed to use the ferry. All it had cost us were several cartons of cigarettes to secure the promise that our Land Cruisers and trucks would be taken across.

Vassi reached through the open car window, pulled Kai to him, and gave him a huge hug. "So, Kai, what's this that you've got going with Lord Ganesh, eh? Well, whatever it is, keep it up!"

As our car proceeded down to the river's edge, I slumped back in my seat. I felt suddenly exhausted from the roller-coaster ride of emotions that the last twenty-four hours had put us through. I couldn't believe our reversal of fortune. How could it be?! The appearance of the ferry on this day at this time felt as though God (or, I should say, Ganesh) had descended onto the river in the form of a machine, like a deus ex machina out of some elaborate, baroque pageant in which a completely hopeless situation is salvaged by the sudden, unexpected appearance of a divine hand. I felt as stunned by this inexplicable show of good fortune as I had felt by the bad news we'd received from the Austrians the day before, the opposite sides of the coin of bewilderment. I began to feel that maybe we were destined to get to Mount Kailas after all, but that we were going to have to earn the privilege. Kai's illness and the impossible seesaw of emotions we had experienced in the last day were the rites of purification and the price of admission that the mountain was demanding of us in order to come close to it. A voice inside told me that we would need continued faith, surrender, and trust. Whatever was to come next, I realized that this clearly was not going to be a predictable road trip along the interstate with regular stops at rest areas for coffee and pie.

At the river's edge we got out of our cars and continued to celebrate our incomprehensible good luck. The river was as gray as the surrounding hills. The current looked to be strong, creating multiple eddies and even small waves, as it flowed to the east. I guessed that it must be at least five hundred feet wide at this place of crossing. If a car or truck had attempted to drive across the river, it would have been swept away within thirty feet.

The source of the Tsangpo is very close to Mount Kailas itself, and for quite some time European explorers believed that its headwaters originated from an outflow on the eastern shore of Lake Manasarovar, the great lake that lies at the foot of the sacred mountain. It carves a slow and deliberate course eastward between the hills and mountains of the plateau before making a sharp turn to the south just above the far northeastern corner of India. Dropping precipitously through a series of spectacular gorges, it turns west once it has reached the plains of India, where it becomes the Brahmaputra, one of ancient India's most legendary waterways. Turning again south through Bangladesh, it converges with the Ganges about sixty miles from Dhaka. Together the waters empty into the Bay of Bengal, which separates India from Burma. The funneled mouth of this joined river system forms a vortex that, like a powerful geographical magnet, draws to it some of the most terrifying weather systems on the planet. Cyclones and subsequent flooding routinely claim thousands of lives every few years.

We watched as two large Chinese army supply trucks were being loaded onto the ferry on the far side of the river. The ferry was nothing more than a flat, steel barge about fifty feet long. On both of its sides it had protective, but flimsy-looking railings from which a multitude of red and white circular life preservers were unreassuringly hung. As the ferry began its slow passage across to us, we could see that it had no power of its own. It was connected by a steel cable to another larger cable that spanned the river and was secured into a massive concrete block on the banks at either side. The purpose of the cable was to stabilize the ferry and prevent it from being swept away by the current. At the stern of the barge was a single, twenty-foot-long, wooden oar that allowed the crew to maneuver the ferry as it made its slow and laborious way across the river. Extending itself incongruously out into the water, moving constantly from side to side, it looked like an elephant's trunk. At either end of the ferry was a pair of curved steel pylons, about ten feet tall, which supported cables that lowered and raised a loading ramp. Isolated against the background of river, small village, hills, and sky, they looked like a mammoth pair of elephant tusks.

As the ferry neared our shore, a thirty-foot rope cable was thrown toward us. We ducked out of the way, but once it had struck the ground, everyone in our group ran over to it, grabbed a section before it could slip back into the water, and slowly began to pull the stern of the ferry over to a cement landing off of which the trucks could drive. Once the ferry was unloaded, our drivers gingerly inched our Land Cruisers onto the barge, and we began floating back to the other side.

The buildings in the small village on the far side of the river were constructed with thick mud walls and flat roofs. Doors and windows had been carved out of the walls, and the ends of logs, whose lengths supported the flat roofs, extended out from the top of the walls. It felt as though we had entered a primitive town in northern New Mexico.

As we sat down on cement benches and half-walls in the town square, we were immediately surrounded by a crowd of townspeople. Like the nomads of the meadow, they appeared to be endlessly fascinated by us. We were all quite giddy to have crossed the river, and we spontaneously began to entertain them with what an embarrassed Kai labeled as "seriously hurting" versions of *Yellow Submarine*, *Runaway*, and *Row, Row, Row Your Boat*. The townspeople loved it and shared songs and dances back with us. Jennifer then reached into her pack and produced a softly molded rubber hand puppet of a goat. The puppet was uncannily realistic, and she began chasing the children around the square with it. At first they would run away from her, out of shyness more than fear, but then they would let her catch them and erupt into yelps of laughter, as the goat nibbled on their arms.

We decided not to wait for our supply trucks to cross the river, but instead drove a few miles out of town, where we stopped for a picnic lunch and a rest. Our trucks would meet up with us once they had crossed the river. Our wait, however, turned out to be several hours long, as the Chinese official in charge of the ferry decided to take a long, drunken lunch break and ordered the ferry to stop running in his absence. With a head full of chang, he became impervious to any further bribes and was starting to get annoyed by our driver's continual pestering to start the ferry up again. They wisely realized that it would not be prudent to antagonize him and left him to his meal and extended nap. It wasn't until the middle of the afternoon that they finally caught up with us.

Countering our exhilaration of having crossed the river was the practical realization that we were now far behind schedule, and so we decided to drive as far into the early night as felt safe. The roads, of course, are not lit, and they are pitted with ruts and holes, and we wanted to balance our new need to "hasten not too slowly" with making sure that we didn't have an accident. We were now on the main road of the Southern Route, and like main routes everywhere, the road had drawn people and settlements to its lifeline. Every thirty miles or so we would pass through another small town. Occasionally we would stop and play with the townspeople. The puppets proved irresistible. Everyone we encountered was warm and friendly toward us. They were also genuinely childlike and playful. The gentleness, beauty, and openness of the nomads and townspeople continued to charm us and open our hearts. It felt as though we were falling in love with these people and their land. Like lovers everywhere, we began to romanticize the perfected objects of our affection. Like lovers everywhere, we were setting ourselves up for an inevitable fall.

In the early evening, the sun still suspended above the distant hills but dropping fast, we entered into a village just like all the other villages through which we'd passed that afternoon. Unlike the other towns, however, there was no one in the streets. The village appeared to be deserted, and the atmosphere in the early evening light felt distinctly forlorn. Where were the friendly faces that we had come to expect, the waves and smiles?

On the far side of town everything changed in a breath. The car that Kai and I were traveling in was in the lead, and as we left the narrow streets of the village back out into the open space of the plateau, we drove right into the middle of a large crowd of people. Our car had to slow to a crawl, and like a family of deer that suddenly senses the presence of a nearby hunter, everyone in our car became still and alert. The energy of this gathered group of townspeople and nomads felt totally different from what we had become accustomed to expect from the inhabitants of the plateau. The people looked dull and vacuous. Their faces were empty of expression, as though something or someone had come and drained away their humanity. They didn't walk with any of the grace and fluidity that we had seen in virtually all the other inhabitants of the plateau. Instead, their bodies staggered jerkily back and forth in our path. It didn't take long for us to realize that they were all very drunk. Nor did they appear to be happily inebriated. They looked instead to be "mean drunk."

Wooden carts were rolled in front of our path and wouldn't move aside. People began converging on our cars and jostling them, as we slowly tried to move through the crowd. A few yards away we saw people fighting with each other. Their blows to each other's heads were nauseatingly real. We could hear the dull thud of fist on flesh. It sounded like a melon bursting as it was dropped to the ground. A short distance away three people were carrying a fallen comrade. His body was comatose. We couldn't tell if this person was dead or just extremely drunk.

Both our car and the car directly behind us got through safely, but the third Land Cruiser was not so lucky. Just as it was about to clear the crowd and carts, someone leapt onto the hood and began to smash the windshield with his fist. He was so drunk, however, that he lost his balance, as the car continued to inch its way forward, and he tumbled to the ground. At exactly the same time, someone standing behind the car threw a rock that shattered the rear window. Both side mirrors were torn off, as our driver kept trying to steer the car through the crowd. Other townspeople were trying to pull the doors open, when our driver finally found an opening in the crowd and accelerated away from the village.

Our supply trucks were forced to stop. Several people in the crowd jumped aboard the trucks and started beating our crew. Eventually they let the trucks pass but kept two of the Sherpas who were traveling with us hostage. One of the town's officials boarded a truck and insisted on being driven out to where we were going to camp for the night. He claimed that one of our cars had struck and run over one of the towns-people, but nothing like that had happened at all.

As with so many indigenous peoples in other parts of the world, alcohol is a poison for the people of the plateau and, evidently, an irre-sistible one. I had never before seen so many extremely drunk people gathered together in one place, and it saddened and frightened me to see how the fermented barley drink had ravaged these kind and friendly people, turning them ugly.

Wanting to make sure that we would not be followed, we drove for at least ten or twelve miles before stopping for the night. For the third time in thirty-six hours we felt completely stunned. We talked among ourselves, trying to piece together the sequence of events, trying to make sense of this unprovoked attack. There was really none to be found. Everything had happened so quickly. Miraculously, no one had been hurt. We had been extraordinarily fortunate that Dawa, our kind and gentle Tibetan driver whose vehicle had been attacked, had remained so remarkably calm throughout the assault. As he was recounting his version of the events, however, he began to tremble and then broke down into deep, guttural sobs. We all held and soothed him and helped him down to the ground, as the fear, upset, and adrenal endorphins slowly drained out of his body. When he was able to speak again, he told us in the softest of voices that what upset him most was his deep embarrassment for his people. His car, his major possession in which he had so much pride and which secured him a position of sta-tus within his community, had also sustained a considerable amount of damage, but that was fate, and he could live with and accept that. The behavior of his people, though, had caused his heart to ache. The way he so readily accepted his fate touched all of us, but the reality of his predicament did not sit so well with us as it did with him. Insurance is an alien concept in Tibet. He would have to pay to fix his car himself. It would wipe out whatever earnings he had hoped to make by participating in this journey and could seriously compromise his future financial status. We immediately began talking among ourselves and decided that we would all contribute to a fund to cover the costs of repair for this kind man, whose composure had averted a situation that could have very easily ended our trip. Had anyone been seriously hurt, either one of the townspeople or someone from our group, we would have all had to travel to the nearest Chinese police post. Most likely we would have had to stay there for days, while the officials decided what to do and whom to charge. We knew that once again we had been extraordinarily lucky. The elephant had evidently not left us at the ferry, but had gotten into our cars and driven along with us as an invisible passenger.

As it was, we still had to negotiate the release and return of our Sherpas. Vassi left immediately with Dawa, another Tibetan driver, and the official from town. The official forced two of the drunken townspeople to come with them, and together these six unlikely traveling companions set out for a Chinese police post an hour's drive away. By the time they arrived, the townspeople had sobered up considerably and quickly broke down and apologized for their behavior. They admitted that no one had been struck by any of our vehicles and vowed to release our Sherpas as soon as they returned to the village.

To the people of the plateau not lucky enough to have been born into one of the wealthy, landowning families, there have traditionally been only two major occupational options (plus an additional, decidedly less attractive one) from which to choose. The majority of people who are born into nomad families will remain nomads all their life. Their traditions and style of life have continued relatively unchanged for countless generations. With very few exceptions there is little difference in the way Tibetan nomads of the late twentieth century live from the way their ancestors lived hundreds of years ago. The second time-honored occupation of choice, especially open to men, is to enter into a monastery and become a monk. Before the Chinese invasion, at least one male member of each family would enter into one of the religious orders. It was an occupation that offered security for life, as well as the possibility for real spiritual development, and the main monasteries and religious sects became both powerful and wealthy.

But up until quite recently, there has existed a third lesser career choice for an inhabitant of the plateau for whom the nomadic and monastic lives hold little appeal, and that is to become a bandit. Especially on the largely uninhabited western range of the plateau, where there are few rules or laws and little ability to enforce them even if they did exist, small fringe bands of wandering *dacoits* led by Tibetan Butch Cassidys or Jesse Jameses would roam and prey on parties of pilgrims and on each other.

For different reasons the Chinese have disapproved of all three of the occupational choices. The nomad families were entirely too independent for the feverishly ideological Red Guards, who descended onto the plateau, like secular missionaries, with visions of a Communist utopia in which the fruits of labor would be communally shared. The nomads love the give and take of barter, but this was looked upon by the Chinese invaders as bourgeois and capitalistic behavior. The religious beliefs of the monks and nuns, which the Chinese fearfully branded as superstitious, threatened that vision even further. At least the Chinese tolerated the nomads. The monks and the nuns they set out to destroy.

Bandits could also not be tolerated within a Communist utopia, and the Chinese have created a system of police posts that dot the plateau every few hundred miles. The traditions, however, even in spite of the repression and attack, die hard. Up until recently the far-western plains of the plateau were much like the American West of the early 1800s. It was a frontier land for independently spirited pioneers. The American pioneers settled. The Tibetan pioneers roam. Religion continues to be the most vital current animating Tibetan culture and society, even if it has mostly been forced underground. Although the organized bands of bandits have largely died out or been disbanded, periodic hell-raising has always been a shadow side of the pioneer spirit and continues to this day. In the presence of alcohol, the old ghosts and ancestors come back to life. Driving into the crowd at the far edge of town, it felt as though we had driven back in time a hundred years and found ourselves in the proverbial wrong place at the wrong time. When the alcohol is fully metabolized and makes its way out of the system, remorse for one's actions and requests for forgiveness from the assembled Buddhas and Bodhisattvas replace the actions of the shadow ancestors.

The Chinese would like everything to be meticulously ordered and scrubbed free of what they view as the contaminations of individualism, religion, and the outlaw spirit. To this end they've attempted to legislate homogeneity in a region that has thrived on diversity of human expression for hundreds of years. By shining what they perceive as the bright light of correct behavior onto the affairs of the people of the plateau, the Chinese hope to reshape Tibetan culture into a Communist society. Even the monks and nuns know, however, that the dark side of human nature must be embraced. A place must be set at the table for our shadow sides as well. For the practitioners of Tibetan Vajrayana Buddhism, the dark side was accepted for what it was and enlisted to become a force for enlightenment and a protector of the teachings, and many of the deities of the Tibetan pantheon have dual personalities, sometimes peaceful and beneficent, other times wrathful and frightening. One of the beauties of the Tibetan Vajrayana is that all the many levels and dimensions of life are embraced and allowed to coexist. In this way the traditional worlds of the monk, the nomad, and the bandit have existed for centuries side by side, the one complementing and completing the other. Together they have formed a unit that represents the whole spectrum of human experience: the heaven of religion as explored by the monks and nuns, the hell of the human passions of desire and greed indulged in with ignorance and suffering by the bandits, and the earthly domain of the nomadic life in between.

⟶

September 11 and 12

The days became indistinguishable, the one rolling into the next, as though time were playing leapfrog with itself. The Tibetan plateau, vast to begin with, seems even larger than it is due to the relatively slow pace at which vehicles can travel. Rivers would constantly have to be forded, the water routinely rising above the wheel wells of our Land Cruisers. The roads were often pitted with a maze of craters through which our drivers had to slowly steer the cars. If they missed seeing one, or if they misnegotiated their path around another, we would be bounced roughly into the air. Our heads would strike the roof and our bottoms would come crashing back down onto seats, whose springs and cushioning had long ago deteriorated. We felt as though we were unmatched socks being tossed about in a dryer. When we entered into yet another river, we wryly changed the description to socks in a washing machine.

Sometimes the road simply disappeared. At best we might find traces of week-old tire tracks that could steer us in the direction of the cleft in the distant mountains that would link us to the next valley. As we neared the connecting openings, the road would begin to rise in a series of truncated switchback turns. The top of every pass was celebrated and marked by a patchwork assortment of prayer flags strung haphazardly together, piles of rocks placed one on top of the other, and yak horns on which prayers of gratitude had been carved. Our drivers would stop at the top of every pass, get out of their cars or trucks, and offer thanks at having safely passed this next milestone on our journey. We would all take advantage of these moments of thanks and leap out of the cars to empty our bladders of the copious amounts of water we were all drinking in our attempts to fend off altitude sickness. Driving again back down the other side of the pass, we would enter into another valley that looked almost identical to the one through which we'd just passed. Each successive valley became just another bead on the mala of the Southern Route. The continuous drone of our Land Cruisers' engines began to sound like the recitations of a mantra.

Occasionally we would pass through a town, but mostly the settlements were set back from the road now, tucked perhaps into a protective shoulder in the mountains or built alongside the shores of a lake. There were very few people to be seen anywhere. Occasionally we might pass riders on horseback or a herd of yaks laden with large, wooden boxes filled with supplies or mounds of wool heading for distant marketplaces. Mostly, however, the scale of the plateau swallowed up any signs of life. Even the towns in the distance, mostly composed of single-story, whitewashed bungalows, blended into the landscape like lichens on a rock surface and were difficult to see.

Yaks clearly outnumber humans on the plateau. Kai commented that they reminded him of a cross between a Brahma bull and Chewbacca, the hairy wookie from the *Star Wars* movies. With their long, matted locks of dreaded hair, they are the Rastafarians of cattle. When viewed from a distance, they exhibited the appealing disposition of a domesticated llama. They would gaze benignly and unthreateningly right at you, inviting you over for a cuddle. Once close, the teddy bear personality could turn nasty. Hooves would snap, and horns would lash out. Despite their size and appearance, these animals could be remarkably agile and fleet. We learned quickly to give the yaks lots of room.

Sound sleep became intermittent and light at best during nights that seemed far too short. The accumulated water of the day kept finding its way into bladders that needed to be emptied every three hours. No matter. The increasing altitude made deep sleep elusive anyway. Dreams were getting more vivid and bizarre. We would wake in the morning looking quite crumpled in body and spirit, as though we'd consumed one drink too many the evening before and had fallen asleep fully clothed in an armchair, and no one wanted to admit to or share the specifics of their dreams. The dark spirits were clearly coming out at night, enjoying the use of our bodies and minds while we slept fitfully, departing again before the first rays of sun.

One evening we camped above sixteen thousand feet, and I awoke in the middle of the night to the fearful realization that I was having difficulty breathing. The pattern of breath that serves me perfectly well at sea level simply wasn't supplying my body with enough oxygen at this elevation. I now had to force myself to breathe long, deep breaths. After three cycles of forced inhalations and exhalations, the panic would subside, but as soon as I would relax my breath back to its normal pattern, the feeling of suffocation would start up again. I had to remain sitting up for the rest of the night breathing consciously and with great attention to this most automatic of processes. People often comment on how travel in Tibet alters consciousness much as does long and intensive meditation practice. As I sat upright in my tent that long night, patiently waiting for the morning light to come, I thought to myself, *Of course, it does, but it's not only the air, the mountains, and the people. Simply to stay alive up here requires that every breath be turned into deep, yogic breathing. A meandering stroll becomes intense aerobic exercise within five steps!*

We became gradually accustomed to the feeling of vast, open space and the lack of human habitation, and so it was doubly surprising when, midway through the next morning, we rounded a hillock to see a Land Cruiser and supply truck not unlike our own in the near distance. As we got closer, it became apparent that both vehicles were in trouble. The supply truck was stuck in the middle of a river that it had attempted to ford, the water almost up to the hood. Its rear wheels were spinning, creating churning but futile eddies of water in its wake. It clearly wasn't going anywhere. It looked like a beached Mississippi River boat from the 1800s, its waterwheel turning to no avail.

The Land Cruiser was in even more serious trouble. Its driver had decided to have nothing to do with the river crossing and had instead opted to nurse his vehicle across a flimsy and precarious bridge. Three-quarters of the way across, the bridge had collapsed, and the rear axle and wheels had fallen through. The small bit of friction between the front wheels and undercarriage and the road just beyond the bridge was all that was holding the car from rolling backward and tumbling down into the moving waters ten feet below. It looked like a wounded animal, resting directly on its haunches, wondering whether or not it was time to relax back and give up the ghost.

Staffed and driven by a Tibetan crew, the Land Cruiser and truck were transporting two Westerners, Raymond and Milena, in the direction of Mount Kailas. Raymond was a retired Tibetan scholar and professor of comparative religion at a university in southern California. He appeared to be in his early seventies and was quite frail, his thin frame and stubbly whiskered face topped by thin, white hair that blew freely in the breeze. His skin appeared to have the healthy coloring of someone who played regular games of tennis on the faculty tennis courts under sunny California skies. Later, however, we would learn that he was in fact part East Indian and part Spanish. Milena was considerably younger and fuller and had a face as round and appealing as the ripest of fruits. Born in Italy, she always wore colorful scarves wrapped around her head, and I never once saw her with anything less than a completely disarming smile stretched across her face from ear to ear. It was impossible not to immediately like this hapless couple.

They appeared to be completely unconcerned about the severity of their predicament and took our sudden appearance and subsequent rescue as the most natural of occurrences. They both seemed almost suspiciously ingenuous and optimistic, especially in the face of such a potentially disastrous situation. Later we would find that we had reason for our suspicions. Raymond had been suffering from mild altitude sickness for many days and had not been able to sleep for three nights. His head had been lightly throbbing the whole time, and he had lost his appetite. This had left him feeling both lightheaded and listless. His nonchalance was more a function of extreme fatigue and the early signs of disorientation than what had first appeared to us as almost superhuman equanimity and trust. Milena, although deeply concerned about Raymond's health, was also determined not to upset him by voicing her concern. Still, they appeared to be living in a charmed capsule, two holy fools who could travel anywhere, do anything, and have everything work out perfectly.

As we worked to help them free their car and truck, I spoke to Raymond and Milena about Kai's and my reason for participating in this journey. They were both visibly moved by our story and by the beauty of the bond they perceived between Kai and myself. Milena began to cry lightly as she heard our story, her smile broadening even further with every word. I looked at Raymond and told him that it had been my dream to come to Mount Kailas for twenty-five years. He took my hands in his, and it was his turn to cry. "Will," he said in the softest of voices, "I have dreamt of getting to Kailas for sixty years."

Underneath the radiant exteriors of these two fine new friends, however, I felt I could detect small but worrisome signs of decay and darkness. As it is with a tiny crack in a windshield that has recently been hit by a pebble, I had the unsettling feeling that if the situation wasn't repaired immediately, it could all too easily turn into a three-foot gash. Raymond later confided to me that he felt he was dying. His dreams were becoming increasingly hallucinatory and dark. He saw himself falling into pits and blackness. He believed that it was his destiny to get to the mountain, but he was becoming ever more convinced that he was not going to be able to walk around it successfully. He would drop his body halfway around the mountain and watch his spirit rise. He simply assumed, in that same accepting and nonchalant manner with which he responded to his car almost falling through the bridge and his consequent rescue by us, that this was simply his fate. He didn't for a moment believe that he was truly suffering from altitude sickness. He felt instead that the dark angel was coming for him. He heard her seductive calls and whispers at night as he lay in the darkness of his tent in a kind of dream state that was becoming increasingly hallucinatory. I begged him to try to get some sleep.

We removed some long planks from a railing at the side of the bridge and began propping up the rear wheels of the Land Cruiser from behind. As we held onto the planks, the car was finally able to secure a bit of traction and lurched forward to safety. Like mountaineers contemplating possible routes up a steep slope, our drivers spent several long minutes studying the river before charting their course and deciding how and where to cross. Guided by the lightest colors in the water, they easily drove the trucks and Land Cruisers safely across, the flowing waters sometimes washing up over the hoods of the cars and causing the drivers to turn on their windshield wipers. Once across, we attached a fifty-foot steel cable from the front of Raymond and Milena's truck to the back bumper of one of ours, and within minutes their truck had been pulled safely to the other side. Our new friends were extremely grateful, and it appeared that our destinies were linked. Even though they rarely camped or ate with us, Raymond and Milena quickly became unofficial members of our group.

The small settlements and towns that we passed were mostly nameless enclaves, small islands of Tibetan life and culture, safe zones into which the political realities of the Chinese occupation and infection had not completely succeeded in penetrating. The town of Saga, however, was substantial enough to warrant a small circle and mention on our map. The unofficial capital of the central southern plateau, it boasted a visible Chinese presence that was jarring and discomfiting. It almost immediately felt as though we had driven onto a Hollywood sound stage in which two separate movies were being shot simultaneously, the actors and extras meandering back and forth freely between their sets during breaks in the filming.

The first set was Tibetan Provincial. The other was Chinese Martial. The contrast between the characters and sets couldn't have been more striking. The Tibetans, almost without exception, bore one hundred–kilowatt smiles. They were friendly and approachable, their faces open and trusting without any trace of guile. Even in the squalid conditions of the town, the Tibetan people appeared to live with great dignity. The women were immaculately coiffed, clothed, and jeweled. Bands of turquoise, silver, and coral hung from their necks, ears, and wrists and were braided together into elaborate headdresses woven into their straight black hair. A soft, gray film of dirt like moondust had settled everywhere in the town: along the streets and walkways, on the walls, windowpanes, and lintels of the homes. Still, the younger women appeared unsoiled and fresh, as though the dust and dirt were unable to stick to their skin and clothes. With great dignity and grace, they sat effortlessly upright on chairs just outside their doors, even as pigs walked aimlessly past, rooting fretfully in the layer of dirt for something of nourishment.

It appeared that the townspeople still had not been able to comprehend fully that the dreams, routines, and sanctity of their lives had been forever shattered by the incursion of the Chinese government. Saga may have once been a small village not unlike the others through which we'd passed. Not any more. The Chinese had built a major military garrison with the requisite armories, satellite dishes, and transport trucks. Soldiers milled around everywhere, looking mortally bored and resentful of their posting. The Tibetans went about their business as though the soldiers were invisible.

The Tibetan people dressed in the brightest of colors and continued to paint the doors and windowpanes of their freshly whitewashed buildings with reds, blues, yellows, oranges, and greens. The Chinese buildings and uniforms were as gray-green as the filmy dust that lay on the streets. The dispositions of the Chinese officials were as dour as the coloring of their clothes. Like bureaucratic arthropods anywhere, their facial muscles had evidently lost the human capacity to smile. They fussed over our passports and papers of transit with sagging jowls and then dismissed us on our way with an expressionless wave of the hand that looked as though they might be shooing a fly away from their food. My heart ached for the Tibetan people as we left Saga. One of the beauties of the Buddhist dharma, as well as the key to its successful proliferation, is that it has embraced the traditions and ways of life of the lands into which it has moved, weaving them deftly into the living fabric of the teachings. The Tibetan Vajrayana itself is the result of the encounter between the eighth-century Buddhist-influenced teachings of northern India and the animistic religious culture of the plateau. In its wanderings the Buddhist dharma knows only to open its arms widely and embrace everything wherever it goes. Its teachings invite transformation into people's lives. The Chinese monolith knows only to conquer and subjugate, to tighten its fist in the attempt to gain control. It attempts to force people to change, to be different from how they are, and the predictable result has been depressing at best. In its moments of worst excess, that result has been truly horrifying and dehumanizing.

But Tibet has no oil or resources critical to the Western powers, and so the systematic genocide and ethnic cleansing of the Tibetan people by the Chinese overlords are deemed an internal situation, beyond the reach, interest, and outrage of Western governments. In a world in which the royal family of Kuwait demands that the American military replace the gold bathroom fixtures in their palaces in Kuwait City before they can return from their lavish villas in Paris and Cairo after the first Gulf War, the honest townspeople of Saga are completely overlooked, as their way of life and dignity are altered forever.

It was hard not to hate the Chinese for what they've done and for the flimsy excuses they've cited to justify their actions. That the exiled Dalai Lama is able to look upon the horrors that have been inflicted on his people by the Chinese as actions of ignorance deserving compassionate response is indeed an extraordinary testimonial to this man and his understanding. Within the Buddhist teachings thoughts of malice and attack are seen to be equally as harmful as the acts they envision. In his attitude toward the Chinese, the Dalai Lama has extended Gandhi's gospel of nonviolent action to include the realm of nonviolent thinking as well. Bear no grudge. Anger and ill will only serve to bring one down to the level of the invaders. They may have the temporary power to take and destroy our land, but don't give them the opportunity to take and destroy our minds and souls as well.

Leaving Saga, I wondered if our group of travelers were any different from the German and British tourists who flock to Greece in the summer months, who only have eyes for the ancient temples, glorious water, and sun, but who conveniently manage to avert their gaze from the twentieth-century horrors that the Communists and the right wing military have routinely inflicted on each other, as well as the people unfortunate enough to be caught in the middle. I remembered many years ago driving up to one of the Hopi villages in northern Arizona in hopes of attending a Snake Dance ceremony. At the entrance to the village a rough, hand-painted sign had been erected. It read: "Because you have not respected our laws and traditions, nor the laws and traditions of your own nation, white people are not welcome at this ceremony." I had felt so embarrassed as I drove down off the Mesa, wanting only to give the Hopi the privacy and dignity they deserved in the midst of a larger society that had taken both away from them.

The townspeople of Saga had played with us. They had loved our puppets. They had crowded around our cars as closely as had the drunken townspeople a few days earlier, but they had done so with love and in friendship. There was not a trace of animosity expressed toward our presence in their town. They were happy we were there. For the first time since arriving in Tibet, however, I felt saddened and ashamed. By not protesting violently against the Chinese invasion of Tibet, my government has been a silent collaborator in the destruction of these gentle people and their culture. For the next hour everyone in our Land Cruiser was unusually subdued and quiet.

As we drove away from Saga, the landscape once again began to change. We left the spacious valleys and mountain rings of south-central Tibet behind and drove onto an even higher and much more open region of the plateau. The valleys that I freshly remembered as having felt so vast and empty now felt small and compressed in comparison. There was more sky than land now, more cloud formations than ground cover. We could see mountains in the distance, but they must have been many scores of miles away. Sand dunes and barren prairie lands extended so far in all directions that it felt as though we could see the curvature of the earth's surface.

We drove for hours, and the distant mountains didn't appear to be getting any closer to us. Our drivers began talking about the last hurdle awaiting us in the distance. We needed to cross the Tsangpo one last time, and they knew of a place where we would have the best chance of doing so. There would be no possibility of a ferry anymore, no mechanical interventions by divine elephants, and we would have to find a place that would allow us to drive across on our own. Our drivers kept assuring us that we were nearing our place of crossing, that we would reach it shortly after lunch, but hour after hour passed, and the mountains came no closer.

The afternoon came and went, and still the mountains were far on the horizon. The light began to fade in the early evening sky, and still there was no sign of water. We kept driving into the darkness and finally reached the river at nine thirty at night. The quarter moon illuminated the land and guided us along our road.

What it also revealed was a gypsy camp filled with supply trucks and Land Cruisers. Raymond and Milena were waiting for us there. A group of ten young Italians had been camped at the side of the river for days. The Austrians whom we had met so many days earlier, and who had tried to make up for all their lost time by traveling as quickly as possible out to Kailas, were there as well. The river was disturbingly high. The Italians had been paralyzed by it and were content to wait, for weeks if necessary, to see if the waters would subside. In the meantime they had broken out their stash of nonprescription drugs and dispensed with most of their clothes in a land where modesty of dress was the prevailing custom. Their Tibetan drivers winced when they spoke of their charges. Earlier that day the Austrians had tried to cross the river. Their supply truck had turned back, but they had been able finally to pull and push their Land Cruiser safely to the far side. It had taken four hours to do so, however—four hours to travel fifty yards. Now their Land Cruiser was on one side of the river, their supply truck on the other, and they were freezing from walking back and forth across the river in water above the waist.

Kai, Aimee, and I lay on our backs under the stars at the side of the river. We held hands and listened to the river's song and watched the night sky's show. In the distance we could hear the Italians. It sounded as though they were all quite drunk and stoned. It reminded me of stories that I had heard of small army bases in southern Vietnam. From day to day the soldiers didn't know what they were doing there or what the morrow would bring. All that they had was time on their hands, this most precious of earthly substances that they only wanted to forget about and crush, numbers on a calendar seeking only the forgiving slash of a blue felt pen. The Chinese presence in Saga and now this rag-tag gypsy camp felt crazy to us, as though the world outside were crumbling right at our doors. We had another river to cross in the morning, and no certainty that we would be successful. As we lay together on the sand, however, we felt safe, as though the embrace of our hands had created a cocoon that would protect and help us in the morning. We were happy finally to be out of our cars. We were all exhausted.

"The elephant's still here with us, Aimee. I can feel him."

"Good, Will. We need him as much as ever."

September 13

We slept in late and awoke to a cloudless sky. I hadn't slept well, and my body felt stiff as I lay in my sleeping bag, not wanting to move. Kai didn't want to get up either. We hadn't washed in days now, and we looked like a father and son alcoholic team unfresh from an all-night bender. We uttered a few grunting noises at each other and turned over, fooling ourselves into thinking that we might be able to fall back to sleep.

Washing had turned tricky once we'd gotten onto the plateau. We might sponge our bodies in the morning from a small basin of heated water, but we never felt clean. The water in the rivers and streams was brutally cold. Kai and I had made the mistake several afternoons earlier of washing our hair in a brook at the side of our campsite. Our ears and heads became so cold that they began to ache violently. We dried our heads and put on wool toques and scarves in an attempt to warm up. For half an hour we sat shivering in one of the Land Cruisers, our heads throbbing in pain.

An hour passed, and still there was no call to wake and begin the day. I peeked out of the opening in our tent. Nothing. Evidently everyone was sleeping in this morning. Oh, well, I thought. We all need the rest, and then I remembered that we needed to get across the river. Kai and I dressed in our working outfit for the day: hiking boots, long thermal underwear, walking shorts, several layers of shirts, heavy down jacket, visored cap, flowered bandana hanging down to protect our neck and ears from the intense sun, glacier glasses to protect our eyes.

The mood in our camp was uncharacteristically unhurried and laid back. People were slowly beginning to stir and rise. The Sherpas had just put water on for tea and porridge. We looked over to where the Italians had set up their camp. In the daylight we could see that it looked as though they had hunkered down for the long haul. They had set up an elaborate covered eating area. Another large tent functioned as an open-air living room complete with rugs, pillows, and musical instruments. They were clearly in no rush to get up and begin moving, hoping perhaps that if only they slept long enough, they would awaken from their dream, and the river would have disappeared. It hadn't. In the morning light it looked even wider and more formidable than it had the evening before.

We turned to see Vassi, Raymond and Milena, the Austrians, and several of the Tibetan drivers huddled in the distance. I immediately had the sinking feeling that they were engaged in one of those conversations whose intensity belied the fact that it was going nowhere. Every few minutes someone else from our group would emerge from a tent in brightly colored clothing made mostly from artificial fabrics: Gore-Tex, rip-stop nylon, or polyester fleece. The contrast of our outfits with the vast blue-gray-beige and blinding white light of the plateau was striking. Stepping out of our tents, we looked like colorful morning flowers, our petals opening in the morning sun. Everyone was drawn to the gravity of the conversation and walked over to find out what was going on. Nobody liked what he or she heard.

The truck drivers had all stayed up late, talking amongt themselves. They were flatly refusing to cross the river and were making plans to turn around and return to Lhasa! They had decided that the river was impassable at its current height and wouldn't risk ruining their trucks by becoming stuck halfway across on the sandy bottom. In truth, it looked as though they might be right. All the rivers that we'd crossed up till now had flowed over small, exposed rocks that gave the trucks solid traction and footing. Since leaving Saga, however, the landscape had changed. There were far fewer stabile granite mountains now and many more shifting sand dunes. The banks of this river looked like a beautiful, sandy beach in the Caribbean. Every time we took a step, our boots would sink at least an inch into the soft, wet sand.

Gradually, however, we came to understand that the solution to our problem was to be found in our pockets. A bit of extra money just might make that river bottom passable after all. The drivers withdrew to consider our offer. We could tell by the animation of their conversation and gestures that it was by no means a done deal. I remember joking to the others that at this altitude it was not a good idea to hold one's breath, but we were all decidedly nervous, waiting for their answer. They returned ten minutes later, much to our relief, with smiles on their faces. Their story had suddenly changed. They felt that they might be able to get across the river after all. In fact, they had thought they could cross the river all along, but no one had wanted to go first! In their conversations they came up with the idea of drawing lots. One of the Italian trucks had drawn number one. Our trucks were second and third. But first they wanted to seal the deal with a hearty breakfast. Eggs and cheese were quickly broken out.

By midmorning we were packed and ready to go. The Italian group actually looked a bit put out at having to break their comfortable camp and move so early in the day, but didn't want to be left behind either. With great panache the driver of the Italian truck climbed into the cab. We all gathered around, prepared to push, pull, and prod the vehicle across the river if we had to. The driver ceremoniously turned the key in the ignition . . . , and nothing happened. He looked as startled as we were disappointed. This clearly was not in the script, and we could tell that he was not pleased with the prospect of having to return the bribe money to us, if he couldn't get his truck started. He kept feverishly turning the key and pumping the gas over and over again. The engine eventually did respond with a weak splutter, but it sounded like the low and labored groan of a sick yak. Eventually even the yak went silent. The driver got out of the truck, opened the hood, and set to work. The other drivers rushed over to help him.

The truck had been sitting idly in this one spot for so many days now that the battery had lost its power, and blowing sand had gummed up the engine. We felt torn between wanting to help the luckless Italians and needing to be on our way, but our own drivers quickly informed us that the numbers had been fairly drawn, and there was no way in which we could now change the order. The Italian truck would go first, or nobody would go! From the clanging sounds and imprecations emerging from underneath the truck and the Keystone Cops routine of all the drivers scurrying back and forth, we realized that we might be here for awhile.

Two hours passed. No change. Still the truck sat there like roadkill, its open hood exposing its damaged innards. I looked up into the clear morning sky half expecting to see vultures circling. The drivers kept assuring us that they almost had the problem fixed, but it all began to sound like a repeat of the day before, when we kept being assured that we were almost to the river. Finally we summoned our own drivers to find out if there might, in fact, be a way to change the order. They brainstormed among themselves for several minutes and then returned to inform us that, yes, there just might be a way after all. The depth of our pockets might once again be able to salvage the situation, this time by superseding the inviolability of the drawn lots. In no time our drivers were in their vehicles ready to go first.

Our Land Cruisers backed up about a thousand feet and accelerated the whole way to the river, hoping that the momentum from their speed would be sufficient to catapult them across. They made a terrific splash when they hit the water, like sumo wrestlers doing cannonball dives from a great height and actually got more than halfway across the river before they began to slow and stall. They kept racing their engines, alternately lurching forward and losing traction, until they reached a sandbar on the far side of the river and were able to drive safely onto the far bank. They emerged victoriously from their vehicles with huge grins on their faces and bowed ceremoniously to the hearty applause from our side of the river.

Our first truck went next. The driver of the truck wanted to get a running start, but he didn't back up anywhere nearly far enough. By the time he reached the river, he was still in one of his lower gears. He looked more like a turtle out for a Sunday drive than a drag racer intent on the finish line. He hit the water with a dull thud and became hopelessly stuck in the middle of the river. The more he accelerated, the further the back of the truck sank down. The other drivers and Sherpas bounded into the river to try to push, but the truck had simply stopped moving. We hooked cables and ropes from the back of our Land Cruisers to the front of the truck's bumper and tried again, but all this did was to cause our accelerating Land Cruisers to sink down up to their rear axles into the sand on the far bank.

Without any consultation, the driver of Raymond and Milena's Land Cruiser took it on himself to save the day, and from out of nowhere he suddenly hit the river at high speed completely out of control. He barely missed hitting the beached supply truck, but got to the other side with little trouble. He appeared definitely put out, however, when only looks of disbelief, rather than the riotous applause he had anticipated, greeted his proud emergence from his vehicle. All the same, we now had five Land Cruisers on the other side of the river.

We quickly set to link the Land Cruisers together with cables and ropes. Coordinated teamwork, however, was not a concept that our drivers were easily able to comprehend. The notion that five vehicles working together were much more potent a force than any one vehicle on its own appeared to be an alien concept to them. Nor did they cotton to the impassioned utterances of a Westerner trying to bark directions and explain to them how to coordinate their efforts and make this all work. Instead, the Keystone Cops antics continued, and it all would have been hysterically funny if there hadn't been so much at stake.

Instead of starting up slowly together, they each appeared determined to be the solitary hero. Completely disregarding hand signals of when to begin pulling, the drivers raced their engines and popped their clutches completely at random. To make matters worse, the connecting cables and ropes were not even stretched out tautly when they took off.

The inevitable result was that in a split second the ropes and cables had all snapped, and everyone had to reassemble in their starting positions and tie everything back up again. Meanwhile, our supply truck was slowly sinking in the middle of the river.

The final irony to the whole farcical show was that it was the Italians who saved the day. As we stood motionless on the riverbank, looking out over the drama unfolding in front of us in stunned disbelief, we heard music coming from somewhere behind us. We turned to look, and there were the Italians, marching in single file toward the river, whistling an Italian laborer's tune in two-part harmony, carrying long, heavy, wooden planks on their shoulders, dressed as though they were off for a morning dip in the Adriatic Sea. The boards were wedged underneath the rear wheels of the truck, the Land Cruisers finally began working in concert with one another, and slowly, inch by inch, the truck was pulled safely across. From our bank we began shrieking in appreciative exultation and relief. From the far bank the drivers embraced each other and, in unison, bowed low like opera stars taking a curtain call at La Scala. The Italians danced in the river.

We then all got in the back of our other supply truck in an attempt to add weight to the rear wheels, made it halfway across the river, got stuck, but were pulled out easily. From the other side of the river the Italian supply truck finally sputtered into life, and within an hour everyone was across. We were ecstatic, as we dried off in the warming, afternoon sun, hugging and thanking everyone.

Then, just as we were about to get back in our vehicles and set out once again on our way, two Tibetan women who looked to be at least in their eighties appeared literally from nowhere. One stood tall and erect. She had a green scarf covering her head and a black gown draped over her body. She wore glasses with thick black frames and even thicker lenses that she couldn't possibly see out of. Her head was tilted back, her eyes staring off blankly into the distance as though locked on some invisible star. Her friend was small and seriously stooped. She looked even older. She had the crimped and puckered face of a winter squash and was mumbling to herself, as she turned beads on a mala that hung from her left hand. In her right hand she supported herself with a rough cane, as she shuffled along slowly, dragging her feet in the sand with every step. Her eyes, in contrast to her friend's, never left the ground two steps in front of her. Together they looked like two-thirds of the weird sisters from a production of *Macbeth* that would have had Western audiences squirming in their seats. They definitely did not look like any other humans that I had ever seen in my life.

Their sudden appearance was baffling. It was as though they'd materialized out of thin air. We were in the proverbial middle of nowhere. There were no towns to be seen, no villages, no nomads' tents on the horizon, nothing. Nor had anyone seen them approaching. They simply appeared and began walking through the assembled grouping of people, trucks, and cars, as though they were completely oblivious to our existence. People began to move out of their way, and they began passing through. Suddenly and abruptly, they changed direction and began walking straight over toward Kai and me. We both froze.

At first as they'd approached us, some of the people in our group and even some of the Tibetan drivers had tried to greet them.

"*Tashi delay! Tashi delay*, honored mother!"

Tashi delay is the standard greeting throughout Tibet and is the approximate equivalent of "Hi, there, how're ya doin'? Good fortune to you!" But it was as though they hadn't heard anything that we said. They kept walking blankly forward as if in a dream or trance. As they came to a stop directly in front of me, I was suddenly able to understand what the old woman was saying.

"*Om mani padme hum. Om mani padme hum. Om mani padme hum*," she kept repeating in a barely audible monotone. "*Om mani padme hum.*"

She was intoning the preeminent mantra or sacred prayer of the western plateau, indeed in all of Tibetan Buddhism. Practitioners will sometimes repeat this mantra for hundreds of thousands of repetitions, slowly and gradually accumulating and drawing the power of the words to themselves. It was this mantra that was carved on most of the yak horns that we had seen on the high passes and that was printed on the prayer flags that fluttered in the breeze. It appeared everywhere on the cylindrical prayer wheels that the devout Buddhist people of the plateau would turn over and over again as they walked past prayer walls in temples or in the middle of the town squares. The Tibetans believe that the vibrations of the prayer can be activated and set in motion through constant movement. Speech is movement. So too is the wind. I had seen phonograph turntables in Tibetan monasteries in the West to which prayers had been attached, turning round and round, the electricity never shut off. We had seen crude, but ingenious, prayer wheels constructed on the roofs of houses in the villages through which we had passed in the last few days. They had been constructed out of tin cans. The cans had been opened at one end and then attached to an oiled, central post of steel. When the wind blew, it would catch in the cans and cause everything to turn, much like the devices that measure wind velocity at airports. Here on the plateau, however, the only purpose of these devices was to hang flags of prayers from the cans. The flags inevitably were printed with the one great prayer: *om mani padme hum.*

This prayer has been conventionally translated in the West as "Hail! The jewel in the heart of the lotus!" These are the literal words perhaps, but the translation conveys very little of the meaning and intention of the mantra. A more instructive rendering might go something like this: "Remember. In the middle of this swirling world of appearances, this tidal flow of circumstances and interactions, there is a special place deep in the center of every human body, of every human being, a place of inexpressible peace and comfort. Touching this place, you know that all is right with the world and that you are one with the world. This place is your birthright. It is valuable beyond description. Now go and find that place! Feel it. Become it. Claim it as your own!"

As I heard these words uttered in front of me, I dropped my head to the level of the old woman's and began repeating them back to her. Our eyes locked on each other's, and we began intoning the mantra in unison. *Om mani padme hum. Om mani padme hum.* The sound of the words and the closeness of our gaze began to affect and alter my perception, and at one point she began to look significantly less old and haggard to me.

After a few minutes she abruptly turned her head and, with her partner at her side, continued walking away into the distance. I wouldn't have known how to explain what had happened if I'd been asked, and fortunately no one questioned me about the encounter. In truth the sudden presence of these two women had been so disconcerting that most everyone had turned away, hoping to avoid any contact with them.

Kai looked up at me uncertainly. The color had gone out of his face. Finally he was able to speak.

"Dad . . . what was that?"

"I don't know, Kai. I really don't know."

It was by now the middle of the afternoon. As we drove a few more hours before setting up camp for the evening, I couldn't stop thinking about these women, and gradually I came to believe that I did know who they were and why they had appeared. I couldn't help shaking the feeling that they were the keepers of the elephant, that they had come to take him back, that we would need to proceed the rest of the way on our own, using our own resources and skills to reach the mountain. It seemed completely far-fetched to think these thoughts, and yet I couldn't stop thinking them. To distract myself I tried to joke and make small talk with my traveling companions in the Land Cruiser. I made light of the experience to myself, writing it off as an aberrant effect of the altitude, but still I would keep coming back to these thoughts, these women, this explanation. Finally I gave in and accepted it as every bit as likely an explanation as anything else. It felt wonderfully comforting to do so. What I knew for sure was that the old woman had taught me all the conversational Tibetan that I would need to know for the rest of the trip. *Om mani padme hum. Om mani padme hum.* I began hearing it in the noise of the engine and in the sound of the tires passing over the sandy road. I joined in and began repeating it to myself.

As the afternoon light began to fade, I let the mantra go and thought again of the two women.

"Honored mothers. Thank you so very, very much. Thank you for the precious loan and for all his help to us. We will be fine now on our own. I can't tell you how grateful I am for what you've done for us."

By the very late afternoon we had entered again into a series of small valleys and had come to our last real river challenge. The water went over the hoods of the Land Cruisers, but we drove effortlessly through. That we would reach Mount Kailas was now certain.

September 14

We woke in the morning feeling remarkably rested, refreshed, and light. The accumulated anxieties of the previous week and a half had fallen out of view in the face of the virtual certainty that we would reach the sacred mountain by midmorning at the latest. Our drivers kept moving about our campsite with large smiles, touching us lightly on the back or shoulder, joking with us, pacing back and forth like someone about to be called on stage to receive an award. They were as excited to get to Mount Kailas as we were.

"No more rivers," they kept saying. "No more rivers!"

Anxiety makes the body ache. As with a guest who's stayed too long, our bodies welcomed anxiety's departure. We broke camp early and set out on our way.

The landscape now consisted of small valleys tightly rimmed by small mountains. It felt like a miniature version of the lands through which we had so recently traveled. The road, or what was left of it, became extremely rough. Sometimes we would travel along the rocky banks of a stream. Other times the road and the stream would become one and the same. The cars lurched roughly from side to side, as we followed alongside the slowly flowing water. Even the persistent bouncing didn't seem to bother us anymore. We knew that we didn't have much further to go. Everyone kept looking to the horizon.

We began seeing Tibetan pilgrims making their slow and patient way to Kailas. We passed a family with two yaks and a horse. On either side of the yaks there hung a primitively woven wicker basket, each one carrying a small child. At the top of a slight pass, standing next to the obligatory prayer flags and rock cairn, was a lone pilgrim. He was dressed in the yellow and maroon robes of a Tibetan monk and was twirling a handheld prayer wheel. I was momentarily taken aback when I approached him, as I could have sworn that he was wearing the same, nonfunctional glasses that the tall woman at the river had been wearing yesterday afternoon. He was chanting mantra.

"*Om mani padme hum. Om mani padme hum. Om mani padme hum . . . .*"

I clasped my hands together in front of me in the traditional Hindu form of greeting and began speaking what I now knew to be the only Tibetan phrase that I would ever need to know.

"*Om mani padme hum. Om mani padme hum. Om mani padme hum . . . .*"

He motioned for me to come closer. He cocked his head slightly, as though listening to make sure that he was hearing correctly and then broke into loud tears, as he grabbed hold of my head and brought our foreheads together. We both kept intoning the sacred syllables. After a few minutes he looked up briefly through his tears and smiled and then pulled our heads back together again. Several minutes passed before I looked up at him. His smile was radiant. His tears had dried, but they'd left a series of salty lines streaking down his cheeks. He blessed all of us, Westerners, Tibetans, and Sherpas alike, and kept smiling every time he mentioned the word Kailas. The drivers told us that he was sending us strength for walking around the mountain.

Shortly after we left him, we descended into a small valley that looked more like a moon crater or a ski bowl in the off-season. We were surprised to see the Austrians at the bottom of the valley. When we had said goodbye to them the afternoon before, they told us that they were going to drive directly to the mountain. It seemed like a strange place to take a break, and in their single-minded and highly efficient haste, it was unlike them to stop for anything at this point. We thought that perhaps they were having car problems, because they were out of their

Land Cruiser examining something under the carriage of their truck. All of us on the Southern Route had bonded quite closely these past few days, and our drivers began steering our cars and trucks over toward them to see if we could help.

As soon as they saw us, they began to shout and gesticulate for us not to come near, but by then it was too late. Our cars and trucks were already starting to have difficulty steering away from the bottom of the valley. As we neared their vehicles, our wheels began to sink down into the supposedly solid ground. We couldn't steer to the right or the left.

The ground turned out not to be solid at all. We had all driven straight into a deceptive bog that was equal parts earth, marsh, and mud, with a bit of quicksand thrown in for good measure. By the time we reached the Austrians, the back wheels of our cars and trucks were spinning wildly in a fruitless attempt to avoid getting sucked into the wet ground. Two of our Land Cruisers made it through, but the other car and both our trucks were becoming hopelessly mired. Mud was flying everywhere from the spinning of the rear tires. As our vehicles became more and more bogged down, the wheels rotated ever more slowly, until they finally just stopped moving. Kai looked at me, rolled his eyes, and let out a groan.

"Did we say 'Kailas was certain?' It looks like we've just walked into our latest Crisis of the Hour."

The intrepid Jonathan was riding in the Land Cruiser that had become stuck. He was the first person to venture out of the car. He took two tentative steps, smiled broadly back at everybody as though to inform us that all was okay, and then on his third step sank halfway up to his knees. Like a person in a dream who is trying to run away from danger but keeps getting stuck in molasses, he began scrambling furiously to free himself from the pull of the bog. It was all quite funny to watch. Jonathan finally got to a small patch of solid ground and wouldn't budge from it. For the first time since leaving Katmandu our seemingly inexhaustible source of the clever pun and facile *bon mot* stood speechless.

Kai was sitting on higher, solid ground with Cindy, the CNN camerawoman. She was pretending to film the events transpiring just below them, and Kai held an imaginary microphone to his mouth, offering color commentary.

"After a moment of panic he's completely safe again! The UN Peacekeeping Force is assessing the damage and coming up with a plan to extricate the machinery! Oh, brother. It looks like a two-hour delay at least!"

Like optimistic prognosticators everywhere, Kai underestimated the delay by more than half. It took us more than four hours to free all the vehicles. In the end we had two Land Cruisers pulling a truck to which another stuck truck was attached. In truth, Kai's estimate would not have been that far off, if it hadn't been for our new friends, the Italians, who in the middle of all this suddenly came bounding over the ridge (having gotten a later start than the rest of us), horns honking, thinking we were all gathered together for a last communal lunch, and drove right into the middle of the bog, smiling and waving at us the whole time. In the end we did all end up having a light snack together.

After our snack we said goodbye for the last time to all our new companions. Raymond and Milena must have bypassed the bog and were probably already in Darchen, the small village from where pilgrims begin the trek around Mount Kailas. The Austrians and the Italians were heading straight for Darchen as well. We were planning on bypassing Darchen and resting and spending an extra day on the shores of Lake Manasarovar at the foot of the mountain.

Continuing on, we passed through more small valleys and skirted several large lakes. The ground stayed solid underneath us the whole time. A well-defined road even appeared. We kept looking to the horizon, hoping and expecting to see the first sign of the mountain around every ridge. The landscape began to look more like the photographs we had all seen of the Kailas region. Colorings of rust, ochre, and even the occasional purple began appearing in the striations of the rock cliffs. Water was once again more abundant in this region, and underground aquifers, spreading out from the rivers and lakes, fed and nurtured the roots of thick yellow and green grasses. We started seeing flocks of birds bathing and lolling by the shores of the lakes. We felt warmed by the reappearance of the vegetation, the birds, and the color. It felt as though life was coming back into the land.

Suddenly Dawa, our Tibetan driver, began shouting and pointing. For the briefest moment he had seen the tip of a snow mountain peeking through a space in the hills and mountains. Just as suddenly, the tip vanished again. Dawa made a sucking sound with his lips, as though to tell us that we were so close to the mountain that we could taste it.

We kept driving through smaller and smaller valleys. It felt as though the mountain was teasing us, like a courtesan who entices you with the briefest glimpse of her thigh. Every time we rounded the next corner, every time we drove over a hill, we expected to see it. Still it didn't appear, and we would all look ahead to see where the next corner was, the next pass through the hills.

Finally, we began climbing up a series of long, graded switchbacks that had been carved into the side of a steeply inclined hill. When we got to the top, it felt as though we had emerged into a whole new world. No more enclosed valleys. No more moonscapes. We had reached yet another level of the plateau with grassy pasturelands spreading out for miles in front of us. In the middle of it all, no more than twenty miles away, completely dominating the plateau like a protective guardian, stood the snowy peak of Kailas, its white pyramidal shape pointing upward toward the sky and clouds in a land of horizontals. Dawa brought the car to a stop and began to cry. Then he began to beam. Through the veil of his smile and tears he started hugging everyone in the Land Cruiser.

We all leapt out of our cars, embracing and yelping like a litter of happy pups. The drivers were on their hands and knees doing prostrations to the mountain. Prayer flags were strung everywhere. Small rock cairns covered the land for acres.

We stayed in this spot for at least an hour before we drove any further. No one wanted to get back in the cars. The drivers and Sherpas scrounged through the tightly packed crates in the back of the trucks and put together a small feast for us all. The hard-boiled eggs, marmalade, and yak cheese tasted splendid.

We talked together of our journey, reminding each other of details from the last few days that others of us had completely forgotten. The challenges that we had faced, and that had caused us so much upset and anxiety at the time, now all seemed uproariously funny. We all agreed that the challenge and adventure of getting to the mountain had been perfect. It made sitting on this spot at this moment all the richer.

Kai and I walked out onto the field and wandered through the maze of cairns. Snippets of clothing, pages of worn manuscripts, and faded pictures of the Dalai Lama had been attached and built into the small pillars of stone that carpeted the land. We came to a small cairn and added our rocks to it. We then lay down on our backs, looking up into the sky. The drivers were beginning to pack up. We would go soon. I hugged Kai and held him close to me. He wasn't embarrassed to hug me back. There was nothing to say.

As I lay on my back I kept looking up at the thick and pliant cloud formations that kept forming and dissolving into ever-different shapes. I remembered back to a time when, as a small child, I would lie on my back in the warm summer grass, staring at the clouds for hours, as a drama of castles, dragons, heroes, and mythic animals slowly played itself out against the backdrop of the blue sky. As I lay on the earth with Kai at my side, I began to see things. At first I saw faces smiling down at me benignly, then a procession of women in long robes carrying candles, whose flames fluttered in the breeze, and finally the beginnings of an animal, whose head covered the entire sky. I kept looking at the animal, watching its features form in the currents of moving air, and then turned to Kai.

"Kai, look . . . quick! In the sky. What do you see?"

He had been dozing, half-asleep, but began to let his eyes roam and his imagination play. His eyes were relaxed and unfocused, as though he was looking at one of those three dimensional images that appear out of a jumbled field of ostensibly random colors, spots, and shapes. Suddenly his mouth dropped open, and he jerked his head toward me. He had seen it too. It had covered the whole sky. The long trunk, the droopy ears, the twin tusks.

For Kailas,
Mountain and Man

We camped that night on the shores of Lake Manasarovar underneath a monastery that seemed to have sprouted like a rocky mushroom from the top of a small hillock. Mount Kailas is sacred earth. Its upward thrust connects the surface of the earth, the arena of human life, to the realm of the sky gods who cavort and play in the heavens and the stars. Shiva himself is said to sit in meditation on the mountain's summit, bringing order to the underlying world through his practice. Manasarovar is accorded the status of sacred water. In her depths lie the unseen, chthonian forces of the psyche that provide the needed checks and ballast for the sky gods, whose romps and capers, much as in Greek mythology, can sometimes teeter on the edge of veering out of control. Like man and woman, the mountain and the lake complement each other. The twentieth-century Indian teacher Sri Aurobindo often stressed the importance of this understanding for the work of spiritual practice, cautioning his students against the hubris of a transcendent spiritual vision that wishes to move only upward, leaving the earth far behind. "You only go so high as you go low. Otherwise you become lopsided and fall off the top."

Just as Kailas can be viewed from certain vantage points as a perfectly shaped pyramid, Manasarovar is an almost perfectly shaped circle. Its dimensions of seventeen miles across and fifty-five miles around the circumference of its shores accord very closely with the numerical *pi*'s demands for the requirements of a perfect circle. Lake Manasarovar is the highest body of fresh water on the planet. It is a huge inland sea, as large as Lake Tahoe in northern California. Only a lake as large as Manasarovar could hold her own in relationship to the dominating presence of Kailas.

For the Hindus and Jains who walk across the Himalayas, Lake Manasarovar is viewed as even more sacred than Mount Kailas itself. The name of the lake comes from the Sanskrit word for mind, *manas*, and the lake is seen as the repository for the latent powers of the human mind that, with proper training and understanding, can blossom beyond the superficial limitations and identifications with which most people content themselves. Especially in the early morning hours, when there is very little wind, the lake speaks eloquently to the possibility of stilling the internal monologue of the mind and plunging deep into the source of consciousness itself. In the Ramayana, one of Hinduism's most revered texts, the lake is described as the agent of transmutation, like the later philosopher's stone of the Western alchemists: "When the earth of Manasarovar touches anyone's body, or when anyone bathes in the lake, he shall go to the Paradise of Brahma, and he who drinks its waters shall go to the heaven of Shiva and shall be released from the sins of a hundred births." Little wonder that with endorsements like these, innumerable Hindu pilgrims have risked everything over the centuries to journey to the sacred lake. At Pashupatinath, the Hindu temple complex in Katmandu, Kai and I had seen paintings of Manasarovar. Mount Kailas appeared in these paintings as well, but only as an insignificant peak in the background.

The gompas that line the lake like jewels on a bracelet are Tibetan Buddhist. Their doors, however, are open to all pilgrims, regardless of their religious preferences: Buddhist, Hindu, Jain, and Bon-po alike. The latest insurgency of pilgrims, the ragtag groups of Westerners who organize convoys of trucks and Land Cruisers, take buses, or even hitchhike to get to the sacred region, are equally welcomed into the gompas as honored guests. As elsewhere, the Chinese destroyed all of the monasteries in the Kailas-Manasarovar region, but most have been slowly resurrected and rebuilt. Some of the original stones from the original monasteries have been patiently salvaged and placed prominently in the new walls.

The aptly named Chiu Gompa (*chiu* means bird in Tibetan) is perched like a bird on a branch atop a large rocky hillock at the northwest edge of Manasarovar. It appears to grow organically right out of the surrounding rocks, and indeed some of its rooms are more carved out of the rocky hill than built on top of it. So naturally does it blend into its surroundings that if you didn't know it was there and weren't looking specifically for it, you could pass by Chiu Gompa without ever seeing it. With its many levels of rooms and its many small spires dressed in prayer flags, it looked like an enchanted castle out of a Tibetan fairy tale.

Because of the earlier delay in the swampy valley, we didn't reach Chiu Gompa until late in the afternoon. As soon as we arrived, I decided to take a short stroll and climb what looked to be a small hill behind the monastery. I knew that the top of the hill would offer a spectacular view of Mount Kailas in the distance, and I welcomed a short hike, no matter how strenuous, after so many days in the Land Cruisers. Kai took one look at the hill, labeled me out of my mind, and opted to rest in camp.

Distances and the passage of time are deceiving in the high, thin air, and as I walked toward the hill, I began to have the unsettling feeling that the more I walked, the further away the hill seemed. I slowly began to realize that the hill was much farther away than I'd judged it to be. When I finally got to the base of the hill and looked up, it looked like a towering mountain. The sun was slowly sinking in the sky, on its way to set behind the mountains in northern Nepal. The sky was immaculately clear and still. I didn't think I would be able to get to the top of the hill before sunset, but decided to climb up as far as possible for the view. I was also curious to see how well my body would function climbing uphill at this elevation.

Within the first twenty steps the answer to my curiosity came through very clearly. Not very well. My heart started to race, and I had to sit down on a large boulder, strenuously sucking in air to supply my muscles and tissues with oxygen. A simple act at sea level becomes a major undertaking at high elevation. To be so physically challenged felt simultaneously exhausting and invigorating. That I had tired so quickly was concerning, however, especially in light of what I knew the next number of days held in store for us. As my heart rate settled back down, I stood up and continued climbing.

It must have taken half an hour to climb a hill that couldn't have been more than 150 feet high. Most of that time was spent resting and recovering my breath. I reached the top of the hill just as the sun was starting to drop behind the distant mountains. The view was indeed spectacular. Below me to the east I could see the whole expanse of Manasarovar spread out like an ultramarine carpet. Its surface was slightly rippled in the gentle evening breeze like the low pile in a Berber rug. I could now see all the way to the far shore and found it sobering to realize just how big this lake actually was. To the south were the mountains leading into Nepal. Their peaks were all dipped in snow like monumental chunks of ice cream lined up on a rocky platter. To the west was Manasarovar's sister lake, the mysterious Raksas Tal. The circular shape of Manasarovar has traditionally been associated with the sun, whereas the crescent shape of Raksas Tal has been linked to the hidden powers of the moon. In the legends of the region, Raksas Tal is seen as the habitation of the bogeyman, the dark shadow to Manasarovar's light. Indeed, many pilgrims shun Raksas Tal completely, like a dark forest in a fairy tale, and there is only one monastery that has been built on its shores. To the north, like a paterfamilias overlooking its brood, stood Kailas. Its snowy face shone pink with alpenglow in the fading light of sunset. I kept turning round and round, looking in all directions. What different worlds each direction revealed. The light, the dark, the lone sentinel, the comfortable crowd.

I felt as though I had never stood on a singly more beautiful spot anywhere on the planet. I wished Kai could have been here to share this view with me.

I was startled to hear the sound of footsteps on rock and turned around quickly to find Aimee almost at the top of the hill. She had started out walking south along the shore of the lake and had then decided to climb the hill. She was as startled to see me as I was to see her, but we ran to each other and embraced, as soon as we recognized who the other was.

We didn't say much, but just held on to each other, as we continued to look out over the lakes and mountains. We kept turning around, not knowing where to focus our gaze. Every vista was more spectacular than the previous one. The few clouds that had formed in the distance were turning pink and purple. The light of the setting sun cast an intense yellow glow wherever we looked.

We walked over to a small flagpole that had been erected on top of the hill. The combination of the altitude, the exertion, and the truly spectacular nature of the spot generated a pronounced feeling of warmth and contentment that spread through my entire body. A thought that I had never thought before formed itself in my mind and found its way into speech. I was fascinated by the sound of the words, because it felt as though someone with whom I wasn't familiar, a part of me whom I didn't know, was thinking and speaking them.

"Aimee, if I could just drop my body and die right now, on this spot at this moment, I would feel completely content, as though my life had been perfect."

She didn't reply, but just held my arm more firmly and rested her cold head on my shoulder. A breeze began to stir, and we knew that we would have to walk back down to camp shortly. We kept walking around the broad, flat top of the hill. Some places offered better views of Kailas or of Gurla Mandhata, the dominant mountain leading into Nepal, to the south. From other spots we could clearly see the lakes on either side. Suddenly in our meanderings, Aimee grabbed my arm tightly and froze.

"Will, look down."

It took me a while in the fading light to figure out what she was looking at, but then I recognized what she'd seen. At our feet were the deteriorated, chalky remains of a body. It was still clothed, but the clothes, like the body, were badly decayed and decomposed. It looked as though it had been here a long time. Had someone carried this body here, leaving it exposed to the elements? Sky burials were a common way of disposing of dead bodies in Tibet. Or had this person woken one morning to the certain knowledge that his time on earth was completing itself, made one last heroic effort to bring himself to this one spot that he loved more than any other, lay down on the ground, and let his spirit and body separate through one last blessed exhalation? It would be like sprinkling one's ashes in a favored spot while still alive.

Whoever it was had lain on his back, his arms outstretched and bent slightly at either elbow. His pelvis had twisted onto its left side, his legs bent at the knees and resting one on top of the other. Not wishing to violate the sanctity of this spot, we withheld our urge to reach down and touch the chalky dust inside the clothes, to confirm to ourselves that the body had slowly decomposed through natural processes and that it hadn't just dematerialized in a blinding moment of transformation. Such a possibility is far beyond most of our abilities to comprehend or even accept, and yet there are many stories from Tibet of advanced practitioners consciously choosing the moment of their death and dematerializing their physical form into what the teachings refer to as the Rainbow Body, a body of light and color. Practitioners who came to understand that the time had come to enter into their Rainbow Bodies would evidently announce their intention, erect a small tent for the purpose of the transformation, and enter into it, after asking that they not be disturbed for at least seven days. When a week had passed, a great celebration was held by their friends, families, and fellow practitioners. Everyone would gather at the tent, take it down, and inevitably all that they would find would be the clothing of their friend, lying fastened on the ground, and perhaps a few short hairs and the trimmings of fingernails. The contemporary Dzogchen teacher

Namkhai Norbu has recounted episodes from his childhood of practitioners attaining the Rainbow Body. It is also widely accepted, even by the attending Chinese, who are extremely uncomfortable with this story, that the twelfth Tengye Rimpoche, while undergoing the most intense interrogation and torture, simply vanished from his prison cell shortly after his capture and incarceration during the 1959 invasion. He was never seen again either by his own people or by the Chinese. To the Tibetans these stories are no more far-fetched or miraculous than the idea that carts could be built to fly through the air, even to the moon, or that we could hold an object to our mouth and speak to a friend living halfway around the world.

As we stood pondering the chalky remains, we were again startled by the sound of footsteps on loose rock. We looked up, and there was Kai! We rushed over to greet him. He had watched our slow climb from the comfort of camp and had felt a strange pull to join us. He was winded from the climb, but clearly exhilarated to be standing with us on this spot. We pointed out the lakes and mountains in the four directions and showed him the body that we had found. For several minutes we all kept turning, until we began to feel slightly dizzy. The temperature was dropping as rapidly as the sun, and we began to feel the chill.

We stood motionless, trying to freeze this moment in our memories. It felt as though we were standing in the middle of a living mandala, a perfect circle of life, in which the ordinarily chaotic and disparate elements of nature had, just for a moment, brought themselves into a perfect balance that revealed their underlying order and connection. The mountains to the north and south were balanced out by the lakes to the east and west. Above us the sky, still alight with the setting fire of the sun. Below us the earth. And standing in the middle of all this, three friends in different stages of life, and a fourth body, unknown to us, who had passed beyond the circle of life altogether. Earth, air, fire, and water, and the phases of human life in between.

We climbed carefully down the hill in the darkening light and arrived back at our camp just as the first stars were signaling the passage into night.

⤝

September 15

We awoke early to a blindingly bright sun that, as it slowly rose over the mountains on the eastern horizon, turned the waters of Manasarovar a deep orange. Flecks of white began flashing and sparkling on the tops of small waves as the air currents heated up, and a slight breeze began to blow over the surface of the lake. Kai and I dressed quickly and walked to the shore.

Four older monks were standing in a line at the side of the lake, their hands folded in front of them in prayer, chanting mantra, invoking the spirit of the sacred lake. They were wearing long orange and maroon robes, and their heads were covered in woolen toques. We were happy to watch them from a respectful distance, giving the sun time to rise fully in the sky and begin to warm the air and land. By the time that they had finished their morning prayers and began walking back to the gompa, the morning chill was gone, and the air felt passably comfortable. It was time to plunge into the lake.

The Tibetans believe that walking the *kora*, the sacred path, around Mount Kailas burns away the accumulated sins of a lifetime, whereas the Hindus believe that a ritual immersion into the frigid waters of Manasarovar can lead to a future incarnation as a god. I took my clothes off down to my undershorts and walked gingerly along the clay and mud beach toward the shallow waters. The soil felt squishy and cold underneath my toes. The water was even colder. Its touch on my legs caused me to pant like a woman practicing Lamaze breathing at a birthing class.

I had to walk out at least 150 feet before the water was deep enough to allow me to lie down on my back and immerse my whole body. Covered in mud with beads of frigid water dripping from my body, I erupted with a shriek and ran back to shore and a waiting towel. Kai was laughing and shaking his head back and forth at the foolishness of his father. He said the look on my face when I had jumped back up had been priceless. The fine mud and silt that had been stirred up from the lake bottom and had stuck to my body had made me look like a primitive creature emerging out of the ooze. I complimented Kai on his imagination as well as on his prudence. He had opted for a sponge bath at the water's edge, gathering water into his cupped hands and dripping it over his head. He looked only a bit cold, not frozen. My teeth chattered violently, as I dried and dressed myself. We walked back to camp and a waiting warm drink.

Later in the morning we set out on a slow walk up to the gompa. Thousands of flat *mani* stones on which prayers had been carved littered the sides of the path leading up to the grouping of small buildings. The same prayers had been beautifully painted onto the faces of large boulders, a sacred version of graffiti. Once again we had to walk very slowly as we climbed the steep path up to the gompa. A young novice carrying a large porcelain basin passed us on his way down to the lake. A handsome monk, his hair pulled back into a ponytail and wearing a dapper yellow V-necked vest, met us at the entrance to the gompa and began guiding us through the maze of rooms. Eventually he led us down into a darkened shrine room lit only by several rows of butter lamps. It took our eyes several minutes to adjust to the dim light.

Framed pictures of the Dalai Lama and other revered teachers, as well as elaborate and colorful Tibetan paintings of deities richly mounted in brocaded silk, completely covered the walls. In one corner of the room stood a small statue of the Buddha, his body golden, his tightly curled hair and eyes blue, his robes orange, seated atop a green, orange, gold, and lavender lotus seat. His right hand reached down in front of him, touching the earth. In his left hand he held a begging bowl that was filled with small coins and bills as offerings.

Presiding over the room was a large, and equally colorful, statue of Padmasambhava, the eighth-century Indian teacher responsible for bringing Buddhism to Tibet. The shrine rooms of Tibetan gompas will often focus on a particular deity or teacher, and Padmasambhava is definitely the tutelary guardian of Chiu Gompa. His presence could be seen everywhere: in numerous small clay figures and prayer flags, as well as in the paintings and large statue dominating the crowded space of the shrine room. Even though he is revered throughout the whole of Tibet, he spent much of his life in the Kailas-Manasarovar region, and he is said to have dropped his body at Chiu Gompa.

As our eyes became accustomed to the light, we began to appreciate the Tibetans' love for color and detail. Other than the brilliant blues of the sky, the Tibetan plateau is almost uniformly monochrome in color. Situated far above the tree line, the plateau harbors very little vegetation. Everywhere you look, for unbroken miles in all directions, you see the gray and beige of the earth. The overriding impression of the plateau is of vast, empty space. Tibetan artwork, on the other hand, is intricately detailed and embraces every color in the rainbow. Animals, buddhas, ritual objects, and highly stylized clouds, mountains, and rivers fill up every square inch of the surface of the traditional thangka paintings. As I stood in the narrow confines of the shrine room, I couldn't help thinking of the contrasting vision of Japanese Buddhism. In a land that is small and compacted, rich in vegetation and densely populated, the artistic expression leans toward understated images of great space and emptiness. Shrine rooms in Japan are particularly free of clutter. So too are the minimal depictions of landscape and people that appear in the single scrolled painting that might hang on a large wall. The most popular color in Japanese Buddhist paintings is black. Both cultures have evidently found it necessary to depict the ineffable nature of highest truth through images and colors that are completely foreign to their culture and land.

We walked back out into the light and passed by a wall of brightly painted prayer wheels. We greeted two pilgrims from the eastern part of Tibet, their long, black hair tied up in buns atop their heads and secured with bright red sashes that hung down their backs. We wandered around the rooftops and the pathways that circled the gompa, climbing elaborately crafted ladders that led nowhere but to a spectacular view of the lake or the mountain. By late morning we had broken camp and began the short drive over to Darchen, the village under the south face of Mount Kailas, from where the kora around the mountain traditionally begins. What a joy only to have to drive for twenty miles!

⤙

For many centuries the village of Darchen has been the staging point for the circumambulation of Mount Kailas. It also gradually developed into a center for the wool trade in southwestern Tibet, but its most fundamental reason for being is its proximity to the sacred mountain. From this spot the pilgrim's journey around the mountain naturally begins and ends.

Shiva is said to live at the very top of Kailas, and there are legends that speak of how Milarepa flew to the top of the mountain to do battle with opponents of the dharma. Other than that, however, no one has ever stood on its summit. In a rare display of sensitivity, the Chinese have repeatedly refused the requests of Western expeditions keen on being the first to climb the mountain and stand atop its summit. They understand how sacred the mountain is to the people of Tibet and know that they would risk an uprising if permission to climb the mountain were ever granted. It would be a bit like turning the hundreds of rooms in the Potala Palace, the largest and most sacred building in all of Tibet, into a Holiday Inn. The pilgrimage to Mount Kailas has nothing to do with conquering the mountain. It is, rather, about surrendering oneself completely to the forces and presence of the mountain, about dissolving the egoic fiction and being conquered and liberated by the mountain in the process. To do this, the pilgrim walks around the entire base of the mountain. The path is thirty-two miles long, and it is all at high elevation.

The Buddhist, Hindu, and Jain pilgrims who gather in Darchen all head west after leaving the town and walk around the mountain in a clockwise direction. The Bon-po pilgrims begin their circumambulation by heading east and circle the mountain in a counterclockwise direction. Such is the foolishness of the fundamentalist mind that issues concerning the "proper" direction in which to walk around the sacred mountain can be taken very seriously. It is not that different from the situation in the West, in which some of the different sects of Christianity bicker endlessly among themselves over their definition of universal love, uniting only long enough to consolidate their shared distaste for people living outside the Christian fold. In Tibet the different schools of Buddhism often held violently opposed positions on the correct way to attain Buddhahood. As in the West, the different schools could at least find common ground in their condemnation of what they pejoratively viewed as the primitive practices of the Bon-po (even though the practitioners of the different Buddhist schools were all mostly descended from Bon-po ancestors).

Approaching Darchen, we came ever closer to the magnificent south face of Mount Kailas itself. It appeared as an almost perfectly shaped white pyramid rising incongruently out of the lower rocky hills and valleys. The closer we approached the town, the bigger the mountain appeared to grow. It hovered over everything, a gigantic, sheltering presence cloaked in a cape of snow with rock buttons and ornaments sewn into the garment. It was impossible to be unaware of the mountain's presence. Even when we turned away from it, gazing back toward the lakes and the mountains of the Tibetan-Nepalese border, we knew the mountain was there. Just to feel this presence, to see it in the clear light of day, even to know that it was there when the clouds came to conceal it, as they did much of the time, felt very special, as though a kind of blessing was being conferred, and it became quickly evident to all of us why this mountain has generated such widespread veneration. It also became very clear that to be in the presence of the mountain was enough, and that it didn't matter one little bit which direction anyone chose to move as they made their way around its base.

The town of Darchen itself felt like half–nomad encampment, half–permanent village. Although there were a small number of more permanent-looking structures in the center of the town, Darchen was encircled in tents that temporarily housed the transient community of pilgrims, as well as the merchants who were drawn there in the summer months to sell supplies to the pilgrims. As the tents moved closer into the center of the town, they became heavier and sturdier, until finally their walls of yak hides or canvas began to be covered with mud, and openings for permanent windows and wooden doors began to appear in the structures.

The Darchen guest house stood almost exactly halfway along this transitory path from tent to structure. After so many days in our tents, we were all looking forward to a solid roof over our heads, a bed under our bodies, and the ability to stand upright in our shelters. Our drivers were particularly eager to spend a restful night inside a real building. Relatively affluent city dwellers in a society that is not free of class consciousness, they had found the long string of tented nights beginning to feel a bit too much like the nomad life for their comfort and self-esteem.

After a brief inspection of the guest house, however, we opted once again to pitch our tents on the outskirts of the town. Uncovered mattresses lay exposed on concrete floors that slanted slightly toward the middle of the room, where a covered drain had been built to catch the flow of any liquids that might penetrate the room. At first we thought this might be a convenient way to keep the room relatively dry in case of flooding. We gradually came to realize, however, that the rooms functioned not only as a resting place, but as latrines as well. This didn't seem to bother our drivers, however, and they happily settled into a room in the guest house while we began searching for level ground for our tents. By the evening our drivers had managed to purchase the freshly skinned carcass of a goat. It looked as though it had probably been bounding around in the village that very morning, rooting for garbage and playing with children. They placed it on the floor of their room and then rustled up a blowtorch, which must have been packed deep at the back of our supplies, because none of us knew we were even carrying one with us. Strategically pointing the blowtorch, they would heat a small section of the goat. Once it was cooked, they would turn the blowtorch off and begin picking at the darkened, cooked meat. If they were still hungry when the meat began to turn too rare and cold, they would turn the blowtorch back on and heat up some more!

By early afternoon our camp was erected, and we had the rest of the day free to rest and explore. We didn't have to walk into the market area to purchase supplies for the kora. Tibetan traders began appearing at our campsite with all different sorts of commodities that we "needed" for our walk: everything from boot polish to cooking kettles to prayer flags. The prices for these objects differed widely from merchant to merchant, but as more merchants kept appearing to vie for our attention, the prices kept coming steadily down. A number of the people in our group decided to rest, and Kai chose to stay with them. Aimee and I, however, set off to wander and explore. Our experience above Chiu Gompa the afternoon before had crafted a strong bond between us, and we began meandering through the maze of narrow streets and alleyways that separated the buildings and created thoroughfares for the people. Aimee told me that the evening before she had dreamt that she, Kai, and I had suddenly merged into one being. We held hands as we walked through the small lanes thick with the smoke of fires and the smell of simmering stews that consisted mostly of meat and water.

A Tibetan lama now residing in California had asked Aimee to make a donation at the gompa in Darchen, and so we set out to find it. We crossed makeshift bridges over streams and passed dilapidated pool tables that had been set up outside in the middle of the streets with hotly contested games in progress. We looked into small shops and stopped in to see if any of the supplies and trinkets that were offered for sale held any interest to us. Some streets led us directly into cul-de-sacs from which we had to backtrack to continue on our way. Others would somehow loop us back onto other streets, over which we'd already passed. It began to feel like a maze that had no exit. It certainly didn't lead to a gompa. After having wandered through the tangled streets two or three times, we began to wonder if the Darchen gompa existed at all.

As we rounded a corner, we were greeted by a short, toothless man with huge eyes and a furrowed forehead, whose etched lines appeared to keep his eyelids pulled perpetually upward. He had a purple robe draped over his left shoulder, and he was motioning to us with his hand to follow him. He kept nodding at us to make sure he had our attention and made the kind of clucking noises with which we might call a cat. At first Aimee and I felt a bit wary of his overtures, assuming that we were about to be hustled. He was insistent, however, in his motions, and they became even stronger and louder when he sensed that we might either ignore him or bolt. At one point he broke into a loud and disarmingly raucous laugh. His laughter seemed so good-natured that we decided to follow him. He seemed like a middle-aged gnome out of an enchanted forest.

He began deftly shuffling through small courtyards and ducking under low lintels, periodically turning around to make sure we were still following him. His feet dragged as he walked, never moving much higher than the ground, and he kept motioning us the whole time with his hand to follow him. We walked through short, dark tunnels that opened onto concealed inner courtyards. We passed through the interiors of homes, where people lay resting or squatted beside low fires stirring soup in large, black, iron kettles. Finally, we entered into a dark and smoky room that was lit only by a single row of butter lamps. He motioned for us to sit down, while he took a seat slightly above us. As our eyes became accustomed to the light, we watched as his features settled and his bearing shifted. The reflected light revealed a face rich with compassion. An intense light seemed to emanate from his eyes. His gaze was steady and strong. As we looked around the room, we began to recognize the pictures of Tibetan deities and were able to make out the shape of a small, but elaborate, altar at one side of the room. On the altar sat sculpted images of the Buddha, bowls of rice in which incense sticks were planted and burning, bells made from semiprecious alloys, malas, and other ritual objects of Vajrayana practice. In the time it took our eyes to become accustomed to the light, we both realized that we were sitting in the Darchen gompa.

For several minutes we all just sat silently together, our gazes burning into one another. The lama looked back and forth between Aimee and me, as though he were trying to decipher something or figure out who we were and why we were here. I began to feel dizzy from the enclosed space and the turbid, smoky air. Finally, Aimee began to speak. Realizing that it was unlikely that he understood English, she nevertheless began explaining that she had been sent here by a Western lama who had requested that she bring an offering of money to the Darchen gompa. He listened intently, nodding his head as though he understood what she was saying, but said nothing in response. When she was finished with her explanation, she moved over to the altar and deposited a large handful of assorted currencies, bills from the United States, Nepal, and China, into a shallow dish, where a few coins and beads had been placed. She came back to her seat, and we kept sitting in silence, staring intently at this kind man, whose body and head appeared to grow larger, as he kept staring back at us. After fifteen minutes we both felt it was time to leave. We brought our hands together at the level of our chests in the traditional gesture of greeting and departure and began crawling back toward the exit. Just as we were about to step into the passageway that led to the lighted interior courtyard, we heard him call quietly after us, "Thank you."

The light blinded us as we made our way back through the maze of rooms and alleys, until we finally reached the place where we had first met this enigmatic man. Aimee told me that she felt the encounter had been perfect. She felt as though we had been led to find the gompa by her lama in California and that she had been able to fulfill his wish.

We stood in the lane for several minutes while our eyes became once again accustomed to the light of the harsh Tibetan sun. From this spot we had an unobstructed view of a large flagpole that was lodged on the top of a prominent hill up behind town. Streamers to which prayer flags had been attached were strung from the top of the pole and extended outward in all directions like fluttering spokes on a wheel. The streamers were then secured into the ground and functioned as ornamental guy wires, both embellishing and securing the towering pole. We could see a small, but steady stream of pilgrims walking up to the flagpole, and we both knew that this was the next place that we needed to visit. We began to make our way through the twisting streets, always trying to move in the approximate direction of the pole, until finally the lanes began to widen, and we left the dense interior of the village. Once again we crossed the stream, passed over an open field, and came across a path that could only lead up the steep hill to the flagpole. We began follow-ing the path upward, walking slowly as it rose, concentrating on our breath as we walked, trying not to exert ourselves in the thin air.

Aimee had prepared for the trip by participating in morning work-outs with the United States Marines in San Diego and was in extremely good shape. I had to walk more slowly than she, but gradually we both made our way to the top of the hill where the flagpole stood. From this spot we could look back down over the maze of Darchen and the lakes and the Nepalese mountains in the distance. Turning around, we were given a tantalizing glimpse of the very top of Mount Kailas peeking up over the tops of the hills that rose to obstruct the view of its bulk. The path beyond the flagpole kept rising through a narrow cleft in the hills, but not nearly so steeply as the hill we had just climbed, and so we decided to keep following it, to see if we could get an even closer and more complete view of the mountain. The afternoon sun shone bright and warm, but a slight and pleasant breeze cooled us as we continued to walk. We kept rounding corners that lured us to keep going further. Primitive stone chortens (small pillars of stacked rocks, placed as reminders of the teachings) had been built at every bend in the narrow path. Scrub grasses and an occasional plant pierced through the crust of the soil, but mostly the land was dry, rocky, and barren. The severe light of the sun made the landscape appear even more austere. Still, it kept on inviting us to keep walking further.

Just when we both felt that it was probably time to return back to our camp, we rounded a tight bend on the narrow path, and a spacious valley unexpectedly opened up in front of us. Up until that point, low, steep hills had crowded the path, creating an enclosed and restricted feeling. We'd kept walking cautiously, constantly on the lookout for small rocks that might come dislodged from the hills on either side and come tumbling down onto the path below. Quite abruptly the confin-ing walls disappeared, as though we had just walked out of the rocky equivalent of a dense forest. The claustrophobic feeling of the path gave way suddenly to a sense of vast space.

It's difficult to gauge distances accurately in the high Tibetan air, but the valley appeared to be roughly two miles in diameter, a perfect bowl with high, gradually sloping walls. In the distance stood a rock wall on the top of which elaborate stupas had been erected. Towering above the wall on a high hill in what appeared to be the approximate center of the valley was a square fortresslike structure. It could only be a gompa. I recalled seeing an old map of the region and remembered that a gompa had once stood on this spot, but I had assumed that it had been destroyed during the Cultural Revolution and never rebuilt.

Aimee and I both stood silent for several minutes, gawking at the scene that had just appeared before us, unsure of what to do next. The day was getting late, and we knew that it would be extremely foolish to try to walk back to camp in the dark. At the same time, we felt that so much of our day had already been divinely guided. It was as though we weren't so much making conscious decisions about where to go next, but were simply responding to a force that was moving us, first right, then left, like the current of a river. We both agreed that we needed to keep moving ahead.

As we kept walking, the moon rose spectacularly over the crest of the eastern wall of the valley. It looked to be about halfway between first quarter and full, and we estimated that we probably had another two hours before the sun would begin to set and the sky start to darken. We kept fixing our gaze on the gompa. It felt as though it was pulling us toward it. The floor of the valley had leveled off considerably, and we began to walk faster. Within half an hour, we had reached the rock wall of stupas, and a few minutes later we found ourselves standing at the door of the gompa.

The gompa was indeed shaped like a fortress, completely square with turrets at all four corners, between which prayer flags had been strung. It commanded a 360-degree view of the valley and was built on the exact spot on which a military garrison would logically have been constructed. From this point nothing could pass by unobserved. On the rock wall facing south was one small square window, out of which a sentinel could keep watch and observe the passage of every animal and human that entered or left the valley.

A small boy met us at the door of the gompa. He was dressed in a dirty, yellow woolen sweater and was wearing a beige fedora hat with a wide protective brim. He had the largest and darkest eyes I had ever seen in a child, and he looked straight at us with complete comfort and ease. His gaze reminded me immediately of the gaze of the lama at the Darchen gompa. Unlike what might conventionally occur in Western culture when two strangers come unexpectedly upon each other, there was no apparent need for him to look away or to avert his glance in the slightest. The presence of this little boy was remarkable.

He motioned for us to sit down on a small rock bench at the entrance to the gompa and then left. After a few minutes he returned with an older man with a huge smile, who greeted us as though we were long-lost relatives whom he had been expecting for some time. His arm was draped lovingly over the little boy's shoulders, and we assumed that he must be both the presiding lama, as well as the child's father. The little boy held his father's draped hand in his own. The lama was dressed in purple robes with a mala hanging around his neck. He held a chain of thick keys in his free hand and walked over to the brightly painted door of the gompa and opened the heavy locks.

The inside of the gompa was completely dark. The air was musty and surprisingly cool, and it felt as though we had just stepped into a large wine cellar. The lama struck a match and lit several butter lamps. As our eyes became accustomed to the faint light, we realized that the interior of the gompa housed the richest collection of Tibetan art and artifacts that we had ever seen assembled in one place. Antique thangka paintings framed in rich brocaded silks covered every square inch of the walls from the floor to the ceiling. Metal sculptures, many of them quite large, were everywhere. A central altar occupied the space at the far end of the room, but still the gompa seemed more like a museum storeroom than a house of prayer and meditation. I walked over and found the small, square window that I had seen from down below in the valley. It did command a spectacular view, and for a moment I fantasized that a cadre of Tibetan resistance fighters might have holed up here during the Chinese invasion, picking off Red Guard soldiers with automatic rifles smuggled in from Nepal as the invaders made their way up the valley with the intention of destroying this monument to what they perceived to be bourgeois attitudes and beliefs. For a moment I fantasized that perhaps the resistance fighters had even been successful in repulsing the invaders and that the collection of art that was housed in the gompa had not been disturbed. This, of course, was a very far-fetched fantasy. This gompa had surely been leveled to the ground, as had all the other gompas in the area, but still I kept wondering where the resident lamas had hidden all the artwork in the weeks and days leading up to the arrival of the Red Guard. Had all this magnificent work been removed to a hidden cave perhaps and stored caringly, patiently awaiting the day that it could once again be displayed publicly in a rebuilt gompa?

The little boy kept watching us with the same unflinching gaze. Other than an extraordinary air of presence that this gaze created, he was almost completely expressionless. His father, on the other hand, was smiling freely the whole time, obviously proud, as he kept pointing out ever more objects of interest in the gompa's collection of art. He told us the names of the Tibetan deities depicted in the paintings and sculptures. He appeared deeply moved with the utterance of each name. After identifying each deity, he would stand motionless for several seconds and would often voice a soft, involuntary grunt of approval or awe at the force or power that the deity represented. He gazed at each figure with a look of complete adoration, as though a mother were admiring the features of her child. His young son continued to be much more interested in us. His intent gaze never left us, as we followed his father around the interior of the gompa.

When we returned to the front door, the lama wished us well in parting. He kept smiling softly in our direction, nodding his head rhythmically. In contrast to his son, he appeared almost shy and wouldn't look at us directly. It was obvious, though, that he was pleased that we had walked up to his gompa. As we started to walk back down the valley, we turned to wave goodbye to the father and son. The lama had his arm once again resting on his son's shoulder, and the little boy once again was holding his father's hand tightly in his own. I wanted to tell them that I too was here with my son, that I too understood the special bond that exists between a father and his boy. I felt that our meeting with this kind man and the son that he obviously cared so much for was deeply auspicious, an indication or symbol that all was going to be well for Kai and me, that our efforts to walk around the mountain would be successful. Acknowledging our wave, the little boy let go of his father's hand and waved back vigorously at us. A smile as equivalently large as his eyes burst forth from his expressionless face. The sun was now low in the sky and was shining directly onto their faces. For a moment the child's white front teeth sparkled in the setting sun, as though they were jewels reflecting light.

We would have loved to have stayed longer with these two new friends, but knew that we only had about an hour of sunlight to traverse a distance that had taken us at least three hours to cover earlier in the day. Fortunately, though, the path was entirely downhill, and it felt as though we were gliding back down to Darchen. Aimee asked me to teach her a mantra, and we kept repeating "*om mani padme hum*" aloud all the way back to our campsite. We reached our tents just minutes after the sun had dropped behind the Nepalese mountains to the south. Kai was happy to see us and looked rested from his afternoon. He had wonderfully enjoyed himself, playing gin rummy with fake money, raising the stakes good-naturedly with every game, until he had accumulated enough money for a college education. Within ten minutes after returning to camp, the sky began to darken rapidly, and the first stars came out of hiding.

September 16

Kai and I awoke the next morning at almost exactly the same time from a deep and seemingly dreamless sleep. As soon as we opened our eyes, we turned to look at each other, burst into broad grins, and then reached over and hugged each other roughly, like two bear cubs at play.

We knew that today was the day that for so many months, and even years, we had been looking forward to. It didn't take long, however, to realize that extended roughhousing in the high altitude was not a good idea, and we quickly lay back to search our minds to see if we could recover our dreams. Recounting our dreams of the night before had become a combination morning ritual/stalling tactic, as we would slowly come out of sleep, not wanting to leave the comfort and warmth of our sleeping bags. The combination of the high altitude and light diet had been a potent catalyst for our dream life. Something had felt different about this night's sleep, however, and we both commented that it didn't so much feel as though we had had dreams that we couldn't remember, but that we simply hadn't had any dreams at all.

We peeked out through the partially opened door of our tent to a cloudless sky. The blue of the sky looked as though it had been stained a deep indigo and more closely resembled the coloring of deep ocean waters than any blue I had ever before seen in the sky. The morning sun was turning everything that it touched a brilliant gold. We had been granted a perfect day to begin the kora.

The moments of anticipation that precede a long-awaited event are especially precious, and no one in our group appeared in any hurry to set out. Instead, we puttered about the camp lazily, as though this moment were a delicious food, whose smell and taste we wanted to prolong and savor. We also had to wait for our yaks and yak herders to arrive before we departed. It is not uncommon for pilgrims to Kailas to secure the services of yaks and herders to help carry the supplies that they will need for the coming days. Just as merchants descend on Darchen during the summer months to provide supplies for pilgrims, so too do nomadic yak herders arrive with their animals in tow, setting up camp in a grassy area just outside of town, where they patiently await those pilgrims who require their services.

In much the same way as owners of dogs in the West often almost comically come, both physically and emotionally, to resemble their pets, so too did the yak herders strike us as a human reflection of their animals. They were certainly unique human beings with their own ideas about grooming and sociability. Many of them appeared wildly unkempt with long, unruly hair that had gradually matted itself into dreadlocks. Like the animals in their charge, they are often highly independent to the point of recalcitrance, extremely unpredictable, and not wholly reliable. They can be easygoing and affable one moment and downright surly the next. They had assured us the day before that they would arrive at our camp by sunrise, but both our Sherpas and drivers cautioned us not to expect them until well after breakfast at the earliest. When they finally arrived, they were indeed a sight to behold, a ragtag confederation of animals and humans who appeared collectively to inhabit a plane of existence unfamiliar to most of us.

The sight of the herders kindled a memory from several years earlier, when I had been living and working on an island in Greece. Late one afternoon I walked down to the harbor and watched a large fishing boat returning to port after being out on the Aegean Sea for several weeks. The men on the boat looked like no men I had ever seen before, and I was fascinated to observe them, as they unloaded their catch. They appeared to inhabit a universe of their own, one which I knew nothing about. Try as I might, I was unable to make even the most rudimentary kind of contact with them. They would gaze off blankly into the distance, apparently oblivious to the presence of the sizable crowds of people who came down to admire their catch.

The yak herders evoked a similar response in me when I first saw them. Our drivers made a point of advising us that, like the yaks themselves, it was probably a good idea to give the herders a good deal of space and not to try to engage them in any way. As it turned out, they were an almost invisible presence over the next few days. Our supplies would arrive at our campsite, but the herders and their animals would then almost immediately withdraw to a distant meadow to spend the night.

By midmorning everything had been gathered and packed, and Vassi called us all together. We huddled in a circle, our hands and arms either draped around a shoulder next to us or grasping another hand or arm in the center of the circle. We kept clustering closer together, and our bodies became increasingly entwined. It was an exquisite jumble of body parts, something halfway between the massing of a sports team before a major contest and the party game Twister, and someone joked that wouldn't it be a cosmic irony if we had come all this way only to enter into a hopelessly entangled knot from which we couldn't possibly extricate ourselves.

Our emotions at that moment were deeply entwined as well. We all felt very close to one another by now, and the round of hugs that had culminated in the human knot was both sincere and heartfelt. In our shared elation I was reminded of Kai's comment before leaving home that he felt 90 percent excited and 10 percent terrified. Kai would later tell me, however, that when Vassi finally told us softly, "It's time to go," he felt a momentary wave of panic surge through his body, as though the number ten now referred to his level of excitement and the number ninety to his fear.

Leaving town to the west, the path was marked and lined on either side by mounds of stones that pilgrims before us had piled on top of one another as their first act of devotion. In places these primitive chortens formed an almost unbroken wall along either side of the path, protectively funneling us, as though we were sheep that might otherwise stray, as we made our way toward the entrance to the great valley to the west of Mount Kailas. The path rose slowly but steadily upward, and in the high altitude the walk felt exhausting even from the beginning. My body was sluggish, as though it hadn't yet wakened or warmed up completely, and I could see that Kai too was struggling to keep up. Within a few hundred yards of leaving camp, he began panting strongly, and I gently reminded him to stay inside his breath, to monitor his breathing from one inhalation to the next, making sure that his pace didn't exceed his body's ability to supply his muscles with oxygen. We talked about walking slowly, but rhythmically, and about watching how our mind could distract us from merging with our natural breath. We both commented that as soon as we became lost in the inner monologue of the mind, we would lose the awareness of our breath, and almost inevitably we would begin walking at a pace either too slow or too fast for our body.

Our talk seemed to help us both, but still it felt as though Kai was having to stop and rest every hundred yards or so. The frequency of his need to rest his body and catch his breath catapulted me once again into worried-father mode. I made a conscious effort to hide my concern, though, and kept on acknowledging him instead for how well he was doing, encouraging him when it was time to get up and move again. In truth, the constant rests suited my body as well. We were clearly in no hurry, and I wanted to savor our time as much as possible. We spoke at some length about how the path itself was the goal. Simply contact the path at its beginning, be aware of it from moment to moment, from step to step, and the conventionally perceived goal will take care of itself. Enjoy each moment and each step. Don't walk so fast that we might miss the beauty of the path and the mountain, the feeling of the air strangely cool and warm at the same time, the incredible silence punctuated only by an occasional breeze, the sounds of birds' wings, the shuffling of our boots, the labored drawing of our breath. I was reminded of the aerobics dictum to never run so fast that it becomes difficult to carry on a conversation. Kai joked that it might take us weeks to circle the mountain at that pace!

Rounding a bend in the path, we came across a pilgrim who was, in fact, taking weeks to circumambulate the mountain. Because he was moving toward us, we immediately recognized him as a Bon-po pilgrim who was walking around the mountain in his customary counterclockwise direction. He was not walking in the conventional sense, however. Rather, he was doing full body prostrations, as he made his slow way. He was wearing a beige, full-length apron that covered the front of his body, and his hands were protected by wooden mittens. From a standing position he would bring his hands together to his chest in a gesture of prayer and then kneel down and touch his hands to the ground. He would then slide his hands forward as he lowered himself, until he was lying face down on the ground, his body completely extended, his arms outstretched ahead of him. At the end of the prostration, he would pick himself up again to a standing position, his feet now at the place where his hands had just been. He would take a moment to recite a prayer and then begin the next prostration. He was traversing the entire kora in this way.

Kai and I sat down to rest on a flat rock at the side of the path and watched him as he inched his way slowly forward like a human caterpillar. His face was radiant, the reddish brown of his skin aglow in the warm morning sun. His smile was large, and there were small tears in his eyes. He would reach Darchen that day, his kora completed. He deserved to be so radiant.

After an extended rest, during which we watched him make a dozen prostrations, we knew that it was time for us to keep making our own way, that we couldn't just remain spectators in the stands. The path began to rise more steeply still, and we walked even more slowly and had to rest frequently. Kai was breathing hard, and his forehead had sprouted small beads of sweat, which had begun to drip down his nose and cheeks. We had walked perhaps a mile and a half from town along this inclined lane of chortens when we came to the crest of a hill, and the path turned abruptly to the right. Much like Aimee's and my experience of the previous afternoon, the landscape completely changed in a moment, and we found ourselves at the edge of a very different world. We were standing at the entrance to a huge valley with sheer walls of rock on either side that must have been fifteen hundred feet high. I had never before thought of rock as possessing richness of color, but the variety of pigments ingrained in this rock was dazzling: greens, blues, reds, corals, and purples emerging out of the dark canyon walls. The colors reminded me of the steep valleys that I had seen on the west coast of Kauai, and the tiered structure of the rocks and sparse vegetation resembled the canyon lands of Arizona or southern Utah. The walls of the valley looked as though they'd been poured in successive layers, like a great rock cake made of molten lava. In the distance we could see a herd of sheep grazing on the meager grasses that sprouted on the otherwise barren and rocky valley floor. We could see a stream flowing lazily through the center of the valley. We had reached the entrance to the aptly named Lha Chu Valley, the Valley of the River of the Gods. Carved mani stones with inscribed mantras were stacked in piles, covering the ground all around us. Mantras had been painted on the rock cliffs on either side of the path. Towering over everything, like a patient guardian overseeing his domain, the snowy pyramid of Mount Kailas stood completely exposed.

We were both tired from climbing up to the crest of the hill, but didn't bother to sit down and rest. We just stood and stared instead. Mount Kailas can be easily seen from a distance, but it's very difficult to see it up close other than by walking the kora. The snowy peak looked as though it was only a few miles away from us. Even though the scale of the valley was huge, the sheltering presence of the snow pyramid made everything seem strangely intimate, as though we had been transported into a miniature world that belied its actual size. I put my arm around Kai's shoulder. He held my hand, just as the small boy had held his father's hand the previous afternoon.

"We're here, Kai. We're finally here."

Several minutes passed before he released my hand and, without speaking to each other, we began once again to move on. As we descended into the valley, I realized that the sluggishness of the morning had left my body. It felt as though I'd just taken a warm shower after an intense workout. A slight breeze was blowing up from the valley, cooling us off after our climb in the hot morning sun. The appearance of the valley and the mountain, as well as the intensity of devotion of the Bon-po pilgrim, had revived us both, and Kai began fairly skipping down the path. Suddenly, though, the toe of his boot caught a rock. He lost his balance and began to stumble. He put his hands out in front of him to brace his fall, but began sliding and tumbling down the path. By the time his body came to rest, he was lying face down on the rocky ground. I was about to make a joke about his deciding to do prostrations around the mountain, but saw that he was quite upset. He dusted himself off as best he could, examined his hands for scrapes and bruises, picked himself up, and then came over to me and burst into tears. I held him and let him cry his tears through. I suggested that we sit down and have ourselves a morning snack.

It seemed that as we'd entered into this huge valley, the enormity of what we were undertaking had suddenly hit home. Kai was clearly shaken by his fall. He kept saying over and over again, more to himself than to me, that it was so "big" here. I kept reminding him not to focus on how big our task was, but just to stay focused in the moment. All that we had to do was open to the next breath and take one step at a time. We talked about constantly remembering that the path on which we stood, the step we were taking in this moment, was the only goal we were trying to achieve. If we became distracted and began to focus instead on how far we still had to walk, we would become paralyzed. Not only would we be unable to move, but we would miss the magic of this very moment. To experience this moment to its fullest was our goal. Let the next moment appear in its own time. If we could attend fully to this moment, then the reappearance of Darchen and the completion of the kora would occur naturally at their allotted moment.

We shared an energy bar that we had brought with us from home and started walking again. The fall had affected Kai, though, and he began to walk even more slowly and rest even more often. Rounding a bend in the valley, we came upon a huge flagpole much like the one that hovers over Darchen. I had heard that this was the site of many festivals and ceremonies that take place throughout the pilgrimage season. It was situated a bit off the path, and I decided to walk over to get a closer look at it. Kai wasn't interested in joining me. The thought of any additional effort had little appeal to him, and I left him resting, as I went to explore the flagpole. I had to climb a small hill to reach it, and I had to admit that even this small extra exertion was taxing to my lungs and legs. When I reached the flagpole, I walked slowly around it in a clockwise direction, a miniature version of the circumambulation around Kailas itself. I looked back down at Kai. He was slumped over a rock, half-lying down, half-sitting up. His face looked strained, even though he was at rest. He was still breathing hard. A wave of doubt, like an unwelcome cold breeze, shuddered through my body. I became suddenly panicky about his ability to complete the kora. My mind began racing about what we would do if he became ill or exhausted and couldn't continue on his own. One thought led to another, and each successive installment kept getting worse. It wasn't until I envisioned him riding on the back of a yak encased inside the Gamow bag that I snapped out of my daydream and was able to chuckle to myself at the insidiously negative power of my mind. Like a thief in the night that comes to steal away our awareness, leaving its calling card of doubt and despair at the scene of the crime, it had broken in again. In the aftermath of every successful theft of awareness that the mind pulls off, the natural balance of mind, body, and being is destabilized, and we're left susceptible to the most egregious of fantasies.

When I got back down to where he was resting, he wanted to know if we could have lunch yet. It was late morning still, and I suggested that we still needed to walk further. Reluctantly, he pulled himself up to standing and started walking again. His feet struck the ground heavily. I joked to him that he sounded like a baby elephant, but he didn't find it funny. He was clearly struggling, as we kept on moving.

We continued in this way for another eight hours. Kai would later say that it had felt like the longest day of his life. After a while we fell into a silent routine of walking a few hundred yards and then resting for about five minutes. We repeated this over and over and over again. We kept drinking as much water as possible and relished our pee breaks as fortuitous, and unscheduled, rest periods. By the afternoon it felt as though we were both in a trance. Kai had been right. It was big here. In fact, it was enormous. My buoyant mood of the morning began to deteriorate with the passing hours and miles. Walking through this magnificent valley, I began to feel increasingly small and insignificant. It was not a comfortable feeling. In spite of the large amount of water I was consuming, I began to feel parched and brittle, emotionally as well as physically. My mind began conversing with itself.

For so much of my life I had sought and striven to discover my true authentic nature, or so I told myself. What I began to realize, however, was that that search had ever so subtly created in me a sense of self-importance, and it felt suddenly that all my striving was being exposed as a charade. I was only a speck of ash pretending to be something important, but in truth this pretense had created an artificiality that the valley was somehow unmasking, as though a light was suddenly being shone into a dark corner of my mind and a well-kept secret was being put on public display. It felt suddenly as though my whole search for authenticity had become tainted by this intruding aura of specialness, that authenticity pursued as an "important" endeavor rapidly becomes unauthentic. By trying to become special, I'd lost my birthright and my connection to those natural forces and energies that are truly important in life. I began to feel a deep sense of unworthiness at having been invited into such an immaculately natural setting, this temple of rock and sky. The phrase *speck of ash* kept taunting me, repeating itself over and over in my mind. *Speck of ash. Speck of ash.*

We passed by a large gompa that had been carved right into the cliff face on the opposite side of the valley. It looked like a miniature toy that might turn up under a Christmas tree for a small child. It was simply dwarfed by the massive rock wall that hovered above it. I had read that the magnificence and scale of the western valley with the white dome of Kailas looming overhead progressively exposed the pilgrim's mind to a kind of psychic meltdown. The inner heat generated by this powerful geographic cauldron would gradually dissolve the hard and stubborn covering of the ego, separating out the impure accretions that had accumulated over a lifetime and beyond, exposing in the end the blessed insubstantiality and transitory nature of human existence. When I had read it, it had sounded like fanciful prose. Fanciful or not, the valley was doing its job on me.

Kai was also right to have been scared. The unraveling of the tightly held belief in one's own unique and personal significance, by whatever means, can be brutal, uncompromising, and finally frightening. By the late afternoon Kai seemed to be faring better than I was. Maybe he had gone through his fear that morning and had come out the other side. Physically he was continuing to struggle, but emotionally he appeared more settled than I did. As I kept walking further, the feelings of elation that I'd experienced earlier in the day at being privileged to be present in this magnificent valley had been supplanted by a profound feeling of trespass, as though I simply didn't belong here. No human did. If the snowy peak of the mountain was a kind of presiding deity carved out of rock, there were innumerable minor deities in its retinue everywhere you looked. The cliffs of the valley were composed mostly of a soft, reddish sandstone, and the water, sun, and wind have over long centuries carved out the most outlandish spires and shapes at the top of the rock walls. Many of these formations looked like identifiable human forms, others like animals, and they were everywhere: lizards, monkeys, Siamese twins, snake empresses, Easter Island heads, all of them natural gargoyles carved out of stone by the forces of nature. So rich is the mythology and sense of the supernatural that permeate this great valley that almost all of these rock spires have been assigned specific names and personages. Hindus see the face and body of the monkey god Hanuman in a large stone outcropping that looks as though it burst fully formed from the rock face. Buddhists see a special cake used as an offering in a huge mound of rock that hugs the path just beneath the dome of Kailas. I felt that this was a land for these kinds of entities, these materializations of deep psychic forces in the form of rock and nature, but not for me.

I looked back at Kai. He was still laboring with every step, but didn't appear to need me for support at that moment. I let the facade of my role as father drop away and sank down into my own feelings. I realized I didn't feel very good. I kept dropping like a heavy stone in water. The problem was not in my body. It was tired, but working okay. The problem was in my mind and emotions. I felt confused. My mind wasn't functioning very efficiently. I was having trouble stringing subjects, verbs, and objects together in their proper order, even in my thoughts. And beneath this I began to feel a despair so deep that I knew it would never stop. Who are we really? And who is this "I" who's working so very hard to proclaim and promote his own self-importance, all the time knowing it's to no avail, realizing that death wins every time and makes a mockery of our efforts?

Kai was far behind me by now, and I decided to sit and wait for him. I walked about twenty yards off the path to a rock whose shape resembled a chair and sunk into its seat. I laughed to myself that it looked as though the gods had pulled up a chair for me to sit down in, as I wrestled with my mind and moods, with recurring doubts and questions that I knew had no simple resolutions or answers. I heard a rock falling from somewhere above and behind me. I turned quickly to make sure that I was in no danger, when a small object about fifteen feet away from me glistened in the sun and caught my eye. I looked over to where the flash of light had come from, but couldn't see anything. As I turned my head back to check on Kai, the sparkling light flickered again, and I stood up and walked over to see if I could locate its source.

What I found, lodged in a small crevice in the rocks, was an elaborately carved silver box. It was round, about the size of a quarter, and half an inch thick. At first I thought that it might have been left here purposely as an offering, but then I decided that it must have fallen from a pilgrim's pack or perhaps been left behind mistakenly after a rest period or a break for lunch. I picked it up and cradled it in my palm. It was heavier than I had thought it would be. The mix of high altitude and intense physical exertion can do strange things to the mind, and in a moment's flash of intuition I knew with utter certainty that the small reliquary held inside it a treasure beyond valuation, the answer to the questions that were tormenting me, and that it had been my destiny to find it. I took it back over to the rock I had been sitting on and, with pounding heart, slowly opened its top.

I fully expected to find a rare jewel contained inside or perhaps a text that could speak to me and help me grapple with my feelings, but as the top pivoted open on its hinge, I saw that the box held nothing but some finely ground green powder. I placed my forefinger in the powder and brought some to my mouth. It had little taste, neither bitter nor sweet. I stirred my finger through the powder to see if something might be concealed. There was nothing. I was dumbfounded. My intuition of a few moments earlier had been so strong and certain. I knew at that moment that this small silver box held something of great importance for me, and all I had found was a vial of dust, nothing but powdered ash.

And then the voice inside of my head began speaking again: *speck of ash, speck of ash, speck of ash* . . . . And suddenly my body began tingling, and I burst into tears.

The tingling was strong and extensive. It felt as if my entire body were just a mass of minute sensations flickering on and off like stars on a cold and clear night. Everywhere I looked there was only sensation and change. I kept searching within this mass of physical flux to find myself, but came up empty-handed, as though I were a bear reaching into a stream for a trout that kept eluding its grasp. For a moment I thought that maybe the powder was a kind of drug, but then the tingling began to subside, and my body began to feel more normal again.

I remembered reading how the Buddha would keep telling his students that body and mind are ultimately insubstantial, nothing but a process of continual change that follows very prescribed laws of nature. So much of our suffering can be traced to our mind's unwillingness to accept this truth. Instead of relaxing into this process of eternal change, aligning ourselves with this current of life, we try instead to solidify a sense of self and gradually come to believe that this "I" is very substantial and very important. But this is like fighting with the current of a strong river, and ultimately we end up by being swept away downstream. If we can only learn to relax and let go of the fictive tyranny of the ego, we find our true selves, and what we find is marvelous indeed. I turned my attention again to the sensations in my body. Everything was subtly moving and dancing. Nothing stayed still for longer than the smallest fraction of a second. Where could my mind take root in this stream of change? How could my sense of self coalesce into something solid and substantial and avoid being swept along on the tide of this most powerful and natural of processes? It couldn't. It too was part of this river of change. As I sat there on the rock waiting for Kai to come meet me, I felt as though an intricate and elaborately woven Persian carpet had been suddenly yanked from underneath my feet, and I had landed with a thud on the cold, concealed earth, and the ground felt wonderful.

I then realized that up until now I'd been viewing this journey as a rite of passage for Kai alone. I now saw that the journey was every bit as much a rite of passage for me as well. As I looked into the interior of the box with its fine green powder, I saw so clearly that any limiting role I identified with had to be transcended before I might truly meet myself face to face. Zen practitioners are often instructed to find their original face before they were born. To find my original face, I needed to let go of all personas and ideas about who I am and simply surrender to the experience of this very moment. The truth about this very moment is that everything is changing. The tingling that had passed through my body hadn't left a single part of me out. It consumed everything. Nothing could exist outside of this matrix of change, certainly not my body, and not my mind either. The Theravadin Buddhists speak about *anicca*, the experience of constant change that, like a fire out of control, engulfs and consumes everything. Walking around this mountain, I could never again fool myself into thinking that I was something independent and permanent, separate from this stream of constant change. Letting go of trying to be somebody, I felt that I'd finally gotten back in touch with my self.

By the time Kai reached me, I was feeling very light. I felt so much love for him in that moment, this young friend who was sharing this journey with me. He could tell that something had happened to me. The sensations in my body reminded me of the times when I would carry someone on my shoulders, set the person on the ground, and then began to feel my body float up.

"Dad, are you okay?"

"Yes, Kai, I'm fine. I really am. How are you doing?"

He looked like a bedraggled pup that had been left out in a rainstorm. "Well . . . ." His opening, drawn-out "well" reminded me of how my father would extend the single syllable of a word into a multisyllabic treatise. "Wu-ayyy-ell . . . my legs feel like they're . . . falling off, my lungs . . . are burning . . . , and I feel so spaced out that I can't . . . string the words of a thought . . . row. . . together . . . in a . . .you know. Other than that, I'm doing great."

We both laughed at the perfection of how he'd jumbled his words and sat down for an extended break and snack. By now it was late afternoon, and we knew we still had several miles to go before we would reach our camp. We were nearing the end of the valley and could just begin to peek around the sharp spine that separates the western flank of the mountain from its massive north face. The sun was beginning to fall low in the sky, and the light was softer and less glaring. In the late afternoon light everything began to look less intimidating, more accessible, more human in scale. The rocks and valley that just an hour earlier had appeared so formidable and harsh looked inviting again, comforting even. I felt that I could reach up and hold the valley in the palm of my hand. The change in the valley's appearance mirrored the shift in my mood that had followed my discovery of the silver box. Let go of everything, and everything is granted and given. Quit trying to be something special, and the truth and uniqueness of our natures are restored.

Without elaborating too much about my discoveries and realization, I showed Kai the silver box and its strange contents. He couldn't even begin to guess what the green powder might be, but we both decided that, whatever else it was, it was a special gift to me from the mountain deities, and that I should keep it with me for the rest of my life.

We arrived at our campsite an hour and a half later to a welcome cup of warm tea. The sun was beginning to set, and we were both cold and exhausted. The yaks and their herders were still far behind us, and we sat down with the other members of our small group behind a makeshift rock wall that protected us from the bitter wind that was beginning to blow up from the valley. Leaning back against the wall, we had an unobstructed view of the north face of Mount Kailas. From this vantage point the mountain looked like a mammoth arrowhead rising upward out of the ground.

As pilgrims slowly make their way around the mountain, they're often astonished to see how the snowy pyramid appears to change its shape, depending on the place from which it's viewed. The perfectly shaped pyramid from this morning, with its gently inclined face, was now gone. The face of the arrowhead was sheer and flat with horizontal striations of black rock peeking out through the covering of snow. It reminded me of the uncarved backside of a Haida totem pole that's never intended for viewing. I felt that if I hadn't gone through my earlier episode with the small, silver box that I wouldn't be able to stand looking at the north face. It was too sheer and uncompromising. I looked around at the others huddled together for warmth. Everyone was warily eyeing the arrowhead.

I saw a grouping of three small stupas on a hill about a hundred feet above us and decided to walk up to examine them more closely. We wouldn't be able to set up camp until the yaks arrived, and I was beginning to feel chilled. It actually felt good to start moving again, but I had to walk very slowly, and it took me at least twenty minutes to reach them.

The stupas were very primitive and possibly quite ancient. They appeared to have been carved out of mud and stone. Embedded in each stupa and sticking upward from its top was a vertical pole that had been made out of a branch of a tree that must have been transported from the distant Nepalese valleys far below. As I looked at the stupas, I realized that they were almost miniature replicas of Mount Kailas itself. It was as though an artist had sat down on this spot and crafted a sculpture of the mountain in much the same way as a traveling watercolorist might stop at the side of a country road, bring out an easel and paper, and paint a picture of a landscape scene.

I remembered that Mount Kailas had often been associated with the mythical Mount Meru, the center of the universe in Hindu cosmology. I also remembered that the vertical pole extruding from the top of the stupas was a common feature in primitive stupas, these earliest of Aryan structures. The vertical pole was like a cosmic spine around which the visible bulk of the world of appearances could organize itself and be held together. And then I remembered how the first temples of India had been elaborate renditions of these early stupas, which themselves were copies of the great mountains of the Himalayas and of Mount Kailas, the embodiment of Mount Meru, in particular.

My mind began racing as pieces of an elaborate architectural puzzle began fitting themselves deftly together. The stupas were one of the earliest human attempts by migrating Aryan artisans to express the sacred principles that governed their lives. The stupas were copies of mountains. The form of the stupas gradually developed into large structures in the lower, more hospitable lands of the Gangetic plain, on which the Aryan peoples would eventually settle, and functioned as places of worship, architectural reminders of the forces of divinity at play in the mountains, the natural habitat of the gods. In Ellora in central India, for example, the silhouette of the aptly named Kailasantha temple looks uncannily like Mount Kailas and its surrounding hills viewed directly from the south.

What, then, of the central pole, the spine around which the mass of the stupa was built? It may originally have functioned as an ancient equivalent of the rods of rebar that hold modern-day concrete structures together and keep them intact. It may also have served as a kind of symbolism of the Great Tree, the mediator between heaven and earth that joins these two realms together as one. As the tree's branches reach ever upward in the direction of the sky, its roots sink ever more deeply into the earth. God and humankind become inextricably linked.

In the great Hindu and Buddhist temple complexes of Asia, the form of the mountain was the dominant feature taken from the early stupas. The central pole was never really incorporated into the design and construction of buildings of worship. As the new Aryan consciousness that first was recorded in the Vedic and Upanishadic hymns gradually spread over distance and time and eventually reached what we now call the lands of the West, the master builders and craftsmen would become more interested in the pole. The overt allusions to the mountain were concealed under elaborate designs and ever more sophisticated building technologies. What came to dominate the Western churches were the spires that reached upward ever higher and higher. The great spires of the Gothic churches of Europe were sophisticated elaborations on the simple tree branch that protruded upward out of the bulk of the primitive stupas.

As I stood on this spot with the risen moon providing more light than the sun that had recently set, a vision of how religious architecture had progressed from its distant origins to its most recent expressions in glass, steel, and concrete began to play itself out on the screen of my mind like an historical movie. In the high mountain air, this vision made great sense. I remembered back to being a young boy, sitting uncomfortably in the solemn houses of worship that I would enter into. I remembered back to being a young man, so much at home in the high Sierra mountains, feeling a deep core in my body and mind beginning to come open, like a long unused door, as I walked and played so high above tree line. In that moment of fading light, I could understand that Mount Kailas was Mount Meru, the centermost and seminal point out of which so much spiritual expression had sprouted and proliferated. I saw the unbroken spectrum of that expression from the primitive stupa at my side to the Kailasantha temple and on to the soaring Gothic spires of the great cathedrals at Chartres and Notre Dame de Paris. Standing in the cold, I felt my body relaxing and becoming effortlessly balanced, as though it were organizing itself spontaneously around an invisible vertical axis. The mass of my body's tissues and organs surrounded this invisible pole, and as soon as the outer mass and the inner core became so appropriately related, I was filled with a deep feeling of peace and contentment. I knew that this central pole or core had no anatomical basis. It was, however, exactly aligned with the directional flow of the force of gravity, this mighty power that relates heaven and earth, that perhaps even brings God down to earth. At that moment I too was mountain and pole. I looked up. My head felt as though it were floating on top of my body, like a fishing bobber floating on the waves of the lake of my childhood. Like the invisible roots of a tree, my feet felt deeply implanted in the ground. The first stars and planets were already beginning to show themselves. I felt that for the first time in my life, finally, I was back in church.

September 17

Neither Kai nor I were able to sleep well. I had drunk so much water, tea, and hot soup the day before in my hopeful determination to keep any symptoms of altitude sickness at bay that I had to get up seven

times during the night to pee! Every hour or so I would feel the growing pressure in my bladder pulling me out of a light and fitful sleep,
bringing me back into my tent from a shallow dream world whose stories didn't make any sense. I'd lie on my mat for several minutes, trying
to ignore the urgent message coming from my bladder for as long as
possible, until it launched me out of the warmth of my sleeping bag,
into my waiting shoes and down jacket, and out into the cold and dewy
night. The air was absolutely still. Tiny beads of condensation floated
in the motionless air like watery fireflies illuminated by the light of the
moon. If you looked closely enough, you could find traces of all the colors of the rainbow in the prismatic dewdrops. The north face of the
mountain was completely lit up. If anything, it looked even more severe
in the moonlight, and I could scarcely bring myself to look at it directly.

In the middle of the night, I began to have trouble breathing. I had
to suck the thin air forcibly into my lungs to ward off the panicky feeling of suffocation that would otherwise begin literally to choke me.
Eventually I had to prop myself up in a sitting position to insure that a
large enough supply of oxygen made its way through the walls of my
lungs to the waiting blood cells lined up impatiently on the other side.
For the rest of the night I slept sitting up. My mind wasn't working well
either, and all I could think was *please, let this night be over.*

Whenever I would come back in the tent after a bladder break, Kai
would be propped up on his elbows.

"Dad, I can't sleep."

"Neither can I. Let's just try to rest as best we can."

Neither of us got much rest. The night felt as though it went on forever, its darkness and stillness as unrelenting as the previous day's emotions, physical challenge, and glaring light. Kai and I were both relieved
to see the dawn's first hints of light finally infiltrate the blackness of this
longest of nights.

We had camped above 16,500 feet. As challenging as our walk to
this campsite had been, we both knew that the coming day's challenges
were going to be more demanding still. Starting off from our camp, we
knew that the trail would rise sharply, until we crested the 18,600-foot

Dolma La Pass, the highest point on the kora and one of the most sacred spots in all of Tibet. The pass had been named for the goddess Dolma, one of the most benign deities in the entire Tibetan pantheon, who is described as being filled with compassion and mercy of such magnitude that she cannot possibly contain it in herself. It pours from her like water as she shares it freely with any practitioners who, through the intensity of their thirst and search, are fortunate enough to locate her. I couldn't decide whether it was a good or bad sign that this sacred pass was named after such a benevolent being. In either case I kept my thoughts to myself. Kai was apprehensive enough, as he slowly layered his body in the clothes he would wear, and both of us were feeling a bit crabby from not having slept well.

We knew that we would be walking slowly and wanted to set out as early as possible. The sun had not yet risen above the encircling mountains, and the air was crisp and cold. Neither of us had much of an appetite, and so we ate lightly and quickly, made sure our water bottles were filled, and slowly began to follow the path away from camp. Our exhalations were clearly visible in the thin, cool air. Even in the early morning light we were wearing our glacier glasses for protection, and my lenses clouded up every few steps. By the time the sun did appear over a dip in the eastern mountains, my mustache was caked with the frozen fluids from my runny nose. The combination of my cloudy glasses, dragon's breath, and coated upper lip proved irresistibly funny to Kai. I was happy to see him laughing.

The path leaving camp was reasonably level, and for the first half mile or so we were both able to walk comfortably, if slowly. After gingerly making our way across a primitive bridge of piled stones and logs that crossed one of the many glacial rivers that carve paths across the valley floor, we began our first serious ascent, and it was clear that we were in trouble. The hill was only a few hundred feet high, and the rise was gradual. Still Kai could only go about twenty yards at a time before he needed to sit down and rest, and I wasn't doing much better. I felt disconnected from my body, almost as though I were walking in a dream. My breath and my legs felt as though they each had contradictory agendas, and I realized that I needed to get them working together in concert as quickly as possible.

The morning before, when we had first set out from Darchen, we had talked so eloquently about the need to walk within our breath, to be aware of and coordinate these two activities with every step. It had all seemed so clear and obvious, and I'd felt pleased with myself for having recognized the linkage between these two functions and for my ability to articulate these insights to Kai. As I kept pushing myself to reach the top of this first hill, however, I realized that I had lost all awareness of my racing breath and that my feet were stumbling to catch up. I stopped walking for a moment and leaned forward into a strong gust of wind that stung my face and pulled the down hood of my jacket back off my head. The cold and unexpected breeze felt like a wake-up call that jolted me out of my dreaminess and brought me squarely back into my body. My breath and pounding heart both slowed down, and in a sudden, sobering moment of clarity I realized that I had better begin literally walking my talk if I wanted this day to turn out successfully.

I started out again, quite tentatively at first, but within a few steps I discovered the secret to coordinating my breath and feet at this altitude. One breath, one step. As I inhaled, my right foot moved forward. As I exhaled, my left foot moved ahead. Inhale, right foot forward. Exhale, left foot forward. My movements were slow, but they were also very steady, and I soon found myself at the top of the hill. The labor of walking suddenly felt so much easier. I was elated.

We took an extended rest at the top of this first ascent, and I congratulated Kai at length in hopes of raising his spirits. In truth, though, he didn't look so good. His face was burned from the wind, and it took a long time before his heartbeat and breath began slowing down. Even in the cold morning air, he was sweating. I reminded him of the need to drink large quantities of water and then talked to him at length about what I'd discovered about coordinating each step with a phase of the breath.

As we set out again, we both made a conscious effort to walk and breathe in this way, and soon found that it did make a significant difference. As we had yesterday, we settled into a slow procession of two. Kai would always walk behind me, as though I were clearing cobwebs from his path. We may have been moving like turtles, but our progress was steady. The sun was now up and peeking through openings in the swiftly moving layers of clouds. It felt good to be able to unzip our jackets. The path kept moving upward but the rise was gradual, and we must have walked at least a mile, resting regularly as needed, before we came to our next serious slope.

As we kept moving closer to the pass, we began encountering more and more Tibetan pilgrims. A handsome young man with a walking stick and long black hair gathered back into a ponytail walked past us as leisurely as if he were taking a stroll on the beach. Strapped securely to his back was a small boy, who was bundled in layers of wool and wearing a heavily felted green hat. He could sense that Kai and I were also a father and son and smiled at us in recognition as he passed us by. A little further on we came across a small group of pilgrims who were sitting on a patch of mossy ground just at the side of the path, taking rest. A very old man with a fleece-lined coat and a white woolen toque motioned for us to come over and join them. His face was deeply weathered and lined, and he had very few teeth left. He was holding an elaborately painted bowl that held a steaming tea or soup. His smile was huge, and his tongue kept darting in and out of the openings between his few remaining teeth. Everyone in his small group was softly chanting mantra.

"*Om mani padme hum. Om mani padme hum . . . .*"

A young Tibetan woman who struck me as wondrously beautiful in both body and spirit was fingering the beads of a mala as she kept repeating the sacred phrase. Mostly she would stare off into the distant sky, as though her gaze was fixed on some invisible star, but occasionally she would come out of her meditation, turn her head, and look directly over at Kai and me. Initially, it felt as though she were looking right through us, as though we weren't even there, but then she would break into a smile as large as the old man's and nod her head at us, as we continued to chant together. Nothing felt as though it could ever be easier than to love these people at this moment. The old man shared his warm liquid with me, and I honestly couldn't tell whether it tasted more like a soup or a tea. They eyed an energy bar that Kai and I were munching with some suspicion, but in the end accepted a bite, laughing uproariously at the unexpected taste in their mouths.

The sun was quite high by now, and I was aware that we'd walked perhaps two miles at most since leaving camp. I knew that we would soon begin another ascent, because the long, gently rising valley that we had been moving through was coming to an end. We could see that within a few hundred yards, it simply stopped, disappearing on all three sides into steep, rocky hills that themselves led up to even steeper mountains. We bid our new friends good-bye and set out again on our way.

Unfortunately, the rest and snack didn't appear to have freshened Kai at all. If anything, his body had stiffened up, and he looked even worse, as he trudged forward, forcing his feet to move ahead in rhythm with his long and labored breath. His breathing had developed a hoarse, rasping sound, and it began to remind me of the slow rattle an ailing animal might make in the final hours of life. I turned around and watched him as he moved, trying to hide my concern. His jaw was hanging slackly open, and his head was tilted toward the side. The outer corners of his eyes were drooping, and the skin around his cheeks looked as though it was sagging. He was clearly laboring not only to keep up, but to force himself to move at all. His feet barely cleared the ground in front of him with each step. No father wants to see his son in so much discomfort, and yet I kept reminding myself as best I could that this was a necessary part of Kai's rite of passage, that the exhaustion he was feeling was a prerequisite for the resolution that I hoped was to come. As I looked back at him again, though, I realized that my thoughts weren't very convincing, and so I tried to force the worry from my mind and returned, as best I could, to focusing on coordinating my breath with my steps.

As we neared the end of the valley, we saw that the path now rose sharply to the left through an utterly bizarre landscape of small granite boulders, many of whose tops were covered over by brightly colored articles of clothing. The sudden appearance of so much color in this land of grays, beiges, and mossy greens was startling. As we came closer to the hill, we could see that pictures and talismans, like accessories to an elaborate outfit, had been lodged in small fissures in the rocks or at the base of the boulders. The first sight of this steep hill brought our forward motion to a numbing stop. It was very weird. The shattered rocks looked like small children that had broken into their parents' closet and drawers and were playing dress up. Because the hill was situated at the end of the valley, there was no wind at all, and the stillness of the air only increased the feeling of eeriness. To make matters worse, the hill looked like it extended upward forever. We couldn't see where it ended. In the far distance toward what we hoped was the top of the hill, the articles of clothing became smaller and smaller, until all we could see was a jumble of small points of color.

Kai caught up to me, took one look at what lay ahead, and began to shudder. He was clearly frightened by the vision of the hill and its steep ascent. In the softest of voices, as though he was afraid that someone might overhear him, he pleaded for some explanation.

"Dad, what is it?"

I remembered from the books I had read that this hill marked an important transitional station on the pilgrim's journey around the mountain. The circumambulation of the mountain was like a process of initiation with distinct stages of psychic unfoldment. The western valley possessed the power to melt down the rigidities and fearful resistances in the pilgrim's mind, and the Dolma La was said to signify the final release from the suffering caused by our illusions. Cresting the Dolma La, the pilgrim was reborn into a new dimension and life. Before that rebirth could occur, however, death must come to cleanse the pilgrim of his or her last clingings and attachments. In the still air the hill smelled of death. The rocks looked like ghosts. The children that I had imagined a few moments earlier began to take on the appearance of troubled orphans.

I explained to Kai that the hill was here to complete the work of yesterday's walk through the great valley and to help prepare us for the final ascent to the Dolma La. This was the hill of final passage, and every pilgrim is asked to leave something of him or herself behind, as they pick their way through the boulder-strewn path. I could tell that Kai's heart was pounding as he listened to my story, and he held onto my hand much as he had the first day, when we walked into the bustle of Thamal in the center of Katmandu.

"Are we supposed to leave something here, Dad? A piece of clothing or something special?"

I told Kai that, yes, this is what we should do and then began kicking myself internally for having been so disoriented this morning when I woke up that I had completely forgotten about the hill and its importance and had neglected to pack anything that I could leave behind. Furthermore, it was important that the article that we would place here be something of real value and significance for us. A tattered sock that we planned on discarding when we returned home wouldn't do. Kai and I were only carrying small day packs on our backs. Our large duffels were trundling along somewhere on the back of a yak a mile or two behind.

Kai took off his backpack and searched through what he was carrying: water, lip balm, sunscreen, a rain jacket, a bag lunch, an extra sweater, an army knife, moleskins, a favorite T-shirt from home. He groaned when he saw the T-shirt, but knew that this is what he must leave behind. At this point he was willing to play by every rule in the book, if his compliance would help him get up and over the pass. He took a last, affectionate look at his shirt and walked over to a naked stone. He put the shirt on the stone as though he were dressing a doll and came back over to me.

"What are you going to leave, Dad?"

As I took off my pack and placed it on the ground, I honestly didn't know. I wasn't even sure what I was carrying with me. I quickly discovered that I wasn't carrying any extra clothing except for my rain jacket, and for a moment I thought that I might have to part with it. As my hand kept foraging at the bottom of my pack, I touched up against a small, metal object. At first I didn't even know what it was, but then froze, as I recognized what I'd felt. In that moment of recognition I knew with certainty that this is what I needed to leave behind. Kai groaned as I brought it out of my pack, but then slowly nodded his head in assent, understanding that I was making the right decision. It was the small, silver box of yesterday.

I explained to Kai that the box had revealed some important insights and that these could never be left behind, but would always be with me. If it's possible to take anything with us on our journey beyond death, it could only be the understanding we've cultivated during our passage through life. I told Kai that it was probably better that I leave the box here. If I kept and treasured it, it might start to take on a counterfeit life of its own. I might then run the risk of having it eventually supplant the insights themselves as the most important feature of yesterday's experience. It would be a tragedy if, at the moment of my death, I had lost the understanding that the box had revealed to me, but clutched the box itself possessively to my body.

Kai listened closely, but I could see that he was wrestling with many different feelings; what looked like a deep sadness over leaving behind these objects that we so cared for was mixed with a pinching fear about the journey still ahead and the strange hill we were walking through. On top of this, he looked as if he were physically struggling just to stand up. Neither of our minds were working that well at this altitude. The thin air was playing havoc with our emotions, and we were both on the edge of tears.

I placed the box on a small stone, silently thanked it for its help, and walked on. It felt difficult to start moving again. Kai was clearly exhausted, and the hill was steep. I had to keep encouraging him to keep moving. I could tell that he wanted to get off this hill, but that his body was barely letting him move. He told me that it felt like there was death all around him.

Almost as soon as he had said this, we came across a Tibetan pilgrim who was lying immobile on his back. I instantly froze, thinking that we'd come across a recently deceased body, but then realized that the pilgrim was engaged in a symbolic death only. He was staring so far off into the distant sky that his eyes had become glazed and unfocused. He was saying mantra, though, and was fingering the beads of his mala. Just beyond him three young men were contorting their bodies, as they crawled through openings in the rocks that looked far too small for their bodies to fit through. The rocky openings scraped against their bodies, like a knife that scrapes scales from a fish's flesh before it's placed in a frying pan. In this way the pilgrims were hoping to strip away their accumulated impurities, before they felt deserving to climb up to the Dolma La.

Slowly, and with many rests, we climbed the hill and emerged into another small valley. Kai was now grunting with each breath and walking more slowly than ever. I kept vocalizing my encouragement to him, but it looked as though he couldn't even hear me. He didn't look well, and I began quietly to curse myself for the folly of this trip. At this altitude emotions proliferate like mold on the underside of a piece of stale bread, and the first seeds of concern soon developed into a colony of full-blown doubt and worry. I felt powerless to resist the emotional tide and watched myself getting swept away, as it built and rose. I had so wanted this day to be a wonderful experience for Kai, a positive memory that he would carry with him and that would nurture him all through his life. What if I'd misjudged the kora? What if it was too much for a young boy? Of all the Westerners who've come to Mount Kailas, there have been very few young boys. I experienced a moment of deep despair and felt like a fool and a failure as a father.

As we neared the end of the valley, the final thousand-foot ascent to the Dolma La came into view. It was far steeper than anything we had had to climb to this point. A switchbacked trail rose up sharply over a series of successively higher hills that finally disappeared into the clouds and sky. We couldn't even begin to see to the top of it, and we had no way of knowing how far we had to climb to reach the pass. I suggested that we stop at the side of a creek for lunch before beginning our climb. I hoped that a rest and some nourishment would help us in our efforts, but Kai was so exhausted that he could hardly eat anything. He just kept looking up at the steep hill on the other side of the river.

After what passed for lunch, we were joined by Kesar, a young Sherpa from our group who asked if he could join us for the final climb. We were both happy to see him. Kai and he had become good friends during the long drive across the plateau. Kesar had with him a small, handheld Tetris game, and he was thrilled at how adept Kai was with it. Kesar was in his early twenties and was married with children, but he and Kai looked to be almost the same age. It was apparent to all of us who were traveling together that Kai and Kesar were like young brothers who loved each other very much.

Using our day packs as pillows, we all lay down on our backs to rest, soaking up the warmth of the intermittent sun, like sea sponges into which water was slowly trickling. After twenty minutes, however, I realized that I was becoming more groggy than rested and sat up and suggested that we all start moving again soon. Kai voiced a resigned and barely audible sigh and took his time in getting up to join me.

We started off walking very slowly, and I reminded Kai to let go of all thoughts of the summit, but simply to remain focused on the step he was taking and the phase of breath he was breathing at that moment. The path was very steep, and we found that we had to slow down even more. Inhale, right foot forward. Exhale, left foot forward. On the exhalations we would often just manage to bring our left foot up to the level of our right foot, but no further. In the first ten yards, a group of young Tibetan men came skipping past us, whistling and singing, gesticulating with their arms. Kai watched their lightness and ease of motion, as though someone were slowly twisting a screwdriver into his body. I told him that, if these young men who had lived their whole life on the plateau were to come down to sea level, they would have just as much difficulty adjusting to the elevation as he was experiencing now, but could tell that my words didn't cheer him. After twenty yards he collapsed down onto a rock, panting like a puppy who had been left too long inside a car with the windows rolled up and the summer sun bearing down. He needed to rest a full five minutes before he was willing to stand and move further.

The well-worn path moved back and forth up the steep hill in a series of switchbacks, like a herringbone strip that had been carved out and cleared between the boulders piled high on either side. After every five or six switchbacks, the path would come to a crest of a hill only to reveal another hill with another handful of switchbacks ahead of us. Every twenty yards or so, Kai would need to rest. As he sat on a boulder alongside the path, his chest would visibly heave as he attempted to get more oxygen, and the pain and strain of his exertion were imprinted all over his face. As the air got thinner and thinner, it became even more difficult to move.

At one point he went to get up after a rest and began to stagger. I felt momentarily sick. It reminded me of what had happened to a friend of mine who had participated in the Boston Marathon many years earlier before the running boom had exploded in North America. He had managed to finish the race, but was so dangerously exhausted and dehydrated at the end that his body had lurched violently from side to side over the last hundred yards, all coordination gone. Fortunately, Kesar was standing very near Kai when he stood up from his rest. When he saw him beginning to wobble, he quickly grabbed hold of his arm to help steady him. Whether Kai was walking, resting, or attempting to stand after a rest, Kesar was now at his side, steadying him and giving him support. These two young friends kept holding each other's hands, as they continued up the steep hill.

During another rest period a half an hour later, Kesar left Kai sitting on a boulder and came over to speak to me. He said that he could tell that I was concerned, but encouraged me to let my worry go, that it was not helping Kai or me. He assured me that Kai would be fine and told me that everyone has a different experience as they walk around the kora, the perfect experience for them. He could tell that things were shifting for Kai, but that he had to be left to himself to sort out his own obstacles. Dolma would see to it. That's what she was here for. She was helping Kai. She was helping me. She was helping him too.

"Kai began his kora," he said. "Only Kai can finish it."

Words have the power sometimes to stun. In the time of the Buddha, people would become enlightened just by hearing the dharma teachings spoken. As Kesar said those simple words, I was flung out of my body, racing backward in time, reliving my life in reverse, until I found myself at Kai's age, strapped into a chair, fighting to land my sailfish, and my father had voiced his concern to our fishing captain over my ability to continue. Dick's reply that I had caught the fish and that either I would land the fish or the fish would go free had meant so much to me at that moment and had stayed with me all these years. I knew that Kesar was right, just as Dick had been right so many years before. This was Kai's kora. The only way I could help him was to let go of any feeling that I needed to. If Kai was truly to have a chance of becoming a man, then I needed to stop treating him like a child. Small children need protection and assistance, but when a boy becomes a man, that same protection and well-meaning assistance only serve to undermine the claiming of his own power.

True to Kesar's perception, about halfway up the pass, I too began to detect a shift in Kai. A quiet and peaceful determination could be seen in his walk. During his rest periods he would sit and concentrate intensely on his breathing, focusing his gaze on the ground the whole time, getting up to move when he knew his body was ready. I no longer had to speak to him, and he no longer spoke a word to me. Inhale, right foot forward, exhale, left foot forward, both of our heads down as we walked, mindful of every step we took, continuing on. His rests became progressively shorter, his walks longer, and I knew he was going to make it.

And suddenly I looked up, and there it was, a hundred feet above us, the sacred Dolma boulder and the thousands of prayer flags that adorn it and mark the pass. There were more flags than I had ever seen before in one place, and the boulder, as sacred to the Tibetans as the Wailing Wall in Jerusalem is to the Jewish people, looked impossibly large and out of place amid the rubble of the pass, as though some deity beyond imagination and full of big mischief had set it there as a final assault on the logical mind.

I shouted into the wind, "Kai, there it is!"

I looked back and saw Kai perhaps ten feet behind me, walking within himself, step by step, clearly spent, the muscles of his face drooping, his arms hanging slackly at his side. He heard me as from a distance, strained to raise his head, and needed several seconds to comprehend what he was actually seeing. Like a flash flood in a dry desert gully, a wave of recognition exploded through him, and his face erupted into an expression of emotion that I had never seen before and have never seen since. It was a combination of disbelief, exhilaration, and the triumphant release of long pent-up pain and terror. His mouth and eyes opened wide through the mask of exhaustion that a moment earlier had been his face, his arms rose spontaneously out in front of him, and like a stick figure in a dream, he walked over to me and threw his arms around me. By the time he got to me, we were both crying uncontrollably. As we continued to hug each other, we let these tears of release and elation and the closeness of a father and a son wash over and soothe us. Our tears felt rich and comforting. I knew that they were Dolma's balm.

After a few minutes we continued on our way, energized by the sight of the pass. Although they continued to walk together, Kai no longer held onto Kesar, and he insisted on walking in front of me as well. At the top, the others in our group were waiting and showered Kai with hugs and heartfelt congratulations. Back home he might have been embarrassed by so much attention, but he wanted to hug everybody back just as strongly. These people were our friends. We had all become so close and intimate by then. Someone had prepared some warm tea. Kai sat on a rock and sipped it between congratulations, and I invited everyone to gather around and participate in a small ceremony. It was cold at the top of the pass, and we all stood huddled together in a semi-circle around Kai.

I began by speaking to the group. "As you all know, this trip has been a kind of pilgrimage for me and a rite of passage for Kai. In traditional cultures the age of thirteen is a time when the aging youth is challenged to perform an extraordinary task as a rite of passage into young adulthood."

And then, turning to Kai, I continued. "And Kai, your climbing up the Dolma La today is just such an extraordinary act." With this acknowledgment, tears began pouring out of Kai's eyes, and my voice broke, and I had to stop speaking. I looked around. Everyone in our group, including the Sherpas, stood there with varying amounts of moisture in their eyes. Many of the Tibetan pilgrims at the top of the pass had moved over closer to our circle. Even though they couldn't understand English, they could see that something of significance was happening, and many of them stood silently with their hands pressed together at the level of their hearts, gazing over at us as the ceremony proceeded.

When I was able to continue, I reached into my pocket and pulled out a gold medallion attached to a leather strand that I had had made up before our trip. I had kept it hidden in an extra pair of socks that I'd hoped wouldn't attract either Kai or a customs official.

I turned back to Kai and said, "As a formal acknowledgment of what you've accomplished, I want to present you with this medallion. On the front you'll see the symbol of the Dzogchen mirror known as a *melong*. You can see that there are three equally spaced sets of three triangular dots apiece. This is a very ancient symbol of a very ancient teaching that actually predates the arrival of Buddhism into Tibet and represents the mirrorlike clarity of awareness, the highest state we as grown humans can aspire to, the condition in which we know that we are one with everything that is. It is this condition above all that I pray you will uncover in your journey through life."

I turned the medallion over and continued. "On the back is the following inscription: 'For Kailas, mountain and man, September 1994, Dolma La Pass, Tibet.'"

I reached over to Kai and put the medallion around his neck. "I want you to know how very proud I am of you, Kai. Congratulations on what you've just done." And again we hugged and held on to each other, not wanting to let go.

After a few moments' silence, Jonathan cleared his voice and said he wanted to speak. Jonathan had come to feel like an uncle to Kai and a brother to me, and we had both come to love his big heart and unexpected wit. Everyone turned to listen to what he had to say. In a soft voice, full of caring, he began addressing Kai.

"Kai, it's been a real privilege to have been part of this journey with you and to have shared this moment with you. If I could, I'd like to offer you a little advice as you now move into manhood."

Jonathan was a natural at working a crowd. He had everyone's interest and attention, and after a pause during which he looked to the ground as though he were searching for the exact words that could convey his thoughts and feelings, he continued.

"Kai, you're growing up now, and as you get older, a time may come when you meet a woman who feels really special to you. When that time comes, you'll know it, and you may feel that you want to live with this woman and share your life. As the years go on, maybe you and this woman will have children together. Maybe you'll have a son. Maybe someday, as your son is leaving his childhood, you'll even want to participate in a ceremony much like the one that you and your father are participating in today. Kai, here's my advice to you."

A ham all the way, Jonathan savored every moment of the pause that preceded his final announcement. "Kai, name your son Maui."

It was perfect. We all erupted into raucous laughter and continued on in a mood of celebration, until it was time again to keep moving on. Jonathan would tell me the next day that the small ceremony for Kai had been very important to him. This had been his fourth attempt at getting to Mount Kailas, and he had felt from the moment of meeting Kai and me in Katmandu that, this time, he was destined to succeed. He had set out very early that day filled with emotion. Finally, after all these years, he would reach the summit of the kora and see and touch the Dolma stone. He had climbed the hill up to the Dolma La with great excitement and anticipation. He knew with certainty that something special awaited him there. But when he reached the top of the pass, nothing had happened. No feelings, no elation, no profound insights. It was just another rock and some flags. He had bitterly tried to hide his disappointment, as the others in our group joined him one by one, but the sting in his heart was real. Without directly realizing it at the time, however, something began stirring in him during the ceremony for Kai. When it was completed, he had wandered off alone. He said he could feel a kind of sweetness and a tenderness entering into his body and his spirit. He walked around to the far side of the Dolma stone, where no one could see him, and in his privacy he felt all the striving and passage of his life come rushing to his face like an underground spring bursting through the crusty surface of the earth. His forehead touched the Dolma stone, and he began to cry like a baby.

After the ceremony Kai added our small string of prayer flags to the ones left by the thousands of pilgrims who had been there before us, and we each cut a lock of our hair and left it at the foot of the Dolma stone. We hugged each other one last time and then knew it was time to continue on our way. We still had a long walk ahead of us to get to camp, but at least it was all downhill. Even so, we had to walk very slowly, as we began to descend the even steeper path on the far side of the pass. Fifty yards ahead of us were the old Tibetan man, the young beautiful woman, and their friends with whom we'd shared a rest and nourishment earlier in the day. They too were ebullient. Like teenagers singing the catchy chorus to a popular song, we shouted out the sacred mantra at the top of our lungs back and forth to each other. They would call, and I would answer. Then we would each elaborate on what the other had sung and send it back as a further challenge begging response. So sacred was this wonderful phrase that our play only gave it more power. In this way we kept on improvising different melodies back and forth, until we eventually had to stop because we were all laughing too hard. This was no time to fall, and we turned our attention back onto our breath and feet as we carefully picked our way down the rocky slope.

By the late afternoon Kai, for the first time on our trip, was far ahead of me, and when I finally arrived in camp, he had already set up both our Thermarests and sleeping bags, and my running shoes were neatly set out and awaiting me at the entrance to our tent.

18 September

The eastern valley was green and gentle. The sun shone the whole morning, as we walked the final few miles back to Darchen. It felt as though we floated more than walked. Both Kai and I felt strong and rested. Our legs were sore; our spirits were soaring. We had completed the kora.

As we entered back into the twisted maze of Darchen's streets and walkways, everything seemed strangely familiar, just as it had been, yet somehow different. One of the alleyways that we followed led us directly past the outdoor pool table. The game was still in progress, as though nothing had changed.

Epilogue:
The Days Between

So often it seems that nothing has changed. We hear phrases like "You can never enter into the same stream twice," but somehow assume that such a statement refers only to something fluid, like moving water, or something clearly ephemeral, like patterns of weather or the cycle of nature's seasons. Rarely do we recognize that it applies equally to all things: our homes, our possessions, our bodies and health, our sons and daughters. Every moment in life is a moment of passage (are these the same words with which this book began?), and every object or event that we can perceive to exist is constantly changing.

Every moment. All the time. Despite this mighty truth, we often cling to the illusion of immutability, hoping that we can defy this ongoing process of passage that is so natural and inevitable. If we deny the truth and experience of change, however, we lock ourselves into patterns of fear and tension that cut us off from the very qualities of love and happiness that our act of defiance sought to create. Partnerships form and dissolve, clouds appear to hide the sun, the pains of transition in labor always signal the imminent birth, our sons and daughters grow up into mature adults. Change saturates every moment of expe-

204

rience in the same way that salt saturates every particle of ocean water.

In light of the inevitability and importance of change, why not fill our days on earth with rituals, both quiet and celebratory, to honor its permeation into every corner of our lives? Births, maturations, deaths, the onset or dissolution of loving relationship: these are the seminal moments out of which we pass into dramatically different phases of our lives, and we create events to acknowledge the significance of these moments. But what about the multitude of less dramatic moments, the long and sometimes uneventful phases that connect the large events one to the other and form the major expanse of our lives? Can we not also create rituals and practices that both celebrate and align us with the reality of constant change and honor what might be called the "days between?" As Robert Hunter, poet and lyricist for the Grateful Dead, reminds us, these days too have a richness and a patina to them:

There were days
There were days
There were days between,
Polished like a golden bowl
The finest ever seen.

Describing the profound moments of passage in a life can be like focusing on the tops of mountain peaks that one has climbed, all the time knowing that the slopes leading up to the peaks, the valleys between the slopes, and the flatlands over which one travels to reach the mountains are all equally valid features in the topography of one's life. In truth, the peak of a mountain occupies only the smallest bit of space. The slopes, valleys, and flatlands are far more extensive both in geography and in life. If significant moments of passage are truly to make a difference in our lives, then the experience of passage itself must be embraced and valued during the days between, the long months and years that come after the events of significance. Otherwise, we run the risk of becoming addicted to the rush of sensation that inevitably accompanies peak moments and of developing a subtle aversion to the greater passage of our life that follows and precedes such moments and which may come to appear so uneventful in contrast. If at the end of our lives all we have to show for ourselves is a dazzling collection of silver boxes, but none of the insight that the discovery of the boxes represented, then our collection will not be of much value for us. It would be a bit like lining the walls of our home with a mounted collection of exotically beautiful butterflies or moths. Although perhaps pleasant to look at, the rows of dead insects also represent the diminishing and snuffing out of life, not its cultivation or blossoming.

The prominent moments of passage in our lives need to be celebrated loudly. The births, maturations, and the bonding of love between people are occasions for the great outpouring of joy among family and friends. The expression of real joy is never silent. Neither is the expression of profound grief that rips through our bodies in the face of the deaths of partnerships and loved ones. Common to both emotions is the spontaneous shedding of tears. Keeping joy and grief silent, muted, and under wraps is an unconscious strategy through which we attempt to deny the inevitability of change. The peak moments of our lives possess an intensity that our bodies are unable quietly to contain. Whether publicly or privately, this intensity needs to be released physically and verbally.

The quality of passage that permeates the days between needs to be equally expressed and honored, but its expression will naturally be more quiet and subtle. Quietly, without drawing any attention to ourselves, we can invite ritual and practice into our lives and celebrate the reality of passage every moment of every day of our lives. As we learn to acknowledge the truth and experience of change, our bodies lose their status as solid objects and instead become an open conduit through which a dance of minute, shimmering sensations passes through in unceasing flow. If we can learn to surrender to the current of the life force that so palpably animates us in this way, we stay relaxed and balanced. In such a relaxed condition the internal monologue of the mind naturally becomes quieter as well. At times it may even dissolve away into complete silence.

Moment to moment, we can learn to pay respects to the truth of change through continually yielding to the flow of tactile sensations that we can feel oscillating in every part of the body down to the smallest cell, through listening to the sequence of sounds that have never been heard before and will never be heard again, and through softening our vision and seeing the inherent luminosity and shimmer of the visual field. What a gift life is! As we practice and become more adept at this process of yielding to the truth of ongoing passage, we discover a silent place deep within ourselves. This silent place is valuable beyond words. *Om mani padme hum.* It speaks to us in a way that words cannot come close to approximating of the nobility and dignity of the human condition. If our formal rituals of passage do not somehow encourage and support our remembrance of this silent place of subtle, wordless shimmer, so natural to each and every one of us, then those rituals have not been wholly effective in accomplishing their goals.

Paradoxically, the process of change is the only reliable constant in our lives. The only thing that we can ever be certain of is that "this too shall pass." Passage is everything. Nothing can remain impervious to its influence. The present moment is constantly shifting its shape from one second to the next. It can never be pinned down or frozen. Any attempts at resisting this process of passage will not only be futile; they will also be accompanied by muscular and mental tension that will remove us from fully experiencing the richness of immediate experience, lock us into beliefs about ourselves and the nature of reality that are not wholly accurate, and ultimately cause us pain.

The great challenge to those of us who decide to work to become ever more aware of the reality of this present moment, however, is that the present moment is a highly volatile and elusive commodity. Its contents are forever in eternal flux. Just when we think we have finally grasped it in the palm of our hand, asserting that this finally is the present moment, we find that it has already slipped through our fingers and has once again shifted its shape. Doubly paradoxically, it is only through aligning ourselves with this process of ongoing change and passage that we are able to apprehend this one eternal constant.

This act of constant alignment with the present moment is not unlike the action of bodysurfing. If we can catch a wave in just the right place, neither too far in front of or behind its crest, then we can ride it joyfully all the way to the shore. If we hold ourselves back when the breaking wave approaches or push off too quickly before it has reached us, however, we either miss our ride or get wiped out every time. When through practice we learn how to stay poised right at the apex of the breaking wave that is our life, we naturally stay very awake and aware. Our minds can then become like the Dzogchen melong, mirrorlike in their ability to be fully present and not to linger over something that exists no more or something that is yet to come. Through such mirror-like awareness we discover who we are in truth.

A Tibetan teacher, Patrul Rimpoche, once summarized the whole of the teachings through the emphasis on remaining vigilantly aligned with the passing show of the present moment:

Don't prolong the past.
Don't invite the future.
Don't alter your innate wakefulness.
Don't fear appearances.
Apart from that, there's not a damned thing.

Apart from this very moment in its dazzling procession of appearances and shapes, its parade of pains and pleasures, what possibly could there be? Because this is our life, why not open to it and experience it as fully as possible?

The benefits that come through acknowledging the truth of constant passage and remaining vigilantly aware of the impermanence of all things are available to all of us all the time, irrespective of our situations or stations in life. For orchestrated rites of passage to be wholly successful, however, we frankly require a bit of luck. We never know when a sudden and unexpected cloudburst may drench an outdoor wedding reception or when a river in an uncharted region may prove too high to cross. Kai and I were first-time lucky in our attempts to reach and walk around Mount Kailas. Jonathan was fourth-time lucky. Raymond and Milena were not nearly so lucky.

After ferrying our cars and trucks safely across the river, we said a last goodbye to Raymond and Milena. Raymond was still clearly suffering the effects of the onset of altitude sickness, but was determined to get to Darchen and begin the kora. He had told us that he had dreamt of coming to Mount Kailas for sixty years and was not about to give up when he was so close to the attainment of his dream. He had also, however, alluded to the possibility of not being physically able to survive the walk around the mountain. He had dreamt of a dark wind on the mountain that he believed was coming for him.

Only after we completed the kora did we learn of what had happened to Raymond and Milena. Clearly aware that they were running out of time, they set out on the kora as soon as they reached Darchen. As they made their way into the western valley and began gaining altitude, Raymond's illness miraculously and unexpectedly began to improve. While his condition cleared, however, Milena became ill. It was almost as though the illness were a malevolent spirit that vacated Raymond's body and took up residence in Milena's. By the next morning she was suffering from altitude sickness that was so severe that she could not go on. They had no choice but to turn around and walk back down to Darchen.

Part of me wants to believe that Raymond and Milena's experience was the perfect one for them to have, that the lessons that they most needed to experience at that moment were only available through their being unsuccessful in their attempts to walk around the mountain. An equally strong part of me grieves for the apparent lack of fortune of these two fine people who had become our friends. I kept asking myself how I might have felt had we not been able to get across the first river and our journey to Kailas had ended virtually before it had begun. How would I have felt if someone had been badly injured in the attack on our cars, and we were forced to turn back to Katmandu? What if we had not been able to get across the final river, or if our cars and trucks had become so mired in the marsh and quicksand that we couldn't proceed? Would I have been so quick to accept that in our lack of success at getting to the mountain, we had been given the perfect lessons that we needed to learn? We can create itineraries for our lives and hold a strong and clear intention for how we would like to see events unfold. If we are unable, however, to accept that changes in schedule are the rule, rather than the exception, we will set ourselves up for inevitable disappointment. Holding to anything—whether it is a planned event, a person, a possession, an attribute of self—runs counter to the law of passage and will very likely lead to upset. In the end, life plays itself out according to its own scripts. As a friend of mine is fond of saying, "Everything's perfect, like it or not." I inwardly cringe every time I hear him say it, but also recognize the truth contained in the words he speaks.

Within this play of life with its inevitable surges, lulls, and dips, the best we can do is to remember to love, care for, and support each other. Isn't this deep bond of caring the motivation for staging rituals of passage for our sons and daughters? Don't all parents everywhere want the best for their children? Our hearts naturally swell with pride during the initiations, the weddings, the bar mitzvahs and bas mitzvahs, the baptisms. Riding atop of the crest of these feelings, we hope to prolong and maintain the caring and the love indefinitely, like a surfer who dreams of catching the perfect wave that takes him every time all the way to the beach. It is easy to feel love at the top of a mountain peak. We get tested when we descend again back down to the valleys and lowlands, where most of us are destined to pass the greater measure of our lives. Does everything become once again too familiar, taken for granted, a bit gray? Or are we able to sustain the insight, vision, and exhilarated love that we felt at the top of the mountain? Our rituals of passage are like the peaks of the mountains. We go there from time to time to fill ourselves as full as possible, to create a reserve on which to draw when we return back down to the valleys of our lives. In the valleys of our lives we can practice the awareness of passage, breath by breath, moment to moment, day after day. If we practice diligently and are successful in our practice, we transport the mountain peak back down into the valley, all the while hoping, once more in the words of Robert Hunter, that love will not forsake the days that lie between.

⤙

I will never be able truly to know what effect the trip to Tibet had on the formation of Kai's life. It's a given now, part of our history, a special memory perhaps. What I do know is that I came away feeling good about how I was able to participate in this event of passage for this young man about whom I care so deeply. I also know that this event turned out to be a powerful moment of passage for me as well. It has continued to this day to feed my certainty about the value of continuing the practice of the days between.

Almost ten years of accumulated days between have now passed since Kai's and my journey. Much has happened in that time, the great majority of it uneventful. I recently had occasion to speak with one of Kai's best friends, and our conversation turned back to the trip we had taken to Tibet. His friend told me that when Kai returned from the trip, he was different. He looked different. He felt different. When pressed to elaborate on that difference, Kai's friend just shrugged his shoulders. He said he didn't know, that there was just something different.

When Kai started classes again at the small school he was attending, his teacher announced a Mount Kailas week, during which the students studied the geography, history, and religious traditions of the region, based on Kai's stories and photographs. At the end of the week they were asked to write a poem describing their impressions of the sacred area. One student wrote about how "mani stones seemed a long ways away from minimalls." Kai wrote about his experiences climbing the hill above Lake Manasarovar and titled his poem "Trek."

Sitting on the top of the hill
Exhausted from the walk up
Staring in every direction
Beautiful scenery takes hold of my vision.
To the side a lake
In front of me an incredible sunset.
In the distance beyond Chiu Gompa
Mount Kailas rises out of the clouds
Like a tooth from the center of the universe.

I have always enjoyed his image of a tooth. A tooth is something that cuts through and is one of our most important tools of transformation. A tooth begins the process that turns our food into human energy and life. Is not our work on this planet to cut through the limiting beliefs and fears, the obscurations and patterns of habit that prevent us from becoming who we truly are, liberating ourselves from the unsatisfactoriness that is otherwise our lot? Like the alchemists of old, aren't we here to break down the sorrows that cloud our heart and create barriers among us, to transform the lead of our limiting beliefs about ourselves into the gold of our true being, our original face?

When Kai's teeth had come in as a child, we noticed that he had an extra premolar. When his baby teeth were replaced by his adult teeth, our dentist told us that this extra tooth would not cause any problems and did not have to be removed. For some unexplained reason this extra tooth of his has always given me a peculiar pleasure. I hope he never loses it. I also hope that he never loses the image of a tooth that rises up from the center of the universe, a tooth that belongs to all of us, a tooth that cuts through everything that stands in the way of our becoming our true selves and experiencing our connection to all that is.

Books of Related Interest

FROM MAGICAL CHILD TO MAGICAL TEEN
A Guide to Adolescent Development
by Joseph Chilton Pearce

THE EDISON GENE
ADHD and the Gift of the Hunter Child
by Thom Hartmann

CHILDREN AT PLAY
Using Waldorf Principles to Foster Childhood Development
by Heidi Britz-Crecelius

MOTHER AND CHILD
Visions of Parenting from Indigenous Cultures
by Jan Reynolds

THE NEW CHILDREN AND NEAR-DEATH EXPERIENCES
by P.M.H. Atwater, Lh.D.
Foreword by Joseph Chilton Pearce

THE BIOLOGY OF TRANSCENDENCE
A Blueprint of the Human Spirit
by Joseph Chilton Pearce

TIBET'S SACRED MOUNTAIN
The Extraordinary Pilgrimage to Mount Kailas
by Russell Johnson and Kerry Moran

RUMI: GAZING AT THE BELOVED
The Radical Practice of Beholding the Divine
by Will Johnson

Inner Traditions • Bear & Company
P.O. Box 388
Rochester, VT 05767
1-800-246-8648
www.InnerTraditions.com

Or contact your local bookseller